Party Ballots, Reform, and the Transformation of America's Electoral System

This book explores the fascinating and puzzling world of nineteenth- and early twentieth-century American elections. It examines the strategic behavior of nineteenth-century party politicians and shows how their search for electoral victory led them to invent a number of remarkable campaign practices. Why were parties dedicated to massive voter mobilization? Why did presidential nominees wage front porch campaigns? Why did officeholders across the country tie their electoral fortunes to the popularity of presidential candidates at the top of the ticket? Erik J. Engstrom and Samuel Kernell demonstrate that the defining features of nineteenth-century electoral politics were the product of institutions in the states that prescribed how votes were cast and how those votes were converted into political offices. Relying on a century's worth of original data, this book uncovers the forces propelling the nineteenth-century electoral system, its transformation at the end of the nineteenth century, and the implications of that transformation for modern American politics.

Erik J. Engstrom is a professor of political science at the University of California, Davis. He previously taught at the University of North Carolina at Chapel Hill. He received his PhD from the University of California, San Diego, in 2003. Engstrom is the author of *Partisan Gerrymandering and the Construction of American Democracy*. His research articles have appeared in numerous journals including the *American Political Science Review* and the *American Journal of Political Science*.

Samuel Kernell is a distinguished professor of political science at the University of California, San Diego. He has also taught at the University of Mississippi and the University of Minnesota and has served as a Senior Fellow at the Brookings Institution. Kernell received his PhD from the University of California, Berkeley. He has written numerous articles and books, including *Strategy and Choice in Congressional Elections*, second edition (1983, with Gary C. Jacobson); *James Madison: The Theory and Practice of Republican Governance* (2005); *Going Public: New Strategies of Presidential Leadership*, fourth edition (2006); and *The Logic of American Politics*, sixth edition (2014, with Gary C. Jacobson, Thad Kousser, and Lynn Vavreck).

Party Ballots, Reform, and the Transformation of America's Electoral System

ERIK J. ENGSTROM
University of California, Davis

SAMUEL KERNELL
University of California, San Diego

CAMBRIDGE
UNIVERSITY PRESS

CAMBRIDGE
UNIVERSITY PRESS

32 Avenue of the Americas, New York, NY 10013-2473, USA

Cambridge University Press is part of the University of Cambridge.

It furthers the University's mission by disseminating knowledge in the pursuit of education, learning, and research at the highest international levels of excellence.

www.cambridge.org
Information on this title: www.cambridge.org/9781107050396

First published 2014

Printed in the United States of America

A catalog record for this publication is available from the British Library.

Library of Congress Cataloging in Publication Data
Engstrom, Erik J.
Party ballots, reform, and the transformation of America's electoral system / Erik J. Engstrom, University of California, Davis; Samuel Kernell, University of California, San Diego.
    pages cm
Includes bibliographical references and index.
ISBN 978-1-107-05039-6 (hardback)
1. Elections – United States – History – 19th century.   2. Political campaigns – United States – History – 19th century.   3. Voting – United States – History – 19th century.   4. Political parties – United States – History – 19th century.   5. United States – Politics and government – 19th century.   I. Kernell, Samuel, 1945–   II. Title.
JK1967.E64   2014
324.973′08–dc23   2014012715

ISBN 978-1-107-05039-6 Hardback

"For whomsoever hath, to him shall be given, and he shall have more abundance:
But whosoever hath not, from him shall be taken away even that he hath."

Matthew 13:12

Contents

Acknowledgments

In exploring the implications of the myriad laws and practices governing nineteenth-century parties and elections, we have taken lessons from a class of Americans with more practical concerns – nineteenth- and early twentieth-century party politicians trying to win elections. These politicians practiced institutional manipulation with the dedication if not the lofty aspirations of the Framers. For them, institutional design was a fine art. Given all the ways we found them manipulating state laws and practices over the course of the nineteenth century to achieve responsiveness, it comes as no real surprise to us at the end to find that they had a hand in dismantling it.

We have also learned a lot from sage contemporaries, particularly those generous friends and family who read part or all of the manuscript. We thank John Aldrich, Richard Bensel, Gary Cox, Gerald Gamm, Dianne Kernell, Georgia Kernell, Scott Mackenzie, Jerrold Rusk, Eric Schickler, Matthew Shugart, and referees for the publisher who gave an earlier draft a careful and insightful reading. We learned a lot and deeply appreciate their efforts. Each will find his or her suggestions in these pages.

Numerous colleagues generously shared data and other information with us. Jerrold Rusk, who occupies a special place in the development of our argument, as noted in Chapters 1 and 2, sent us statewide data on congressional and presidential elections. Charles Stewart and Stephen Ansolabehere, who were researching related historical issues at the same time, provided numerous clues on sources. Happily, we found mutual opportunities to fill in holes in our collections of legislative returns. John Wallis not only created a phenomenal resource in his state constitutions online database (http://www.stateconstitutions.umd.edu/), he also repeatedly guided us in its use.

Of all the many data requirements, compiling partisan vote shares for state legislative elections outstripped all of the other data-collection work combined. Only for one state, Nevada, can one go to a single source to find the partisan share of total popular votes cast for state legislative candidates. All of the other states required compiling each legislative district's election returns and summing partisan totals. None of this information was available for our time period in machine-readable form. This required entering more than 200,000 election returns. Without the generous support of the National Science Foundation (NSF) (award #1036260, for FY 2005), this phase of the research would have been impossible. The University of California, San Diego's Committee on Research repeatedly funded the research after we exhausted NSF support.

We were blessed with extraordinary research assistance. Scott MacKenzie, now a professor at UC Davis, took over the final stages of data collection and merged the original data with Inter-University Consortium for Political and Social Research's district and election-returns files. Moreover, Scott became the "reader over our shoulder," fixing inferences and writing style and reminding us of data constraints as well as forgotten opportunities. Had Scott not daily kept the project on course, this book would have foundered long ago. More recently, Scott Guenther, who is presently writing his dissertation, came on board and started contributing immediately.

Nicole (Fox) Willcoxon began entering election data for us as a sophomore. Her attention to detail and ability to break large, complex projects into a series of manageable tasks allowed her to offer instruction to everyone she worked with. By her senior year, she ran the project. Everyone, including us, reported to her daily to submit our work and draw our next assignment. Other undergraduates who cheerfully worked on this project include Novette Buenaflor, Jenny Hwang, Andrew Jan, and Max Simon.

Dozens of librarians and archivists in more than twenty states generously entertained our requests for state legislative elections records. Several individuals stand apart. Lloyd Velicor at the Wisconsin Historical Society sent dozens of legislative manuals through interlibrary loan after checking each one to ascertain its information. He also tracked down the location of election returns for eight other states. Mary Hughes Greer, a freelance researcher, uncovered dozens of election years' returns in the Wisconsin, Michigan, and Maine collections. Another exceptional individual is John Mifflin, who, after finding incomplete records for Washington in the standard secretary of state files, managed somehow to track down each missing district's returns. We still have not figured out precisely how he managed this over a two-month period.

Erik Heidemann's e-mail messages describing his ordeal and feats of endurance inspired our student workers, to whom we read his missives as they keyed in election returns. Erik found the original county reports for Idaho hidden away in an unheated room of the state historical society. He undertook days of transcribing in dim winter light, dressed more appropriately for snowshoeing than armchair research. This excerpt from one of his e-mail messages ended any temptation to feel self-pity for the team toiling away in sunny Southern California:

I started the "scrolls" today. Let me tell you about the scrolls. Whereas it took about an hour to transcribe each election from the ledgers, it will take much longer to do the same from the scrolls. The scrolls are county scrolls – not one big scroll for each election like I anticipated. They are horrible to work with. I have to use 10–15 paper weights to find the elections of interest. They are not uniform throughout either, meaning that the scroll pages for one county are not necessarily sequential to that of another county.

Other generous archivists and researchers include Johnathan Bruner, a student at the University of Chicago; Keith Edwards, a student at the University of Denver; Debbie Greeson and Margaret Knecht at the Kansas State Historical Society; Brian Graney at the New Mexico Records Center and Archives; Nancy Horn at the New York State Library; Sandy Levy and Cynthia Requardt at the *Baltimore Sun*; Lupita Lopez at the Washington State Archives; Steve Nielsen at the Minnesota Historical Society; Nancy Peluso at the Connecticut State Library; Karen Shafer, a student at Arizona State University; Genevieve Troka and David Cismowski at the California State Archives; Noah Waisberg, a student at Brown University; Dave Wendell at the Oregon State Archives; and Martha Wright and Steven Towne at the Indiana State Archives.

We wish to thank the Missouri Historical Society for permission to reprint Abraham Lincoln's letter to fellow Whigs in Chapter 2; the Carnegie Society for permission to reprint nineteenth-century travel times across the nation for Chapter 3, and the University of Chicago's Special Collection Library for permission to reprint the Democrats' 1864 broadsides for Chapter 3. Cambridge University Press has kindly permitted the reproduction of Gerring's party ideology scores for Chapter 3; the University of Massachusetts Press has permitted the reproduction of Gamm and Smith's presidents' public speaking graph for Chapter 3; and Blackwell Publishing has granted us permission to reprint our previously published article, "Manufactured Responsiveness: The Impact of State Electoral Laws on Unified Party Control of the President and House of Representatives" 2005. *American Journal of Political Science*. 49(3): 531–549 in Chapter 4.

Prologue

During the last decade of the nineteenth century and the early decades of the twentieth century, elections in America changed dramatically. From the late 1820s to the end of the nineteenth century, national elections were hotly contested affairs waged by militaristically organized state and local political parties dedicated to mobilizing massive voter turnout. Frequently, presidential elections were narrowly decided. Even so, thin victory margins could reverberate throughout the nation's elective offices into numerous narrow victories. Early in the next century, political parties weakened and played a diminishing role in campaigns. Voter turnout declined sharply. Although presidential candidates won more decisively, their success failed to pull as many fellow partisans into Congress or the state capitals.

In an exchange published in a 1974 issue of the *American Political Science Review*, two leading political scientists of America's electoral history sparred over the secular and structural forces that had transformed America's elections. Walter Dean Burnham launched the exchange with an article (1974a) in which he argued that it reflected nothing less than a bourgeois revolution. Fearful of the Populist agenda, the corrupt appetites of party leaders, and the easily manipulated votes of massive numbers of recently enfranchised immigrants, America's emerging capitalist class infiltrated and wrested control of both political parties and government, whereupon it eviscerated state and local party organizations and curtailed participation by what had been a keenly engaged electorate.

Jerrold Rusk followed in the same issue with a lengthy comment (1974) in which he critiqued Burnham's cinematic conspiracy theory and proposed an alternative and simpler, yet fully capacious, explanation. Declining turnout, diminished party organizations, and shortened presidential coattails were the direct result of Australian ballot reform, which virtually all of the states had adopted during the last decade of the nineteenth century and first decade of the twentieth century. It replaced public submission of a party-supplied ticket with the secret vote of a state-supplied ballot listing all of the eligible candidates. Perhaps anticipating Burnham's response, Rusk further argued that rather than an instrument of elite takeover, party leaders in many states ushered in ballot reform as a practical solution to some pressing organizational problems, problems that we examine in detail later in the book.

In his rejoinder, Burnham acknowledged that ballot reform proximately preceded the dramatic changes in voting and elections but dismissed this "mechanical" variable as insubstantial and, in all likelihood, one of the tools elites enlisted to demobilize the electorate. In any event, he concluded, to analyze the minutiae of state election laws and to sort out their effects on elections would be a daunting task:

Of course, we all await the multivariate analysis based upon total universe recovery to which Professor Rusk alludes. Those of us who work in this area know only too well the immensity of preliminary data recovery and combination this will require – to say nothing of the very real problem not merely of identifying the date and nominal scope of a legal change, but of measuring its effectiveness as concretely applied at various points in time. (Burnham 1974b: 1054)

Blissfully ignorant of Burnham's prescient warning, we naively undertook to assemble more than a century's worth of election laws for all states. Moreover, to test the scope of these rules on election outcomes – and because state legislatures enacted, modified, and eventually dismantled the nineteenth-century electoral system – we needed to analyze voting for state legislative elections, the only set of elections that had still not been collected. By the end of our nearly decade-long data collection, Burnham's characterization of the exercise as a "total universe recovery" no longer strikes us as a florid overstatement. We are ready, finally, to join this conversation.

I

An Era in Need of Explanation

For more than half a century, politics in Washington has involved some form of divided party control. Only seven of sixteen presidential elections from 1948 through 2012 found the same party winning the presidency and both chambers of Congress. Complete party turnover from one party's unified government to the other's happened only once, in 1952. Relaxing the comparison of party turnover and turning to control of the presidency and the House of Representatives, the two institutions where every seat faced election, the opposition wrested control of both institutions in only four of the eleven elections in which a party controlled both institutions going into the election.

One might be tempted to regard modern divided government as the Framers' legacy to future generations. They designed the new Constitution to prevent the concentration of power that might be used by a tyrant or a majority of the citizenry to abuse the rights of political minorities. Along with federalism, the Constitution created an elaborate network of checks and balances in the national government that they reinforced with different modes of election, electoral calendars, term lengths, and constituency aggregations.

However closely modern American politics may appear to satisfy the Framers' intent, the Constitution's design cannot in itself account for our modern predicament of divided government. There was, after all, a lengthy period in America, not long removed from the Constitution's framing, when unified party government was the rule rather than the exception. In thirteen of the fifteen presidential elections from 1840 through 1900, the winning presidential party also won a majority in the House of Representatives. One of the two exceptions came in the anomalous 1876 election, when Democrats won a majority of House seats as well as a popular vote majority for president but lost the White House in a contested electoral vote count. During this era, the party winning the presidency even captured or retained control of the Senate on all but two occasions – a remarkable achievement given that only a third of the chamber's membership came up for reelection during a presidential election year, and that state legislatures, not voters, selected this chamber's members. When divided party control did occasionally arise, it was almost always the product of a midterm election and harbingered the opposition's success in the subsequent presidential election that restored unified government.

Even the era's otherwise robust federalism could not fend off the unifying party forces. The party victorious in the presidential election always improved its numbers in the state legislatures and gubernatorial offices. Nor was unified control of government during the nineteenth century simply the by-product of a hegemonic party or landslide elections. Rather, elections were hotly contested and highly competitive. But even these narrow victories generated systematic swings in party control of offices from Washington to the state capitals.

How could nineteenth-century national and state election outcomes differ so greatly from modern results? After all, with the exception of the Seventeenth Amendment providing for direct election of senators in 1913, these elections dealt with the same offices in the same constitutional setting of separated powers. What happened in the twentieth century to break the tandem movement of party fortunes across executive and legislative branches and across the federal system? These are fundamental questions. Answers to these questions should not only help us better comprehend the electoral dynamics of both eras but also identify those dynamics that break up seemingly stable institutions and reconfigure them into something quite different.

We argue that this era's pervasive and sharp partisan swings in electoral fortunes were largely the product of electoral institutions that determined how (and when) voters cast their ballots and how those ballots were then distributed across legislative districts. Beginning in the 1830s and continuing until near the end of the century, political parties printed and distributed ballots listing their candidates for the offices being contested in the current election. Presidential ballots typically found either the name or image of the party's presidential and vice presidential candidates heading the ticket, followed by the party's House nominee, any statewide candidates, state legislative, and in many states, even candidates for local offices listed at the bottom of the ballot. The party ticket discouraged voters from engaging in split ticket voting, although as we shall discover in Chapter 2, they might unwittingly submit a bogus ballot introduced by a disgruntled, typically local party faction that substituted one or more candidates it preferred over the party's nominees. These exceptions notwithstanding, the party ticket system effectively introduced massive coattail voting tying the fortunes of party candidates to the success of their party's presidential nominee at the top of the ticket.

A second set of institutional rules distributed votes for legislative seats in such a fashion as to maximize the rewards from winning a plurality vote share. Party politicians aspired to draw and redraw districts to maximize the small shifts in the vote in competitive districts and states, of which there were many. This could produce massive swings in partisan fortunes across a range of national and state elected offices. Through districting laws, rules for selecting U.S. senators and those for choosing electors to the Electoral College, among others, many state parties transformed their states into nearly winner-take-all electoral systems. The net result was an electoral system where marginal changes in the national presidential vote produced outsized changes in the partisan balance of Congress and state governments.

This electoral system was largely dismantled by the beginning of the twentieth century. The main event came as state legislatures adopted Australian ballot reform en masse. This reform instituted two monumental changes to the electoral system. It delegated to state government responsibility for creating and presenting to voters a ballot containing the names of all eligible candidates. And it placed voters in a private booth beyond the watchful eye of the party representatives. Voters could now easily split their votes among candidates from different parties. The result was more pronounced candidate-centered elections and weakened presidential coattails. This was an extraordinary alteration of America's democracy. How the new electoral system altered politicians' incentives and voters' information constitute our principal concerns in Chapters 4, 5, 6, and 7. Why party politicians would so completely, so apparently abjectly surrender their prerogatives begs for explanation, which we undertake in Chapter 8.

Layout of Book

The book proceeds by analyzing the mediating impact of state institutions on elections for every significant political office, from president to U.S. House representatives to senators to governors to state legislators. We start, in Chapter 2, by laying out in greater detail the puzzle of pervasively responsive elections that motivates our inquiry. Unlike past research that locates high turnout and close, hotly contested elections in passionate voters, we view these and other distinguishing features of this electoral history as a product of the election strategies of political parties operating in a particular set of electoral institutions.

In Chapter 3 we examine the standard bearer at the top of the ticket. If, as we argue, presidential elections provided the common cue for voters across the nation, we should find voters evaluating the presidential candidates on some common criterion – the economy, war, the current government's performance, or even scandals revealed during the campaign. These concerns need not dominate voters' attention and choices, but they must be systematically factored into those choices. Otherwise, random responses to the candidates across the states or, alternatively, a presidential vote that is strictly a by-product of voters' responses to state and local campaigns would fail to generate the systematic swings capable of changing party control at every level of government throughout the country. Did nineteenth-century presidential elections follow national issues and conditions? For our argument to hold, the answer must be yes, even if minimally. Our analysis establishes presidential contests as a focal point on which all elections were contested and decided.

The first set of coattail effects we investigate are those for House elections (Chapter 4). Although rarely cast as such, the vast literature on modern House elections is devoted to accounting for why the public's response to national events is so muted in congressional elections. Incumbents dominate their local contests; even those incumbents whose political party the public judges unfavorably. In the nineteenth century, on the other hand, House elections appear to more closely track presidential elections and national issues. In this chapter, we develop a structural model of congressional elections to explain this otherwise perplexing trend. Specifically, we trace the influence of presidential coattails and swing ratios fostered by the strategic design of congressional districts to magnify small advantages in the election. Both strongly account for the correspondence between outcomes for the presidency and the House throughout the nineteenth century.

In Chapter 5 we examine Senate elections before and after the implementation of direct elections. Although explicitly fashioned by the Framers as a bulwark against the impulsive desires of voters, indirect Senate elections throughout most of the nineteenth century systematically responded to presidential elections and national issues. The responsiveness of indirect Senate elections is doubly surprising given that Senate candidates were never explicitly listed on the ballot. The role of national forces was mediated by the rules for electing state legislators and in turn by the procedures developed by these bicameral legislatures to select U.S. senators (i.e., nonbinding primaries, joint selection by state legislative chambers). The passage of the Seventeenth Amendment allowed national forces to bypass these state-level mediating institutions and accelerated the responsiveness of Senate elections to national issues.

In Chapter 6 we turn to state legislative elections. The responsiveness of state legislative elections is especially intriguing both in the extent to which these elections were subject to the same structural influences and in their indirect effect on other elections through changes in state electoral laws and the election of U.S. senators. These offices typically fell toward the bottom of the ticket. This would make it easier for voters to split their vote by ripping off the bottom half of the ticket. Also, local rivalries occasionally led to the appearance of dueling party tickets in a district. One party faction, feeling injured, in the district's nominating conventions would print a look-alike ballot that substituted one or more alternative candidates for the lower, less visible offices. With a sizable share of rotten boroughs, marginal changes in party shares would be less consequential for partisan shares of the state legislature. Finally, with bicameral legislatures, we have pairs of chambers that have the same constituency and whose candidates resided on the same ticket, but differed in other potentially consequential ways. The lower chambers, most commonly referred to as the assembly, were larger than the senates, with their members elected to shorter terms and their districts recalibrated more frequently to population changes. Why did some states create rules that insulated and led to one-party dominance (as in the South) while other states wrote rules that accelerated responsiveness to national forces? The literature offers next to nothing on the electoral politics and institutional choices made by these legislatures, a problem we rectify in this chapter.

Chapter 7 examines gubernatorial elections. As the executives of state government, these politicians directed state policy-making in an era when few issues moved up the federal ladder and most state legislatures met part time (B. Campbell 1995). Moreover, governors were central cogs in the state party machinery. They dispensed the ever-important state patronage, oversaw the implementation of election laws, and were the titular head of the party ticket in non-presidential years. Gubernatorial elections also featured a wide range of institutional rules. Some held elections in non-presidential years. Others subjected the governors' office to term limits. These variations in electoral rules shaped the linkages between governors and national political issues.

In Chapter 8 we conclude by analyzing the forces that prompted the dismantling of party ballot regime. Although the party ticket solved the coordination problem of competing for multiple offices in multiple jurisdictions, it also created a series of collective problems for politicians and party leaders. Although leaders needed their supporters to cooperate, these supporters often had incentives to renege on agreements or shirk their obligations. And party leaders had no legal recourse to enforce cooperative behavior among its members. In this concluding chapter, we explain how these strains and stresses of the party ticket system led party leaders down a path of decisions that ultimately dismantled responsive elections.

The Data and Geographical and Temporal Boundaries

Party ballots constituted the critical, distinguishing feature of the nineteenth-century electoral system, but it spawned other consequential rules that comprised the electoral system. These include ballot form, election dates, districting practices, term lengths and limits for state offices, and the presence of nominating primaries. Virtually all of these state rules changed over time, in many instances frequently. Compiling rule changes required scouring state constitutions and statutes, Blue Books, legislative histories, state political histories, and archival newspapers. The result of this effort is a record of every significant change in America's election laws from 1840 to 1940 (except for laws related to suffrage and excluding the South). These are available to interested readers in the Appendix and in a file recording all relevant changes in state constitutions at the following Web site: http://pages.ucsd.edu/~skernell/styled-6/index .html.

With one very large exception, the electoral data were drawn from the ICPSR archives. The exception – the partisan breakdown of voting for both chambers of the state legislatures – had never been compiled. Throughout the nineteenth century, state legislatures resided at the center of America's federalized electoral system. They made the laws that defined their state's electoral system. We searched for these long forgotten election returns in their era's Blue (and Red) Books, in other state legislative manuals, in secretary of states' official reports, at state government archives, and, where official returns were missing, in political almanacs and historical newspapers. We have attempted to unearth results for all of the relevant elections during the century-long period of our study. Our collection, though incomplete, represents the most comprehensive collection of these election returns available. These data are also available at the Web site provided previously. The combination of detailed information on state electoral rules and comprehensive vote results opens a new window into the development of America's electoral institutions and their impact on parties, elections, and governance.

The South

We have omitted the eleven secessionist states of the South from our data collection and statistical analyses. This section of the country was at various points either in rebellion, occupied by federal troops, or beset by waves of violence and intimidation at the polls during "Redemption." From the late 1880s on, a regime of highly restrictive electoral rules disenfranchised whole blocs of the electorate, turning the South into a one-party region that was nonresponsive to national political forces.[1] Including the South in estimating the effects of the party ticket and other rules on elections would obscure the responsiveness of elections in the rest of the United States. Moreover, the disenfranchising institutions of literacy tests, poll taxes, and white primaries were being installed at the same time as ballot reform, rendering hazardous any effort to disentangle their effects. We are mindful, however, of the pivotal role the South played in national party politics. Candidates and party leaders within both national parties factored in the region's electoral votes and heavily Democratic congressional delegations as they contemplated nominations and campaigns.

The Century of Transformation, 1840–1940

Our collection of electoral rules and election returns begins with 1840 for those states already in the Union, and the election following statehood admission for the others. The election of 1840, marking the beginning of the "third party system," is convenient for a couple of reasons. In numerous respects, 1840 marks the culmination of a twenty-year transformation in the nation's

---

[1] Closely connected to the emergence of the one-party South, the book does not include a direct analysis of suffrage related laws. The motivation behind these laws, and their impact with regard to voter turnout, have been expertly charted by political scientists and historians (e.g., Keyssar 2000; Kousser 1974).

electoral system. By 1840, intense party competition between two nationally organized political parties was in place. "The primacy of political parties was the dominant fact of this political era (and of no other). Parties defined the terms of political confrontation and shaped the behavior of most participants in the many levels of political activity," Silbey observes (1991: 8–9).

Despite continuous tinkering in state legislatures and constitutional reform conventions, the electoral system would not fundamentally change until the wave of Australian ballot reform lapped onto America's shores in the 1890s. The party-centered organization of American politics began to unravel as ballot reform replaced the publicly voted party ticket with the privately voted, state supplied ballot.[2] We continue the analysis through the election of 1940 to capture the potential effects of other reforms, including nominating primaries and direct election of senators, and to establish an adequate time series after ballot reform to reliably estimate its effects.

[2] Throughout our discussion we use the terms "party ballot" and "party ticket" interchangeably.

2

The Puzzle of Responsive Elections

The presidential election of 1880 is most often remembered for its violent aftermath. The assassination of President James Garfield, just six months into his administration, by a jilted job seeker, casts a long historical shadow over the election. But what many political scientists will find more intriguing about 1880 is the election itself. It featured one of the highest voter turnouts – 80 percent of eligible voters – and narrowest presidential vote margins in American history. The 8 million presidential votes broke in favor of Garfield by just more than 2,000, yet they were distributed efficiently, allowing him to eke out a narrow Electoral College majority and keep the White House under Republican control. But perhaps the election's most remarkable feature is the breadth of the Republican victory in Congress and across the nation.

Republicans retook control of the House of Representatives for the first time since 1872. Whether Republicans would wrest control of the Senate from Democrats would not be officially decided until the state legislatures convened the following January. Yet Republicans had ample cause for optimism. Of the twenty-seven non-Southern state legislatures elected that year, Republicans won a majority in both legislative chambers in twenty states and split control in two others. Among these wins were bicameral majorities in six legislatures served by lame-duck Democratic senators. Early the following year the final wave of the Republican victory lapped into Washington with the election of the narrowest possible Senate majority – that is, requiring the Republican vice president's tie-breaking vote. Considering the Framers had carefully designed the upper chamber to withstand "impetuous" swings of public sentiment by staggering terms and setting up indirect elections, these results are all the more striking. And yet we can see in Table 2.1 that this outcome was unexceptional for the era. From 1840 until the implementation of the Seventeenth Amendment in 1914, the party winning the presidency also captured or retained control of the Senate on all but two occasions.

TABLE 2.1. *Party Control of Congress and the Presidency*

Session Beginning	President	Senate	House
1841	W	W	W
1845	D	D	D
1849	W	D	D
1853	D	D	D
1857	D	D	D
1861	R	R	R
1865	R	R	R
1869	R	R	R
1873	R	R	R
1877	R	R	D
1881	R	R	R
1885	D	R	D
1889	R	R	R
1893	D	D	D
1897	R	R	R
1901	R	R	R
1905	R	R	R
1909	R	R	R
1913	D	D	D
1917	D	D	D
1921	R	R	R
1925	R	R	R
1929	R	R	R
1933	D	D	D
1937	D	D	D
1941	D	D	D

As linked as the outcomes in Table 2.1 appear, they still understate the extent to which congressional and state elections tracked the presidential vote everywhere but the South – especially during the last quarter of the nineteenth century. In the aftermath of the 1876 election, Republicans ended Reconstruction and withdrew federal troops from the South. By 1880, the Democratic Party held sixty-seven safe House seats and all twenty-two Senate seats in the eleven former Confederate states. This large bloc of seats unavailable to Republicans makes Garfield's success in pulling congressional majorities into office on his coattails all the more impressive.

To better appreciate the responsiveness of elections to presidential voting, we have listed the outcomes of non-Southern congressional and state elections in Table 2.2. (As noted above, we exclude the uncompetitive South from the statistical analysis throughout the book.) Even these figures are somewhat stacked against revealing pervasive presidential coattails. Beyond House elections, the totals in Table 2.2 include offices that were not elected during the presidential

TABLE 2.2. *Presidential Vote and Election Results (Non-South): 1860–1940*[*]

Year	President Party	Percentage Margin	House of Representatives (Non-South) Democrats	House of Representatives (Non-South) Republicans	Governors (Non-South) Democrats	Governors (Non-South) Republicans	State Legislatures (Non-South) Democrats	State Legislatures (Non-South) Republicans	State Legislatures (Non-South) Split	Senate (Non-South) Democrats	Senate (Non-South) Republicans
1860	Republican	10.4	45	106	4	15	5	15	3	15	31
1864	Republican	10.1	**41**	134	1	18	1	20	4	11	39
1868	Republican	5.3	59	120	8	18	6	18	2	7	37
1872	Republican	11.8	73	159	8	17	4	19	3	13	39
1876	Republican	−3.0	74	134	12	15	11	11	5	19	34
1880	Republican	0.1	74	175	7	19	5	20	2	15	37
1884	Democrat	0.3	**105**	132	13	14	7	18	1	12	**41**
1888	Republican	0.8	86	**154**	9	20	6	20		15	37
1892	Democrat	3.1	**138**	124	18	14	10	13	10	**22**	38
1896	Republican	4.3	63	196	4	26	1	22	11	12	46
1900	Republican	6.2	69	193	4	30	4	25	5	7	56
1904	Republican	18.2	43	**245**	8	29	2	30	2	10	58
1908	Republican	7.4	80	213	12	25	3	27	5	10	59
1912	Democrat	18.6	**189**	129	20	17	13	18	6	**29**	44
1916	Democrat	3.1	115	213	16	21	9	23	4	**32**	42
1920	Republican	26.2	34	**295**	4	32	2	30	3	15	**59**
1924	Republican	25.2	82	**244**	12	24	4	28	3	19	**54**
1928	Republican	17.5	68	**262**	7	29	3	31	1	17	**56**
1932	Democrat	17.8	**213**	115	27	8	15	11	9	**37**	36
1936	Democrat	24.3	**235**	87	27	8	18	7	8	**54**	16
1940	Democrat	9.9	**168**	161	18	18	9	17	7	**44**	28

[*] The entries for the president reflect the popular vote across all states. The other columns reflect party control of the respective offices in non-Southern states. Minor parties or independents were excluded. Bold entries for House of Representatives and Senate indicate the party that controlled a majority in the full chamber. In 1916, the Republicans won a plurality of seats in the U.S. House but the Democrats retained majority control with support from Progressives and a Socialist.

Sources: President and U.S. House (Rusk 2001); State Governors and U.S. Senators (*Congressional Quarterly's Guide to U.S. Elections* 975); State legislatures (Dubin (2007).

contest, such as two-thirds of Senate seats. Similarly, the election calendars of numerous gubernatorial and some state legislative elections did not correspond with the president's November, even-year schedule.[1] Despite the presence of numerous decoupled elections in Table 2.2, one can still easily discern a close association between presidential voting and partisan outcomes in Congress and the states.

The 1880 election was a squeaker, but it was no fluke. The second half of the nineteenth century was rife with elections that found similarly small tremors in presidential votes triggering "quakes" throughout the office structure. In 1876 Democratic candidate Samuel Tilden won the national popular vote by an estimated three percentage points but lost the Electoral College vote after the Republican candidate Rutherford B. Hayes was awarded electors in four disputed states: Louisiana, South Carolina, Florida, and Oregon. Even though the election occurred at a time when the Civil War remained a fresh, painful memory for voters, the Democratic Party enjoyed strong gains in both state and national elections. It even established parity in party control of non-Southern state legislatures. In 1892, another three-point win again awarded Democrats control of the House of Representatives and numerous victories in the state capitals. The latter included a majority of the governorships, and in ten of thirty-three non-Southern state legislatures, they held majorities in both chambers and managed to divide party control in ten more. This, in turn, rewarded Democrats with sufficient new Senate seats to take over control of the chamber.

These nineteenth-century elections strike us as extraordinary and puzzling. How did such narrow shifts in popular votes precipitate massive turnover in political power throughout the country? Certainly, one can point to instances during this era in which historic crises understandably stirred up voter revolts. The pressing national issues enveloping the 1860 and 1896 campaigns, for example, provide a clear rationale for the victories Republicans racked up throughout government. Yet one can also find other, less eventful elections in this era, such as 1880 or 1892, which similarly swept the losing presidential candidates' partisans out of office.

In 1880, for instance, the campaign was waged feverishly, but one cannot easily discern an issue that put Republicans over the top. Garfield, a former general and longtime congressman, had secured the nomination at the Republican convention as a last-minute compromise. Although a well-connected party insider, his limited national visibility cast this favorite-son nominee of the Ohio delegation as the quintessential dark horse. Democrats matched Republican's military strategy by nominating their own Civil War hero, General Winfield Hancock. Little in either candidate's political career hinted at serious commitment to any particular party program or policy. In fact, Hancock's boosters trumpeted an absence of such commitments in commending him to competing factions at the Democratic convention (Ackerman 2003). Both

---

[1] In subsequent chapters we take staggered terms and electoral calendars fully into account in analyzing the responsiveness of these offices' elections to the presidential vote.

sides endorsed tariff and civil-service reforms. And Republicans, once more, waved the "bloody shirt," but the issue did not rise above stock rhetoric which Democrats mostly ignored. "There are good reasons for believing that Gen. Garfield's administration will be, like the present one, moderate in policy, though we must regret that civil service reform and free trade have been equally thrust into the background during the campaign, and are evidently not for the moment eagerly desired by any considerable proportion of the American people" concluded one European correspondent's election postmortem (*New York Times*, November 4, 1880).

In keeping with the absence of pressing issues, the national presidential vote swings in this era were a modest 0.1 percentage point in 1880, 0.3 in 1884, 0.8 in 1888, and a whopping 3 percentage points in both 1876 and 1892. And yet all were followed by a widespread removal of the losing party's federal and state officeholders. The occurrence of such landslides within state governments would be easier to understand for the twentieth and twenty-first century elections, where presidential candidates feverishly campaigned on issues hoping not only to win but also to pull in a cadre of partisans and create a mandate for their policies. More recent presidential campaigns have given us the New Freedom, New Deal, Square Deal, New Frontier, Great Society, and a "chicken in every pot." Yet on closer inspection of the record in Table 2.2, twentieth-century swings in party fortunes appear less impressive than did those in the previous century.

Compare the results of Democrat Woodrow Wilson's victory in 1916 by 3.1 percentage points with those springing from the Democrats' nearly identical popular vote victories in 1876 and 1892. Unlike the earlier era's office sweeps, in 1916 Republicans lost the presidency but retained control of a majority of the governorships and both chambers of twenty-three of the thirty-six state legislatures. Simple regression analyses of the presidential votes and seat shares in Table 2.2 confirm that the nineteenth-century vote yielded greater seat returns for each set of offices. Ordinary least squares regression estimates of the relationship between the Democratic presidential vote share and the party's seat share in the House of Representatives are 2.1 percentage points prior to 1900 and 1.7 afterward. For governorships the slopes are 3.8 and 1.7; for unified Democratic control of state legislatures, 3.2 and 1.3; and for the party's share of Senate seats, 1.7 and 1.4, respectively.[2]

Throughout our discussion we refer to election outcomes as *responsive*, in which small shifts in a party's share of the presidential vote are accompanied by large gains or losses in other elections.[3] Moreover, this responsiveness was

---

[2] All coefficients are statistically significant, but given the paucity of observations, the pre- and post-1900 estimates are not statistically different from each other.

[3] Democratic theory and ordinary usage associates responsiveness with the quality of political representation. Responsive representatives act in accord with the welfare of their constituencies. Throughout our discussion, however, we employ a narrower, more technical definition of responsiveness.

pervasive. The repercussions of the party's presidential success could be felt in elections throughout the federal system. The results in Table 2.2 show that the party winning the presidency almost always won a majority of seats in both chambers of Congress and a majority of state governments. In the election of 1880, in sixteen of the nineteen states where voters preferred Garfield over Hancock, Republicans won control of both the legislature and governorship. Similarly, in all but two of the nineteen states won by Hancock, Democrats captured control of state government. Modern elections stand in stark contrast. In 2004, by contrast, in only about a third of the states did the party winning the statewide presidential vote also capture unified control of state government.

Searching for clues for the pervasive responsiveness of the nineteenth century, we consulted both modern political science and standard narrative histories of presidential elections. By and large they proved unhelpful. The primary conditions students of comparative elections identify to explain responsive elections largely fail to account for their pronounced presence in America's nineteenth-century elections. Unitary, parliamentary systems, particularly those with representatives partitioned into single-member plurality districts are commonly associated with highly responsive elections (Morgenstern, Swindle, and Castagnola 2009). This classic type of institutional configuration is commonly referred to as the Westminster model, which we will revisit later in the chapter. With its presidential system and healthy federalism, the only structural feature the American electoral system has in common with the Westminster model are single-member, plurality elections.

Another, frequently cited contributor to responsiveness is nationalization. "The more nationally oriented the politics of a country or the more nationalized the forces prevailing in a given election," concludes Tufte (1973: 547), "the greater the [responsiveness]." Where the electorate is nationalized, issues will break similarly for the parties' candidates across electoral districts. This in turn increases the chances that even small partisan swings in the vote will win a disproportionate share of offices. Yet, here too, America's nineteenth-century elections fail to hew to expectations. Despite immigration-fueled population growth and diversity, a poor communications and transportation infrastructure appears to have kept Americans centered on the parochial concerns of community and region.

Two veins of electoral history offer clues about the sources of nineteenth-century responsiveness. The first investigates "critical elections" (Schattschneider 1942; Key 1955; Burnham 1970a; Nardulli 1995) – landslide presidential elections that appear to have prompted a massive realignment of voters' party loyalties. The elections of 1860, 1896, and 1932 belong on everyone's short list of elections that realigned party affiliations. All were accompanied by highly charged policy questions that separated the parties and broke in favor of the winner. Although what these exceptional elections can tell us about responsiveness during normal times is limited, they do remind us that nineteenth-century voters appear to have been capable – at least on occasion – of focusing on

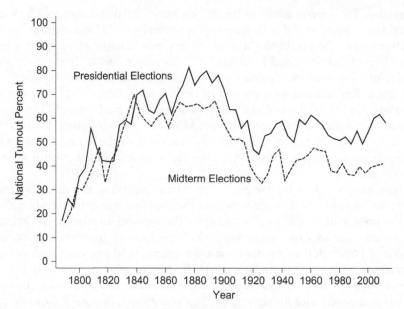

FIGURE 2.1. Turnout in National Elections, 1879–2012.
Note: Data for 1788–1998 comes from Rusk (2001). Data for 2000–2012 comes from the "United States Election Project," retrieved from http://elections.gmu.edu.

national issues. Whether policy disagreements over a limited national agenda normally conferred a competitive advantage to one of the candidates is questionable. We devote Chapter 3 to investigating the role of policy issues and administration performance in generating national swings in party fortunes.

A second vein of electoral history that examines important precursors of electoral responsiveness emphasizes the ethnocultural basis of party support and presidential voting. Here, identity politics quadrennially stimulated keen party competition, intense voter loyalty, high turnout, and narrow electoral margins.

Nineteenth-Century Elections as Identity Politics

Alexis de Tocqueville was only one of many nineteenth-century visitors from Europe who marvelled at the enthusiasm with which Americans engaged in their young democracy's civic life. Ordinary citizens opined freely about national politics and did so with a notable lack of deference to their elected officeholders. They backed up their opinions by voting. By the early 1830s almost all adult white males held the franchise, and by all accounts, the vast majority exercised it. As shown in Figure 2.1, more than three-quarters of eligible voters on average cast ballots in presidential elections from 1868 until early in the twentieth century.[4] This compares to less than 60 percent in the modern era. What makes this figure so impressive is that many nineteenth-century voters must have found voting highly inconvenient. The 1850 census reported nearly two-thirds of Americans living on farms, with another signifi-cant fraction living in small towns or hamlets, which might be some distance from the county courthouse or the nearest polling place. Stacked against these real costs were seemingly modest benefits. The outcome of most elections had a negligible impact on the welfare of a vast majority of those who voted. Why would Americans living in "island communities" (Wiebe 1967) dispersed across a vast landscape care so much about national elections to endure what for many was the considerable inconvenience that voting entailed? And could whatever motivated them to go to the polls help account for the era's responsive elections?

The case for identity politics spans the entire century under study here. It begins with nativism and antislavery in the 1840s and 1850s (Carwardine 1993) and stretches all the way to the adoption of the Eighteenth Amendment prohibiting the sale of alcohol in 1920 (Szymanski 2003). "Conflicting and mutually exclusive dispositions toward cultural pluralism among subgroups structured partisan combat and gave psychological meaning to party identifi-cations in the late nineteenth century," writes Kleppner (1979: 237). He then projects these fundamentals onto the political arena by observing that "Party battles did not reflect a broad consensus over fundamentals but an irreconcil-able conflict over the very nature of the society." Hays (1981: 254) extends identity politics beyond towns to the national stage: "The nationalization of 'constituent parties'... rested largely on ethnocultural identity." And finally, the "intense feelings of partisanship" these cleavages incited "produced high turnout rate, stable coalitions, and close outcomes" (Kleppner 1981: 140). All of these are commonly cited as distinguishing features of the era's elections, and the last as being an essential ingredient in responsive elections.

No student of America's electoral history has been more impressed by the participation of citizens in the nineteenth century, or for that matter, more troubled by its sharp turn-of-the-century decline, than Walter Dean Burnham. Citing the era's exceptionally high turnout rates and normally close division of the two-party vote, he asserts: "The 19th century American political system, for its day, was incomparably the most thoroughly democratized of any in the world. The development of vigorous party competition extended from individual localities to the nation itself" (Burnham 1965: 24). The takeaway for us is that the era's exceptional democracy created fertile ground for responsive elections.

In Burnham's history intense partisan commitment motivated vast numbers to march to the polls to reaffirm their fealty to one of the political parties.

---

[4] We qualify this figure because appearances could be deceptive; by some estimates, up to seven percentage points of these turnout rates consisted of some form of fraudulent votes (Rusk 1974).

Of course, the kinds of individual-level data required to probe motivational basis of participation – or even to establish, as virtually all historians of the era assume, that voters were strong partisans – do not exist.[5] Although acknowledging "scant" evidence, Burnham (1965: 18) buys into ethnocultural history's depiction of Americans as holding ardent loyalties that "had their roots in a cohesive and persistent set of positive and negative group referents."[6] He does not consider that participation might have had less to do with voters' motivation than with the concerted efforts of political parties to mobilize them. Below, we argue that America's nineteenth-century politicians had compelling reasons to expend extraordinary effort and resources to identify and transport loyal voters to the polls. In our scheme political parties replace Burnham's voters as the central actors.

Without survey information, Burnham is forced to dissect election returns for clues about the motivational underpinnings of elections. In an imaginative, albeit problematic, statistical analysis, Burnham estimates higher participation and stronger partisanship among nineteenth-century voters than among their early twentieth-century counterparts. For Burnham, partisanship and participation are intimately connected; the former motivates the latter.[7] He estimates that from about two-thirds to three-quarters of the eligible electorate consistently cast ballots for their party's candidate list.[8] These voters constituted the parties' core constituency. When parties faltered, they did so because these core supporters stayed home and not because they switched sides. Lopsided outcomes, Burnham (1965: 22) observes, are "associated with a pronounced and one-sided decline in turnout." For Burnham the "abundance of core" voters allowed party politicians to forgo persuasion and instead concentrate their energies on mobilization. Later in the chapter, we offer a different rationale for mobilization and high turnout based not on intense partisanship but on the strategic calculations of party politicians who decided whether to invest resources in mobilizing certifiably reliable voters. By *certifiable* we are referring to the ability of party agents to observe voters showing up at the polls and voting correctly.

By the end of the first decade of the twentieth century, turnout was sharply declining and Burnham's indicators – roll-off in voting down the ballot, midterm election drop-off in turnout, and split-ticket voting in presidential

---

[5] Actually, limited individual-level data have been unearthed in county directories. For thirteen Indiana and Illinois counties these sources list local residents' party affiliation in biographical sketches. See DeCanio (2007).

[6] Earlier in his voluminous writings, Burnham appeared more inclined to emphasize social class over ethnicity and religion as the basis of the electorate's politicization, but whatever its foundation, high turnout, he consistently argues, sprang from voters' intense democratic spirit.

[7] Ironically, however, Burnham's causal narrative of the largest partisan swings, those that come at critical elections, is told wholly in terms of mass partisan conversion of classes of voters.

[8] According to Burnham's ecological analysis, roughly 10 percent floated between the parties, with the remaining 15–20 percent not voting.

elections – were registering diminished voter enthusiasm. In the 1920s turnout in presidential elections had declined to its modern levels of about 60 percent. No longer did parties concentrate their energies in identifying enthusiastic voters and ushering them to the polls. Torchlight parades gave way to advertising and "educational" campaigns based on literature presenting the candidates' issue positions and touting their integrity – at least their comparative advantage over the opposition's rascals (McGerr 1988, Summers 2000).

Voters had not changed, but according to Burnham and others (Josephson 1938; Kleppner 1981), a new set of actors that sought to rein in the growing and highly politicized electorate had ascended to power within both parties and government. During the 1890s, Burnham (1965: 24) writes, "American industrializing elites were, and felt themselves to be, uniquely vulnerable to an anti-industrialist assault which could be carried out peacefully and in the absence of effective legal or customary sanctions by a citizenry possessing at least two generations' experience with political democracy."[9] Similarly, Kleppner (1981: 141) concludes that

by the late 1870s modernizing corporate elites demanded more of the political system than inducements to growth and negative safeguards against restriction. They sought the capacity to intervene actively to consolidate and rationalize the corporate system.... The assault on party organizations, the efforts to strip them of some of the functions they performed, and the exaltation of "independence of party" into a secular ethic were all aspects of the effort to rationalize and stabilize the public policymaking process ... [to] make sure that the new electoral system was one [with] ... the displacement of parties as instruments of mass mobilization and of popular government.

By the end of the nineteenth century these elites had "penetrated" and taken "control" of both major political parties. Unnerved by populism and the specter of Democratic bosses marching the swelling immigrant mobs to the polls, Republican business elites took advantage of their party's 1896 landslide victory throughout the country to rewrite electoral laws to tamp down mass democracy under the banner of good government reform.[10] Voter registration laws and poll taxes, ostensibly targeting fraud, disproportionately weeded out less-skilled (as in English language skills) and more easily manipulated citizens. During the late nineteenth and early twentieth centuries, waves of reforms – civil service, secret ballot, nomination through primary elections, and nonpartisan local elections – shrank the electorate either directly or indirectly by stripping political parties of resources essential to successful mobilization.

---

[9] Later, Burnham (1974) proffers a less concertedly conspiratorial effort of party elites. This milder, more generational version of the argument contends that the shift from mobilization to education came more gradually and reflected as much societal changes as political reforms.

[10] Beyond ballot reform, these reformers successfully pushed for voter registration laws.

This history represents an extraordinary turn of events. Economic elites succeeded in knocking party bosses off their horses, not by exposing corruption and other venalities, but by instituting barriers to participation. Although Burnham's story is consistent with the motivations he attributes to the emerging corporate elite, it offers little direct evidence as to who these elites were and how they managed to eviscerate party machines – the same organizations that for decades had effectively turned out legions of supporters.

An Institutional Explanation for America's Responsive Elections

In contrast to Burnham's epic history populated with its politically engaged citizens who, after being courted by party bosses for decades, are ultimately confined to passivity by capitalist barons, we present an electoral history rooted in the nation's electoral laws and rules. Our explanation emphasizes the role of political institutions in shaping campaign strategies that recruited voters and subsequently in allocating the resulting votes across offices. The process by which a presidential candidate's victory was efficiently manufactured into extensive lower office victories involved two specific sets of electoral machinery. The first consisted of party ticket voting – specifically, publicly casting a party supplied ballot listing the party's presidential and lower office candidacies. A second set of machinery then allocated these votes across legislative offices in a manner that maximized the winning party's share of seats. Here, we are referring to congressional and state legislative districting laws. Where the political parties in a state were competitive, small changes in popular votes from one election to the next could dramatically shift party control of the state legislature as well as the state's congressional delegation. These institutions jointly produced some of the most responsive elections ever recorded.

The presence of electoral machinery producing strong coattails and disproportionate office victories to the plurality winner was no historical coincidence. Voters, publicly casting party supplied tickets, offered politicians the opportunity to seek out and commit supporters and assure that they voted. All of this required a great deal of effort and no small expense in canvassing the citizenry and subsequently ushering those identified as supporters to the polls. And where victory was too close to call, the marginal costs could escalate sharply as the parties ferreted out their supporters who were least likely to vote or as they compensated uncommitted voters to show up and deposit their party's ballot. Whatever the ante, the institutional mechanisms that heaped offices on the plurality winner prompted party politicians to go all in when they decided that doing so gave them a good chance of winning.

The Institutions Manufacturing Responsive Elections

Coattails: Presidential Votes → Ballot Form → Votes for Lower Offices
Vote-Seat
Conversion: Votes for Lower Offices → Swing Ratio → Winning Lower Offices

Coattail Voting and the Party Ticket

By the mid-1840s submission of a party supplied ticket had largely replaced voice voting as the standard means whereby voters declared their preferences at the polls. The party ticket appeared in the 1820s as an efficient remedy to the increasingly cumbersome viva voce declarations of a growing electorate. Partisan newspapers published tickets and party hawkers handed them out to voters near polling places. As with voice voting, citizens continued to vote publicly. This gave a party's poll watchers the opportunity to both guard against opposition shenanigans and check that pledged voters honored their commitment – in many instances, commitment based on financial considerations.

During presidential elections the ticket's standard format featured the presidential nominee's name and/or image; during midterm and off-year elections, the party's gubernatorial or some other statewide candidate would be prominently displayed. Typically, the head of a ticket was followed by the names of all the party's candidates to lower offices. Figure 2.2 displays a typical nineteenth-century party ticket. The great majority of these ballots consolidated national and state elections onto a single paper form, although political parties in a few states, such as Ohio for some period (Bensel 2004), printed separate forms for state and federal offices. A different electoral calendar might keep local races off the ticket, but where election calendars were the same for all offices, the presidential ballot might list candidates for a dozen or more lower offices.[11]

The result was strong presidential coattails. The term "coattail voting" was already familiar when young Abraham Lincoln, serving his only term in the House of Representatives, took to the chamber floor to chastise Democrats for criticizing his party's nomination of a popular military figure for president: "The Democratic gentleman from Georgia says, we [Whigs] have deserted all our principles, and taken shelter under General [Zachary] Taylor's military coat tail . . . He has no acquaintance with the ample military coat tail of General [Andrew] Jackson?" (Safire 1978, 125).

Coattail voting refers to the degree to which a voters' preference for a candidate to a major office, such as president or governor, influences their choices among candidates for other offices. In the modern setting, coattail voting represents a kind of affinity relation voters draw between a party's standard bearer and others who wear the same party label. In the nineteenth century, voters did not need to make this connection; the party ticket forged one for them. Indeed, the party ticket discouraged voters from thinking about their vote in any way other than supporting the party team of their preferred presidential candidate. A voter inclined to support candidates from different parties faced an ordeal. He might literally split the parties' tickets and submit

---

[11] A consolidated ticket listing all offices presented a logistical challenge, as a different ballot was needed for every combination of races. One town's ballot would differ from the one next door; even within communities, different tickets might be needed where the boundaries of state legislative districts split communities and county and city council offices were districted.

FIGURE 2.2. National, State, and Local Ballot: 1876 Massachusetts

the different fragments that contained his preferred candidates.[12] Or he might scratch out a candidate's name and pencil in his preference. Otherwise, the ticket system induced coattail voting as the default outcome.

Electoral Calendars

Coupling candidates on a coattail required that they all stand for election at the same time. Not all states, however, held congressional and state elections on the same day as the presidential election. Contributing to the decentralization of nineteenth-century elections, states were free to establish the times of their elections (James 2007; Stonecash, Boscarino, and Kersh 2007). This patchwork electoral calendar was a direct result of the Constitution's federal election provision: Article I, Section 4 assigned state legislatures the responsibility for choosing the "Times, Places, and Manner of Holding Elections." Consequently, states retained wide discretion in deciding when to hold elections.[13] Figure 2.3a shows that before the Civil War, numerous states exercised the option to separate congressional and state elections from the presidential election.

Where candidates stood for election at the same time, the impact of presidential coattails was direct. But the presidential campaign also intruded into the fall elections prior to November, particularly those held in September and October. Figure 2.3b displays a majority of states conducting fall elections (September through the presidential election) for different offices. A variety of evidence suggests that both voters and the political parties treated voting on these two nearby dates as if they were twin prongs of the same election. Turnout in September and October congressional elections was 6 percent higher during presidential election years compared to those states' midterm elections. Political news coverage in Cleveland, Ohio – an October state until 1886 – throughout each of the 1840, 1860, and 1876 election cycles focused almost wholly on the presidency and the presidential election (Kernell and Jacobson 1987). When Abraham Lincoln admonished fellow Whigs (see Box 2.2) to recontact every first-round voter to make sure they turned out in the presidential election, he made the point that calendar broken tickets simply represented the election's second stage.[14]

---

[12] In our searches through library archives and Ebay listings, we have found few incomplete tickets. All that we did spot had the bottom of the ticket torn off. To our knowledge no state laws during this era either proscribed ticket splitting or prescribed a procedure for voting a split ticket.

[13] In 1792, Congress narrowly circumscribed the dates for selecting presidential electors. States were required to choose electors "within the 34 days preceding the first Wednesday in December of each presidential year" (*Congressional Quarterly's Guide to U.S. Elections* 1975: 208). Congress went one step further in 1845, consolidating the selection of presidential electors onto a single date: the first Tuesday after the first Monday in November. According to Argersinger (1992: 44), the practice of repeat voting prompted the consolidation: "With elections scheduled on different days in different states, illegal voting by repeaters became common and in 1840 and 1844 both parties organized gangs of voters who went from state to state."

[14] In Chapters 4, 5, 6, and 7 we find that a significant but also significantly weaker coattail effect for fall elections held prior to the presidential election.

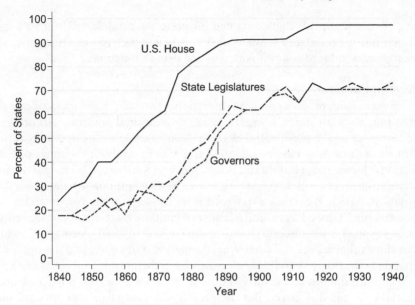

FIGURE 2.3a. Electoral Calendars: November Elections

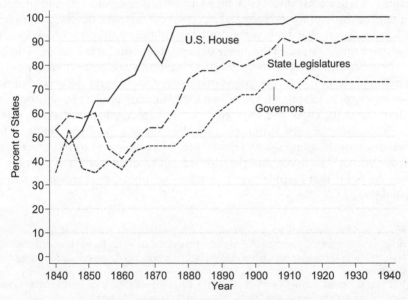

FIGURE 2.3b. Electoral Calendars: Fall Elections

By the latter part of the nineteenth century, states increasingly moved their congressional and state elections to coincide with the November federal election. The impetus for greater consolidation came with enactment of a federal law in 1872 requiring congressional elections to be held (with minor exceptions)

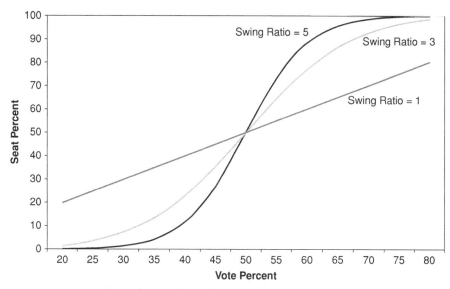

FIGURE 2.4. Hypothetical Swing Ratios In Two-Party Competition

on the first Tuesday after the first Monday of November. Over time, election calendars for both the House and state offices converged on the presidential election date with only minor exceptions (e.g., Maine).

The increasing consolidation of the electoral calendar over the nineteenth century raises a number of important implications for responsiveness. Most important, it heightened the value of mobilizing voters. As much as anything else, the trend toward consolidated calendars may account for the feverish campaigns that prevailed throughout the last quarter of the nineteenth century.

Converting Votes into Seats

Coattail voting represents only the first cog in the electoral machinery that transformed presidential votes into partisan control of Congress and the state governments. Presidential coattails and national issues will decide party control of a legislature only if they cover pivotal votes in individual districts. In tipping narrow losses into narrow victories electoral rules may be decisive. To gauge the efficiency with which the electoral system converts votes into control of offices, political scientists have devised the swing ratio. Briefly, the *swing ratio* measures the *degree* to which a marginal change in the party's share of the vote changes its share of legislative seats. The greater the impact of vote changes on seat changes the larger the swing ratio.

Figure 2.4 presents swing ratios for several hypothetical election outcomes. A swing ratio of 1 indicates, of course, the linear one-to-one correspondence between vote and seat shares (proportional representation). The greater the share of seats a party gets on crossing the 50 percent threshold, the larger the swing ratio. For instance, a swing ratio of 3 translates into a 15 percent seat advantage, when a party wins 55 percent of the popular two-party vote. For a swing ratio of 5, the advantage in seat shares climbs to 25 percent.

So according to this metric, responsive elections occur when elections are competitive and vote margins shift uniformly across districts. After comparing the swing ratios of a number of two-party systems, Tufte (1973) concluded that the classic Westminster-styled parliamentary election represents the ideal electoral arrangement for generating responsive elections. In such a system a relatively homogeneous electorate weighs the appeals of two programmatic political parties and shifts its aggregate vote preferences similarly across districts. For the post–World War II era, New Zealand and the United Kingdom averaged swing ratios of 2.3 and 2.8, respectively (Tufte 1973).

The Westminster model generates the kinds of swing ratios we seek to account for in America's nineteenth-century elections. But this model only deepens the puzzle of America's responsive elections. Aside from the presence of plurality districts, the Westminster model and America's electoral system have little in common. The former presupposes a homogenous national electorate, mirrored in the districts that shift together with the national political breezes. The United States, we learn from ethnocultural history, does not fit this mold. American society was heterogeneous, with regionalism accentuating ethnic and cultural identities. America's national parties were loose confederations of state and local parties cobbled together with ambiguous campaign appeals and creed rather than party manifestos.

So how do the swing ratios for America's nineteenth-century elections waged by decentralized national parties compare? Extraordinarily well, it turns out. Removing the politically unresponsive South, America's nineteenth-century elections swamped those of the classic Westminster systems. The dramatic changes in swing ratios over the course of American political history can be seen in the annual plots of U.S. House elections from 1850 to 2004 in Figure 2.5.[15] In the 1880s and 1890s congressional elections consistently produced ratios of 5 and higher, indicating a 5 percent swing in the partisan distribution of seats for each 1 percent shift in the national vote. These results present a striking anomaly for the Westminster explanation, which neither Tufte, nor to our knowledge, anyone else has sought to resolve. By the 1920s the swing ratio plummeted from over 5 in the 1880s to well under 3, where it has remained.

Underlying the late nineteenth-century's large swing ratios were the vast number of close elections throughout the non-South. At no time or place was

---

[15] Swing ratios can be calculated longitudinally and as in Figure 2.5, cross-sectionally where it is calculated as the expected change in the Democratic seat share given a one percent change in the districts' Democratic vote. Throughout the book we estimate the time-series relationship of an office's vote as a function of the *presidential* vote.

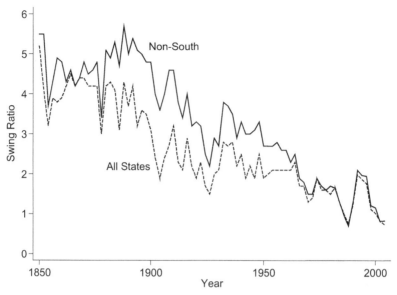

FIGURE 2.5. The Swing Ratio in U.S. House Elections
Sources: 1850–1980, Brady and Grofman (1991); 1982–2004 authors' estimates

competition keener and elections for Congress and for the state legislatures more competitive than during this period. With numerous state and congressional districts evenly balanced between the parties, a slight shift in national opinion could tip numerous districts to the other party's column (Brady 1988). In the 1880 Pennsylvania congressional elections, the Republican percentage of the statewide vote was a narrow 53 percent, yet they managed to capture nineteen of the twenty-seven House races. The boost from Garfield's candidacy pushed Republican candidacies over the top, but it was the pre-existing tight competition across numerous districts that allowed his coattails to be decisive.

A variety of possible causes could have promoted continuously tight elections throughout this era. Party politicians' ravenous appetite for patronage, a highly divisible good, might have tightened competition in a couple of different ways, depending on local circumstances.[16] Unlike ideological goods, patronage and money gleaned from government employees and customs house coffers were fungible. Factions that opposed each other on other issues found in spoils reason enough to coalesce behind a common banner. And it helped cement awkward alliances within the governing party administration. As the slavery issue pulled the Democratic Party asunder during the last days of the Buchanan administration, the president lavished patronage on the party's warring northern

[16] By some estimates, President Cleveland dispensed 350,000 federal appointments during his second administration (James 2006).

and southern wings in what proved a futile attempt to keep Democrats together (Nichols 1948).

Yet patronage was so coveted, it frequently became the bone of contention within the parties. The vast majority of the numerous factional fights at state party conventions involved either disagreement over the distribution of state and federal patronage or nominations of those who would supervise its distribution in the future.[17] It sometimes took the form of a majority faction, apparently confident that alone it could win the next election, rejecting other factions' aspiring candidates in order to reserve more of the spoils of victory to itself (Riker 1982).

Risk-Accepting Districting Strategies

Another likely source of close elections during this era might lie in the manipulation of electoral districts. As parties competed for offices and the rewards they conferred, majority parties in the states tweaked district boundaries and other rules in an effort to squeeze as many victories as possible from small vote pluralities. Unlike modern state governments, which redraw congressional and state districts at regular ten-year intervals under the watchful eye of the federal courts, their nineteenth- and twentieth-century counterparts enjoyed far greater latitude in deciding when and how to redistrict.[18] For every year between 1872 and 1896 at least one state redrew its congressional district boundaries (Engstrom 2006; 2013). In Ohio as party control in the legislature swung back and forth, new party majorities made enacting a new congressional district plan their first order of business. The legislature redrew the state's congressional districts seven times between 1878 and 1892.

In addition to freedom in the timing of drawing district boundaries, states enjoyed much greater discretion in how to draw districts. In this era before court-mandated one-person, one-vote requirements, state legislators were not bound to create equally populated districts. For House districts, controlling state parties sought to maximize their seat shares by drawing numerous competitive, yet winnable, districts. In Maine in 1884, the Republicans redrew the state's four congressional districts and won every district for the next five elections with an average victory margin of only 4 percent (Engstrom 2006). In 1886, Ohio Republicans drew new congressional district maps that secured them fifteen of twenty-one seats (73 percent) with only 53 percent of the statewide vote. This efficient gerrymandering strategy maximized the number of seats state parties won with a given vote share and accentuated the electoral system's overall competitiveness (Cox and Katz 2002).

---

[17] We return to this issue with evidence in Chapter 8.

[18] The U.S. Supreme Court ruled the malapportionment of state legislative districts unconstitutional in the 1962 decision *Baker v. Carr*. The Court extended this ruling to U.S. House districts two years later in the *Wesberry v. Sanders* decision (1964).

Systematic Partisan Swings across Races

Single-member plurality districts imply no more than locally competitive two-party contests (e.g., Cox 1997; Duverger 1954; Rae 1967; Schattschneider 1942). In order for presidential coattails and national issues to alter partisan control of Congress and the state governments, candidate appeals and national issues needed to similarly swing voter sentiment across districts. The evidence presented throughout this book is that they did. But this introduces the question, "What forces were at work in nineteenth-century America generating systematic national partisan swings? On initial consideration, nineteenth-century presidential campaigns appear to have offered weak cues for stimulating voters to weigh national issues. For much of the era the national economy consisted of regional economies with different dominant products and markets loosely stitched together. And unlike their twentieth-century counterparts, this era's presidents played a distinctly subordinate role in formulating domestic policy. All of this leads us to question whether and how presidential campaigns channeled national forces and swung party fortunes.

Pressing national issues rarely dominated national elections. Exceptions were occasional wartime issues, the extension of slavery into the territories; and a depression that dominated the 1894 and 1896 elections. Moreover, the electorate was heterogeneous and much of it geographically isolated. Region, state, and community separated voters and would appear to have prevented national forces from generating similar partisan swings. America's decentralized political parties, which reserved nominations for the constituency party, reinforced localism and regionalism.

The slavery issue deeply separated Southerners' responses from those of voters throughout the rest of the nation. Other national issues, where salient, could also elicit regional responses. These included public works and war with Mexico during the antebellum era and, after the Civil War, regulation of the railroads, currency, tariff, immigration and temperance. Yet responsive elections, pervasive across the country, were commonplace. Finally, the reverse pattern in early twentieth-century presidential elections deepens the puzzle. Just as the president's policies and performance were becoming standard campaign fare, presidential elections began having a noticeably weaker impact on congressional and state elections.

The Reformed Electoral Regime

During the late nineteenth and early twentieth centuries, elections were dramatically transformed. Ballot reform brought an end to the party ticket. It was replaced by a state supplied ballot marked by voters in a private voting booth. As ballot reform disassembled the machinery of responsive elections, one may fairly question why those politicians who thrived with the party ticket would ever agree to reform.

Historians and political scientists have entertained two possibilities to account for reform. Though they appear antithetical, both could be true. The traditional explanation has irrepressible progressive reformers prevailing over the rear guard efforts of machine politicians. The second is more complicated. Party politicians grasped popular ballot reform as a way to solve serious internal management problems that had became increasingly severe toward the end of the nineteenth century. In addition to giving state agencies, a state printed ballot ruled out down-ticket substitution of candidates preferred by a local party organization. The various regulations that states enacted to administer the new state ballots also served the purposes of party politicians by setting entry barriers for independent candidacies and splinter-party and fusion-party movements (Argersinger 1992).[19]

Just how intractable these problems had become is difficult to know. The historical record offers numerous anecdotes of self-destructive party breeches. The presence of alternative ballots presumably caused some voters to split their ticket unwittingly. In 1882, Kansas Democrats managed to distribute sufficient bogus ballots to win the gubernatorial election for the first time (Argersinger 1992). Another common practice for breaking into the party ticket took the form of "pasters." Bolting factions seeking to elect a local favorite instead of the party's nominee would supply voters with the standard ballot with a tab pasting in the local favorite's name over that of the party's official nominee. Figure 2.6 displays a ticket with a paster neatly attached, presumably by the bolting organization.

These subterfuges became so widespread, parties took countermeasures. To ward off corrupted ballots, parties printed their ballots on colorful paper and in some instances perfumed the paper, allowing poll watchers to sniff out bogus ballots. Contending with a rash of factional rebellions, San Francisco's Democratic machine took the precaution of oiling its tickets so that pasters would not adhere (Bensel 2000).

The increasing consolidation of offices onto a single ballot compounded the collective action tensions inherent in the party ticket system. The ticket required cooperation, but the strategic interests of local politicians and their backers often diverged from their state and national counterparts. As calendars converged, they magnified the rewards of running with a standard bearer with long coattails but also the risks of running against an opponent sporting similarly long coattails. Throughout our discussion we will allude to some of these problems and suggest how they might have motivated reform, but we save for the Conclusion a full assessment of the external forces and strategic considerations that led party politicians to dismantle the party ballot system.

---

[19] Petition requirements varied greatly. Some made it next to impossible for even established third parties to field candidates. California's ballot petition required the number of signatures equal to 5 percent of the previous election's vote. Moreover, many of the petition forms were complex and easily disqualified (Fredman 1968).

Democratic Ticket.

FOR GOVERNOR,

MARTIN V. B. EDGERLY.

For Railroad Commissioners,

THOMAS C. GREY,
ALDEN B. SMITH,
HENRY A. EMERSON.

For Representative in Congress,

JEWETT D. HOSLEY.

For Councilor,

JONATHAN H. DICKEY.

For Senator,

HIRAM PARKER.

For County Officers,

JOHN Q. JONES, Sheriff.
DON H. WOODWARD, Solicitor.
OBED G. DORT, Treasurer.
MURRAY V. WRIGHT, Register of Deeds.
LEWIS J. COLONY, Register of Probate.
AARON D. HAMMOND, ⎫
REUBEN L. ANGIER, ⎬ Commissioners.
SAMUEL D. BEMIS, ⎭

FIGURE 2.6. Splitting the Ticket: Paster

The Australian Ballot

The ballot reform movement swept the nation starting in 1888. By 1910 all (non-Southern) states had replaced the party ticket with some form of the Australian ballot. The two distinguishing features of the reform were private voting and a state supplied ballot listing the various political parties' candidates for each of the offices.

States differed both in the timing and type of reform ballot they adopted (see Table 2.3).[20] Of the different formats, the favorite of progressive reformers was the office bloc (Figure 2.7a). It prevented automatic or easy party voting by forcing voters first to identify the office and then, within that office's bloc, choose a candidate.[21] Its main alternative, which as of 1900 three-quarters of the state legislatures favored, is the party column ballot. Aligning a party's candidates for the various offices into a single column, this format made it easy for those wishing to vote a straight ticket to do so. In many states the party column ballot included a party box at the top that allowed voters to cast a straight ticket with one mark (Figure 2.7b).

In addition to these basic forms, numerous variations were tested and discarded during the early years. Figure 2.7c shows an office bloc format, which departs significantly from the reformers' plan by allowing voters to declare a party preference. Where voters wrote in a party preference, their vote would revert to the party in those races where they failed to select a candidate. This ballot, first adopted in Colorado, fell into disrepute when critics charged that party workers were trying to identify individual voters by their handwriting.

Maine devised a ballot format (see Figure 2.7d) widely acknowledged as most likely to induce straight ticket voting. Unlike the party column ballot, this ballot offered voters no space for checking their preferred candidate, but ample space for checking the party column. Voters who wished to split their ballot had to erase the name of the candidate in the column they checked and write in the name of the preferred candidate. Finally, a format that began auspiciously with early adoptions in Connecticut (1889) was the *shoestring* ballot. This involved the state printing party tickets on the same-sized common stock paper, making it relatively easy for a voter to substitute one ticket for another. Party workers distributed these tickets, and the fact that

---

[20] Following closely on the heels of the Australian ballot, party nominating conventions were reformed out of existence during the first two decades of the twentieth century. Although the first direct primary appeared in 1842 in Crawford County, PA (albeit limited in scope), the major push for nomination reform started at the turn of the century. The first state sanctioned primary was in Minnesota in 1899, initially only covering part of the states and a few elective offices. Nevertheless, the reform quickly gathered steam, and by 1910 nearly half of the states had adopted a statewide direct primary law, and by 1920 almost every state had converted over.

[21] Some secretaries of state and election boards employed differently sized and shaped boxes to force voters to concentrate on locating offices and then candidates, presumably reducing voters' propensity to vote the straight party ticket.

TABLE 2.3. *Adoption of Australian Ballot Reforms*

Year	State	Ballot Form
1888	Massachusetts	Office Block (**OB**)
	Kentucky	OB; Party Column (**PC**) (1892)
1889	Indiana	PC
	Minnesota	OB
	Missouri	PC
	Montana (1889)	OB; PC (1895); OB (1939)
	Rhode Island	OB; PC (1905)
	Wisconsin	OB; PC (1891)
1890	Maryland	PC; OB (1901)
	Oklahoma (1907)	PC
	Vermont	OB; PC (1906)
	Washington (1889)	OB; PC (1891)
	Wyoming (1890)	OB; PC (1911)
1891	Arizona (1912)	OB; PC (1895)
	California	PC; OB (1911)
	Colorado	PC; OB (1899)
	Delaware	PC
	Idaho (1890)	PC
	Illinois	PC
	Maine	PC
	Michigan	PC
	Nebraska	OB
	Nevada	OB
	New Hampshire	OB; PC (1897)
	North Dakota (1889)	OB; PC (1893)
	Ohio	PC
	Oregon	OB
	Pennsylvania	PC; OB (1903)
	South Dakota (1889)	OB; PC (1893)
	West Virginia	PC
1892	Iowa	PC
1893	Kansas	PC; OB (1913)
1895	New York	PC; OB (1913)
1896	Utah (1896)	PC
1905	New Mexico (1912)	PC
1909	Connecticut	PC
1911	New Jersey	OB; PC (1930)

Note: Dates in parentheses identify states admitted after ballot reforms began. The following states initially limited the new ballot to certain localities and later applied it statewide: Kentucky (initially applied only to Louisville, statewide 1892), Minnesota (initially towns more than 10,000, statewide in 1891), Missouri (initially towns more than 5000, statewide in 1891), Wisconsin (initially towns more than 50,000, statewide in 1893), and Maryland (initially applied to Baltimore, statewide in 1892). New Mexico (1905–1927) and Missouri (1897–1921) provided separate ballots for each party, but these were printed and supplied by the government, and included secrecy provisions. We code these as party column ballots. Multiple ballot forms listed in order adopted. For more details on ballot laws, see Ludington (1911) and Albright (1942).

GOVERNOR.	Mark One.
Charles T. Apgar..Prohibition	
Samuel E. Brigges..Socialist	
Arthur Fuller..Democratic	
Henry Zabriskie..Republican	

LIEUTENANT-GOVERNOR.	Mark One.
Howard Arnold..Republican	
Clarence P. Snyder..Socialist	
George Van Derzee..Prohibition	
John W. Young..Democratic	

FIGURE 2.7a. Early Reform Ballot Designs: Standard Office Bloc

REPUBLICAN.		DEMOCRATIC.	
O		O	
	Governor, Henry Zabriskie.		Governor, Arthur Fuller.
	Lieutenant-Governor, Howard Arnold.		Lieutenant-Governor, John W. Young.
	Secretary of State, Edward Marshall.		Secretary of State, Steven Byrne.
	State Treasurer, S. Frederick Crocker.		State Treasurer, Timothy Gregg.

FIGURE 2.7b. Early Reform Ballot Designs: Party Column with Straight Ticket Option

a ticket listed only one party's candidates presumably discouraged split ticket voting.

Although reform solved some of party politicians' headaches, on the whole, the Australian ballot appears to have been well designed to accomplish reformers' goal of weakening state parties. By making balloting secret, voters were removed from the steady gaze and influence of party workers. Second, by listing all of the candidates on a single ballot, voters found it easier to cross party lines in selecting candidates for different offices.

As party politicians lost their ability to commit voters, they could no longer recoup the enormous expense their mobilization strategies required. They might

To vote a straight party ticket, write within the blank space immediately here-under the name of the party you wish to vote for.

I hereby voted a straight._____ ticket except where I have marked opposite the name of some other candidate.

If you have vote a straight ticket above and place a cross mark (X)opposite any name below, such cross mark (X) will be counted for that candidate and the vote cast for the candidate on the straight ticket for the same office will not be counted, etc.

FOR GOVERNOR.		Vote for One.
Charles T. Apgar.	Prohibition.	
Samuel E. Briggs.	Socialist.	
Arthur Fuller.	Democrat.	
Henry Zabriskie.	Republican.	
FOR LIEUTENANT-GOVERNOR.		Vote for One.
Howard Arnold.	Republican.	
Clarence P. Snyder.	Socialist.	
George Van Derzee.	Prohibition.	
John W. Young.	Democrat.	

FIGURE 2.7C. Early Reform Ballot Designs: Office Bloc with Straight Ticket Option

usher an opposition supporter to the polls. A bought voter might swear fealty and commit apostasy behind the curtain. Even sincere supporters might switch to another party's candidate lower down the ballot. Voter fatigue became a legitimate concern of down ballot candidates fearful of falling off the coattail. Candidates soon learned that though they could not depend on presidential (or gubernatorial) coattails to carry them to victory, they could, by dent of personal effort in their own behalf, prevail at the polls. Consequently, political parties devoted fewer resources to mobilization, and voter turnout declined. Split-ticket voting became more pronounced as presidential coattails shortened and voters were lured away from party voting by candidates' blandishments. Close elections gave way to safe, incumbent-dominated districts. Sharp swings in party control occurred less frequently, and when they did occur, they were accompanied by readily identifiable, disruptive issues, such as the Great Depression.

<table>
<tr><td>REPUBLICAN.</td><td>DEMOCRAT.</td></tr>
</table>

REPUBLICAN.	DEMOCRAT.
For Governor, Henry Zabriskie of Rockland.	For Governor, Arthur Fuller of Saco.
For Representative to Congress, Levi G. Hinds of Kennebunkport.	For Representative to Congress, Peter A. Ferguson of Berwick.
For Clerk of Courts, Nathaniel Hart of Eliot.	For Clerk of Courts, William Perkins of Skowhegan.
For Sheriff, Robert C. Freeman of Eastport.	For Sheriff, T. Jefferson Stokes of Dill.

FIGURE 2.7d. Early Reform Ballot Designs: Maine's Party Column Without Box for Individual Candidate Selection

Risk-Averse Districting

These changes in the voting booth also introduced intolerable risks to campaign strategies based on voter mobilization. Legislative districting designed to reward thin, broadly distributed pluralities with the maximum seats became too risky. Because party operatives lost their ability to monitor voters at the polling booth, drawing districts with razor-thin districts increased the dangers of mistakes. Soon, the modern districting strategy of hedging against uncertain election outcomes by padding districts with extra party votes became commonplace.

Many state legislators lost interest in districting altogether. Ohio, which redrew its congressional districts almost biannually during the Gilded Age, failed to redistrict at all between 1914 and 1952. Congress failed to reapportion the House in the 1920s, and without the prompting of a federal reapportionment only two states (Pennsylvania and Colorado) bothered to redistrict in 1922 (Hasbrouck 1927). This meant that the vast majority of House district boundaries remained frozen between 1914 and 1932. Even when a new

Census gave states additional congressional seats, some states took advantage of federal rules allowing them to place newly gained seats into at-large elections. Rather than draw new district boundaries, Illinois elected two House members in at-large elections from 1912 to 1946. The result was an electoral system less susceptible to presidential coattails and safer for incumbents. Moreover, the budding careerism of congressional incumbents may have led them to successfully persuade state legislators to draw safer districts.

The Party Ballot's Implications for Political Parties

Given the compelling benefits the party ballot conferred on political parties, candidates and voters, it is difficult to imagine a different electoral system that would have been as well adapted to 1840s America. Toward the close of the second party system, usually marked by Andrew Jackson's election in 1828, the number of popularly elective offices increased sharply – most with short terms.[22] During the same period, the electorate expanded dramatically to include virtually all white males. So many citizens in turn publicly announcing their choices for so many offices surely gave rise to the invention of the party ballot during this period.

In assessing the more general challenge pervasive democratization posed for the next generation of party politicians, McCormick (1966: 344) explained, "These reforms added greatly to the difficulties of party management, for they complicated the nominating and campaign functions enormously not only by multiplying the numbers of officials to be elected but also by adding to the types of constituencies from which those officials were to be chosen." Until the turn of the century, when Progressive reforms professionalized many offices, converting them from elective to appointive, voters in many states faced elections every year. As one Midwestern politician groused, "We work through one campaign, take a bath and start in on the next" (Keller 1977: 241). As taxing as continuous campaigning might have been for party workers, they would have faced a far greater burden directing people how to vote without the party ticket consolidating the plethora of races to a single contest. The party ballot made America's democracy manageable.

Party ballots further slashed communication costs by concentrating the campaign and voters' attention on the most visible candidates, the presidential contestants. Whether ward heelers hovering over a dozen voters or members of the national party committee contemplating where to send literature and speakers, all party workers concentrated their energies on the common goal of winning the presidential election. The party ballot similarly simplified the voters' task. Instead of selecting among the myriad names and offices, they focused solely on the presidential election.

---

[22] With so many and so frequently elected offices, one is reminded of Patrick Henry's favorite Antifederalist slogan, "Tyranny begins where annual elections end."

Beyond saving democracy from itself, the party ballot system favored certain campaign strategies over others. Consider, did the party ticket prescribe that candidates and parties should woo uncertain supporters with promises and stances they favored, as prescribed by the median voter theorem, or should candidates and parties concentrate their energies in mobilizing the party faithful? With the success of thousands of elected officeholders at risk as well as the welfare of many more thousands whose jobs depended on their incumbency, we can be sure that party politicians weighed these options carefully and precisely.

In Chapters 4 through 7 we will examine candidates and campaigns adopting one or the other of these courses as they nominated candidates and conducted campaigns. Their successes and failures clearly point to the superiority of mobilization. The reason is embedded in the rules by which party ballot elections were conducted. Specifically, public voting a party ballot assured a turned out vote would reliably go into the candidate's tally. Votes based on campaign appeals were more complicated and uncertain, especially on those issues where voters in a constituency disagreed. Once we understand how thoroughly the electoral system favored mobilization, many of the features of America's nineteenth-century parties and campaigns, features that might strike modern observers as odd or even offensive, will make perfect sense.

Mobilization Strategy

The relationship between the expected closeness with which a voter views an election and the likelihood of their going to the polls is well established in modern voting research (Aldrich 1993; Cox and Munger 1989; Rosenstone and Hansen 1993). Many voters find campaigns more stimulating if the candidates are running neck and neck in a horse race competition. Others who feel strongly about some issue will find close elections more motivating as they perceive the outcome consequential for their policy preferences. Some may even come to the improbable belief that their vote might prove pivotal. But even without such belief, a close race holds intrinsic interest for many voters and increases their propensity to vote (Rosenstone and Hansen 1993). For purposes of discussion, we refer to this as the *attitudinal* basis for the relationship between closeness and turnout.

Voters are not the only actors observing and reacting to close elections. Candidates and their campaigns may become fixated on closeness as the election approaches. With finishing a close second offering the loser zero return on investment, the logic of plurality elections (Cox 1999) dictates that the closer the expected vote the stronger the incentive for campaigns to ratchet up their effort.[23] Each side will raise and spend more money, intensify voter

---

[23] These actors should be highly responsive to perceived closeness, particularly in plurality elections. Coming in a close second in these winner-take-all elections in that generates zero return on investment (Cox 1999).

contact, advertise more heavily, and where feasible, they might even bid for votes directly through bribes and other quid pro quos. Conversely, where candidates and campaigns foresee that they or their opponent has little prospect of winning, they may slacken their effort to conserve resources.

Campaigns will engage in those activities that offer the best chance of victory. In modern elections this mostly means advertising. Under the party ballot regime, it mostly meant voter mobilization. By *mobilization* we are referring to a campaign's effort to increase the prospective supporter's utility of going to the polls. Mobilization may take different forms in either increasing the benefit or reducing the cost of voting. The rationale for mobilization as the preferred campaign strategy during the party ticket era is compelling. With casting a party ticket a public act, campaigns could assure that only reliable votes for their party would be mobilized. However expensive mobilization might be, and as we shall see, this era's elections were enormously expensive, a reliable vote cast for the candidate trumped less costly but also less reliable efforts at persuasion.

Where the attitudinal basis of turnout in close elections attributes voting to heightened voter interest, the mobilization basis shifts the motivation to strategic party politicians who decide to induce more voters to go to the polls by providing selective incentives. Where voter enthusiasm can boost turnout in both electoral regimes, the parties' strategic mobilization was largely limited to the party ballot era. If this argument is correct, we should be able to observe its dynamics in the states' turnout rates according to closeness of presidential vote in the pre- and post-reform eras.

Testing Mobilization on Turnout

Assuming that the attitudinal effect of an election's perceived closeness was the same in the pre- and post-reform eras, we hypothesize: *Given the greater efficiency of mobilization in the party ballot era, the relationship between closeness and turnout was stronger in the pre-reform than post-reform regime.* The party ticket system is peculiar among electoral systems in pooling multiple plurality elections on a single ballot. Having a "single" vote contribute to multiple pluralities both increased the reward of securing that vote and reduced the marginal cost of mobilization. Presumably, the more offices on the party ticket, the more valuable the vote will be. This provides a second hypothesis for testing mobilization on turnout: *The greater the number of offices sharing the ballot with the presidential candidate, the stronger the relationship between closeness and turnout.*

In Table 2.4 we test these predictions by separately calculating pre- and post-reform eras' presidential vote turnout as a function of the number of key offices on the party ticket or after reform, occurring at the same time as the presidential election, and the closeness of a statewide presidential vote. Because the number of offices in play had no significant effect after ballot reform in a preliminary analysis, we have collapsed all post-reform elections into the single

TABLE 2.4. *Presidential Turnout as a Function of Closeness and Number of Offices on Party Ballot*

OLS (with Fixed Effects)

DV = Percent Voting among Eligible Electorate

	DV: Turnout
Reform Ballot	-4.65^{***}
	(1.57)
Ballot Length	2.73^{***}
	(0.52)
Competitiveness (Dem.-Rep.)	-0.05
	(0.05)
Competitiveness^2	-0.004^{***}
	(0.001)
Reform Ballot × Competitiveness^2	-0.06
	(0.07)
Reform Ballot × Competitiveness	0.002
	(0.002)
Reform Ballot × Ballot Length	1.53^*
	(0.87)
Ballot Length × Competitiveness	0.01
	(0.04)
Ballot Length × Competitiveness^2	-0.003^{***}
	(0.001)
Length × Reform × Competitiveness	-0.03
	(0.04)
Length × Reform × Competitiveness^2	0.004^{***}
	(0.001)
Poll Tax	-4.21^*
	(2.23)
Women's Suffrage	-8.75^{***}
	(1.04)
Literacy Test	-0.24
	(1.56)
1860 Dummy	0.27
	(2.00)
1896 Dummy	7.73^{***}
	(1.66)
1912 Dummy	-9.48^{***}
	(1.65)
1932 Dummy	-0.26
	(1.70)
Constant	74.06^{***}
	(0.98)
Observations	694
R-squared	0.36
Number of states	35
State FE	YES
Year FE	NO

Standard errors in parentheses. * $p < 0.1$, ** $p < 0.05$, *** $p < 0.01$.

closeness-turnout relationship.[24] Our dependent variable, state turnout of the presidential vote, is the share voting among eligible voters in a state. As new voters entered the electorate (e.g., women's suffrage), the eligible electorate expanded significantly shortly after ballot reform. Suspecting that these newly enfranchised voters were less likely to vote, we included dummy variables to adjust the relationships for those states and years for which these conditions were present.[25] Because the stimulative effect of closeness on turnout should fall off on both sides of the plurality pivot, we have specified this variable as a quadratic function of the difference in popular vote share between the major parties. To test the second hypothesis we have added a third interaction variable, *ballot length* – the presence of races for the House of Representatives, governor, and state legislature on the same day as the state's presidential election. We also include dummy variables as controls to represent Burnham's critical elections, and as a precaution, the three-way presidential contest of 1912 (which frequently confounds time-series analysis of voting patterns).[26]

The consistent, statistically significant relationships in Table 2.4 allow us to reject the null variant of both hypotheses. These relationships show party mobilization boosting voter turnout in close elections. To see these complex interactions more clearly, Figure 2.8 plots the quadratic relationships between closeness and turnout for five different types of ballots – the reformed ballot and four types of party tickets according to the number of offices in play in the November election. The functions identify two important relationships that vouch for the impact of nineteenth-century party organization. First, although close elections are associated with higher turnout in both ballot regimes, closeness appears to have consistently boosted turnout more under the party ticket.[27] Moreover, moving from close to lopsided elections, the falloff in turnout was especially severe for the earlier era – again, a pattern consistent with the presence of strategic politicians carefully calculating the utility of mobilization.

---

[24] Little research has examined the impact of the number of offices in the election with turnout. Boyd (1981, 1986) concludes that the presence of a gubernatorial candidate on a state's ballot with the president increased turnout. Cohen (1982) fails to find a significant relationship for the presence of governor races in presidential election.

[25] State-level turnout and party vote share data from Burnham, Clubb, and Flanigan (1972a) and Rusk (2001). Turnout is based on linearly interpolated census state population estimates taking into account the percent of voters eligible for that particular year (e.g., gender, greater than the age of twenty, race). Data for literacy test, poll tax, and women's suffrage laws from Lott and Kenny (1999).

[26] Moreover, we test a variety of control variables and model specification, including fixed effects on both year and state and inclusion of lag dependent variable. None of the alternatives significantly altered the relationships between closeness and turnout presented here.

[27] Although Figure 2.8 consolidates all reformed ballots, we can from Table 2.4 calculate the effect of ballot length under this regime. The results suggest here, too, that the number of offices slightly increases turnout across the range of close elections. Yet even the highest turnout levels under reform ballot elections fail to reach those under the party ticket when only the presidential race was in play.

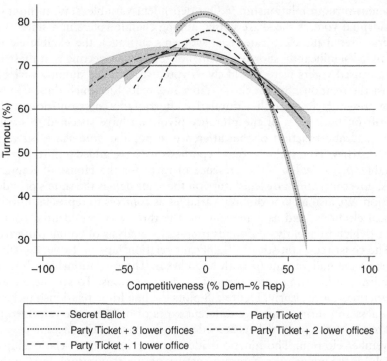

FIGURE 2.8. Turnout as a Function of Closeness of the Presidential Vote

Second, the more offices that were in play during the party ballot, the stronger the closeness-turnout relationship. When presidential candidates ran in a dead heat in the state and theirs was the only election, the estimated turnout was 74 percent. Turnout increased to 77 percent with one of the other offices (almost always a House election), 80 percent when two additional offices were in play, and slightly more than 82 percent when the party ticket included all four offices.[28] State parties committed fully to mobilization in close, long ballot elections. Now let us see how the era's politicians achieved these historically high voter levels of voter participation.

The Historical Record of Mobilization
Mobilization began early in a campaign by identifying firm and potential supporters, pretty much as present-day candidates do in their early benchmark surveys. Although nineteenth-century candidates and their advisers did not have the benefit of sampling technology, in many instances they had something better – platoons of workers fanning out into the constituency to measure the preferences not of a sample of voters but of the full population. One study of campaign intelligence (see Box 2.1) found forecasts of the 1828 presidential

---

[28] These estimates are based on the dummy covariates set at zero.

BOX 2.1. Ohio Politicians Predict the 1828 Election

The historical record offers few clues as to the extent to which nineteenth-century candidates labored under strategic ignorance. Yet accounts of politicos and pundits alike tallying newspaper endorsements and carefully gauging attendance at campaign rallies do survive. Some candidates kept their ear to the ground (a nineteenth-century dictum) by engaging in more active forms of voter research, including canvassing voters well before the election. Since then, as now, information about voters has great strategic value, campaigns kept such information confidential; consequently, much of it is lost to historical investigation. There is, fortunately, at least one exception of an instance of careful, pre-polling voter research surfacing into public view. Buried in the July 9, 1828 issue of the *U.S. Telegraph* is a report from Andrew Jackson's Ohio organization about their candidate's chances in the presidential election four months later.

In July, members of Jackson's campaign committee in Cincinnati canvassed its local operatives and issued an early day press release detailing vote estimates for the presidential race in each congressional district. The news story's author referred to the report's informants as "men of political knowledge and integrity... from every [congressional] district in the state." Their predictions offer a special, perhaps unique, opportunity to shed light on the quality of voter research and the degree of candidates' political competence long before the development of scientific voter surveys.

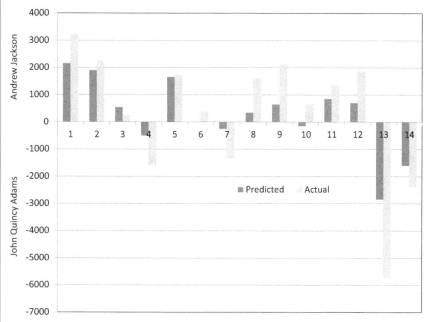

FIGURE BOX 2.1. Predicted and Actual Andrew Jackson Vote Margins in 1828 Across Ohio's Congressional Districts

(*continued*)

How well did they do? Not badly at all. Citing the "mass of evidence," the news report concluded a "probable and almost certain prospect of Jackson getting the vote of Ohio." Specifically, the politicos' individual district tallies summed to a statewide Jackson victory margin of 7,150 votes. Four months later, he won by 4,143 votes from among the 131,049 cast. Translated into vote shares, the committee's point estimate of 52.7 percent for Jackson proved 1.5 percentage points too high, well within the acceptable tolerances of modern surveys that occur on the eve of the election. Moreover, the closer one looks, the better the predictions appear. The bar graph below plots these vote predictions against the actual vote for each congressional district. In only one district, the 10th, did an informant predict the wrong winner, and margin of error was razor thin. (Note that with the exception of the 3rd district, the forecasts conservatively predict a narrower margin than actually occurred.) Considering that these politicos were predicting actual vote margins that depended on turnout as well as voters' stated preferences, their predictions were remarkably close.

From Kernell (2000)

---

vote in Ohio as accurate as those available to modern consultants armed with survey research technology.

In his 1874 governor race, Samuel J. Tilden compiled the names of Democrats in every school district with whom he maintained contact – 50,000 in all. For the tight 1884 election, Indiana's state Republican Party had more than 10,000 "district men" keep tabs on every voter (Silbey 1991). For the 1900 election, shortly after ballot reform eliminated party poll watchers' ability to check which ballots were being cast, the Pennsylvania Republican Party was still compiling a massive list of 800,000 voters, but it had to add a type of voter classification to take the secret ballot into account. Canvassers now scored each voter as "habitual," "reliable," "doubtful," "wavering," or "accustomed to 'fumble in the booth'" (Keller 2007).[29]

Armed with this information and subsequent intelligence, every worker (many on the public payroll) returned to the hustings on Election Day to orchestrate a massive turnout of their supporters. Undoubtedly, some only needed to confirm that a loyalist had voted. Other voters required repeated reminders. Voters, in turn, complained of being hounded by party workers until they caved in and agreed to dutifully follow the worker to the polls. Where polls were distant, workers provided transportation. Then there was the apparently sizable class of voters who required some more tangible form of compensation: liberal provision of Election Day libations was standard practice throughout much of the nation.[30] An extensive menu of party quid pro quos

---

[29] The party was still engaged in extreme mobilization nearly a decade after reform, but it prudently added a voter classification of "fumbler" in anticipation that some "supporters" might fail to pull the party lever.

[30] In some communities the practice triggered a backlash that resulted in Election Day bans on alcohol sales that survive into the twenty-first century.

for votes might include intervention on behalf of those who had run afoul of the law, expediting naturalization of recently arrived family members, a load of coal for winter, a day labor job for a constituent out of work, and many others.

Finally, there were the *floaters* – voters who in hotly contested elections knew they had a marketable commodity. During the last quarter of the nineteenth century, a vote's common market value in a tight statewide presidential contest was a \$5 gold piece – worth more than \$100 today! – but as polling day approached and both sides foresaw a razor-thin result, the market value of a solid vote might double or even triple. In the 1884 election a Democratic postal official intercepted a Republican national treasurer's letter to Indiana party officials directing them to "put a trusted man with necessary funds in charge of . . . [five targeted floaters] and make him responsible that none get away and that all vote our ticket." The funds took the form of bags of \$5 gold coins.[31] Republican candidate Benjamin Harrison won the state by 2,348 votes.

Until the 1880s presidential campaigns offered voters entertainment: torch-light parades escorted by plumed knights; "huzzah" cheers and grandiloquent speeches; giant balls of string and leather rolling from village to village and other imaginative attention-getters; a festival atmosphere; and free-flowing alcohol. What appears to the modern student of elections as little more than the meaningless sparks spun off frenetic campaigns were in reality carefully orchestrated events designed to attract far-flung, entertainment-starved rural voters who might have to travel all day to reach the polling place.

Mobilization appears to have far exceeded efforts at persuasion, the more prominent activity of modern presidential campaigns. Campaign issues were always present and at times dominated campaign rhetoric, but instead of attempting to persuade voters, they were more often employed to rouse supporters out of complacency. Opponents' policies were vilified; party faithful had to show up on Election Day to 'save the republic'. Consider Michael Holt's depiction of the Whigs' strategy entering the 1844 presidential campaign:

[Horace] Greeley and other Whig leaders confidently believed that an issue-oriented campaign would produce a triumph in 1844 because it would reinforce the partisan identity and revive the partisan zeal of the men who had voted Whig in 1840 but abstained thereafter. Such a strategy aimed not to convert Democrats but to mobilize Whigs. . . . Hence, Whigs freely admitted that party rallies and Whig speechifying sought not to change the minds of Democratic voters but "to rouse the lukewarm" among their own and "cause their attendance at the polls." (Holt 1999: 165)

---

[31] In upstate New York, parties regularly took out newspaper advertisements listing the going price of a vote (Cox and Kousser 1981). The extent of voter bribing remains elusive. Evidence of widespread use of bribes in modern elections in Lebanon, which has a confirmable party ticket vote closely resembling America's nineteenth-century party tickets, shows just how susceptible confirmable votes are to bribes. A 2009 public opinion survey found more than half of respondents affirming that they had sold their votes (Corstange 2012).

Durable campaign slogans reflected the goals of rhetoric to trigger enthusiasm rather than appeal to fence-sitting median voters. With the economy in recession during the 1880 election, Republican leaders decided it was time to wave the bloody shirt once more against Democrats, casting them as the party of secession. Another durable, energizing Republican campaign refrain involved, in the words of a contemporary close to party politics, periodically twisting "the Pope's big toe" (Kleppner 1979: 215).

By the turn of the century, historians report that both Democrats and Republicans had heavily curtailed their torchlight parades and other kinds of mass rallies (Summers 2004). In many communities, they also appear to have lost their enthusiasm for scouring the countryside for votes.[32] Campaigns began emphasizing "education" over mobilization (Summers 2004; McGeer 1988). In the decades following ballot reform, turnout dropped sharply across the states. As party voting became less reliable and possibly, as some historians argue, voters increasingly became detached from party cues, campaigns were compelled to switch from mobilization to persuasion. This included instances of candidates defecting from their party's state or national platform and taking an issue stance more closely matching the preferences of the local pivotal voter. By the early twentieth century "campaigns would be routinely conducted on merchandising principles," argues Jensen (1971: 175), with less use of "party symbols."

Regulating Access to the Party Ticket

The list of nominees on a typical party ticket was the compilation of results from a series of largely disconnected party decisions. Nominees for local offices might be handpicked by the local boss or they might require a bruising fight among local factions. Party designees for county and congressional offices came from party caucuses of interested partisans residing within the office's boundaries. The politics of nomination in state conventions assumed every imaginable form over the years and across states. Some conventions handpicked candidates in an orderly manner, by acclimation or in the proverbial "smoke filled" rooms; elsewhere, nominations resulted from free-for-all proceedings and abruptly concluded sessions. However selected, once assembled on the party ticket the nominees rode to success or failure together.

Where party leaders in the communities and states controlled nominations, they could use them to build alliances among factions and recruit candidates

---

[32] Being fully rational agents, party politicians figured out that the only commitment they could monitor in the new post-reform era was to vote or not vote. And because the former led to an uncertain outcome in the voting booth, party politicians turned to the one voting decision over which they could confirm the outcome – not to vote. Accordingly, they set out to find opposition loyalists, who were inclined to vote, and bribed them to stay home (Cox and Kousser 1981). Where this occurred, and we do not know how prevalent this practice became, it served to depress the vote in close elections.

who could effectively promote their party's presidential candidate. An orderly selected ticket offered the means to an efficient, coordinated state campaign. Party leaders might also fashion a candidate list with an eye to burnishing its appeal to voters. As the vocal Progressive reform movement gained steam, local bosses reputedly "perfumed" their portion of the ticket with one or several prominent reformers. Although these "morning glories" might well repay the party nod with ingratitude, they would have already made their contribution by helping elect the full ticket, loaded with "Muldoons," men of suspect integrity who would follow the boss's orders wherever it might take them (Kent 1933).[33]

Party leaders collected and disbursed campaign funds, recruited and scheduled stump speakers, and coordinated the activities of an army of party workers. Above all, party leaders sought to enforce the active contributions of those who stood to benefit from victory. Yet such enthusiastic efforts could not be assumed. The party ticket was, after all, a classic collective good. As such, its beneficiaries might be tempted to free ride. A candidate listed inconspicuously halfway down the ballot – such as register of deed candidate Murray Wright in Figure 2.3 – could reasonably surmise that his efforts would contribute negligibly to the party's success. Would he not be better off sitting discreetly on the sidelines while his colleagues campaigned frenetically? Similarly, some ward captains, confident that their party would prevail locally, might slack off the maximum effort required to generate a local landslide that would help push the ticket's statewide totals past the plurality post.

State and local party leaders vigilantly monitored campaigns to ward off shirking. One solution involved getting the candidates' contribution up front and in cash. In those communities where professional party leaders called the shots, nominees paid a tax for their place on the ticket. During Tammany's heyday the going rate for state assembly nominees was $500 and for a state supreme court nominee, $17,500, which was the office's annual salary.[34]

A more serious threat to the collective enterprise occurred when a politician or local organization sought to defect. An unpopular presidential candidate might harbinger disaster for a local party organization. The modern tactic honed by all incumbents burdened by an unpopular standard bearer involves proclaiming one's independence and emphasizing "home style." This option was unavailable to earlier generations of officeholders. They could, however, engage in subterfuge. This might involve distributing ballots in which their candidate's name had been pasted over the official party nominees (see Figure 2.3).[35] On a larger scale – say a whole local party organization – the defectors

---

[33] Yearly (1970) similarly finds that "except for occasions when political tickets required hasty 'window dressing' or the unusual lustre of some amateur's reputation or funds, bosses seldom permitted significant positions to come to men with less than a decade of party experience."

[34] Some bosses reputedly auctioned nominations to the highest bidder (Riordon 1963).

[35] In towns, cities and counties where factional conflict was a chronic problem, party leaders would go to great efforts to ward off these hard to detect defections. In Sacramento, California

had a more viable option, one that did not involve the voters knowing (nor state party leaders suspecting) they were casting an altered ballot. The local faction might simply print an ersatz party ticket that was indistinguishable from the official party ticket except that some candidates' names were substituted for those of official nominees. A local Democratic slate saddled with an unpopular standard bearer might print out a bogus Republican ballot that listed themselves under the Republican presidential candidate. Voters, keying on the presidential candidate, would be none the wiser. Although systematic evidence of this practice eludes modern research, it became a common complaint of party leaders. In the Conclusion, we consider the possibility that factional conflict followed by reneging had become so serious late in the nineteenth century that party politicians sought a solution in a the state supplied ballot that presented voters with only those candidates certified as the party's nominees.

Seeking to ward off free riding and defection, vigilant party leaders sought out those candidates that had demonstrated loyalty or that could be expected to seek another nomination in the future. An individual's budding ambition for public office provided leaders with leverage to prod them to heroic efforts on behalf of the party ticket. In one election cycle, according to his personal logs, James Garfield delivered more than forty speeches for fellow Ohio Republicans.[36] Nominating caucuses and state party conventions favored candidates who had demonstrated fealty and industry. In 1840 Illinois's recently formed Whig party took no chances that its nominees might backslide to their former parties or strategically commit apostasy. It insisted that all state legislative candidates on the ticket sign a loyalty oath to the presidential candidate and platform (Leonard 2002: 217). In machine cities, where bosses controlled entry and advancement of party activists, party loyalty was unquestioned. It resided in "the long and often ignoble apprenticeships which the somewhat patriarchal organization of the political machine entailed.... District leaders, captains, and the holders of high elective or appointive office were ordinarily men with fifteen to twenty years of service."[37] In the 1880s, members of New York City's Republican Party associations participated in candidate selection only if "they agreed to abide by some forty two pages of regulations

---

in 1871 the regular Democratic organization was so intent on preventing pasting they invented a "tapeworm ballot." In this design, "The names on the Democratic ticket were printed in intertwining wavy lines which made the use of 'pasters' impossible" (Petersen 1970: 17; see also Leach 1917: 14–28). Rarely does one find efforts to manipulate the ballot extending beyond local, county and state legislative elections that encompassed small numbers of wards and precincts.

[36] Continuous party service had left his wife pointedly counting on one hand the days they had actually lived together during the previous couple of years (Peskin 1978).

[37] Yearly (1970: 126) adds, "Fifty-seven of Chicago's political leaders whose careers began in the years preceding 1886 averaged just over fourteen of party service, and random samplings in Philadelphia, New York, Baltimore, Philadelphia, and Boston during the last quarter of the nineteenth century indicate about the same thing."

and signed a pledge to 'recognize the authority of the association'" (Keller 1977: 240). Where the political parties controlled entry onto the ballot, they could subdue factionalism and unite fellow partisans behind their standard bearer.

Electing the party ticket – locally, statewide, and nationally – was, of course, the singular purpose of these seemingly unbridled, exorbitantly expensive campaigns. Where the presidential candidate's position on a salient national issue was viewed favorably by a state's voters, the party would trumpet his policy commitments. But the converse was apparently not true. When the party's nominee was associated with the wrong side of an issue, and his candidacy endangered the party's success, the state party and other candidates were not in a position to disown the head of their ticket. For better or worse, the ticket formally wed them to the national standard bearer and to each other.[38]

Implications of Mobilization for Parties as Organizations

For present-day elections political parties often amount to little more than teams of elective officeholders who share an ideological affinity with fellow partisans. Modern politicians self-select into their party and become officeholders largely through their personal entrepreneurship. During the nineteenth century, however, aspiring politicians seeking office approached their political party as supplicants. They would gain admission to the ticket or be ignored according to their expected contribution to the party's collective goal of having more tickets submitted than the other party could muster.

Successful voter mobilization entailed coordination of hundreds, even thousands of paid workers performing the myriad tasks that a successful nineteenth-century campaign required – recruiting candidates, raising revenue, staffing campaigns, canvassing voters, getting out the vote, and keeping a sharp eye on each polling place's ballot boxes. When state and national offices were in play, some of these activities would be shared and duplicated by local and state organizations while others, such as assessing state workers and contractors and configuring a balanced ticket, gravitated to state party officials. The national party assumed a minor role in campaign financing until the last decade of the nineteenth century, when the national Republican Party began tapping large contributions from Wall Street and corporations (Summers 2004). After the

---

[38] In some states the parties distributed multiple ballots that separated voting for the president – specifically, voting for the Electoral College delegates – from state and congressional races (Bensel 2000). Unfortunately, no systematic inventory of these split party tickets is available. They may reflect efforts of state parties to avoid the risk of an unpopular nominee. Also, where local party units were assured victory, they might extort concessions – say, control of the distribution of patronage – from state leaders or even their presidential candidate as a condition of mobilizing local turnout (Schattschneider 1942). For years, New York City's Democratic machine tussled with its party's national administration over control of the Custom's House. At times it acted on its threats to make a minimum "maximum effort" on Election Day.

assemblage of state delegations at the national convention nominated the presidential and vice presidential candidates, national party officials orchestrated modest presidential efforts, and responded to state requests for literature and stump speakers.

Winning an election today essentially confers a private good to the victor. In the nineteenth century, by contrast, the party ticket conferred a collective good for all those who occupied a place on the ballot as well as the hundreds more whose efforts were rewarded with patronage jobs and lucrative government contracts. As noted above, America's decentralized political parties were especially ripe for free riding, profligate use of resources, and outright reneging on commitments. One solution to this kind of thorny coordination problem is hierarchy – a central authority monitoring and enforcing agreements across the dense, multilevel network of party actors whose efforts had to mesh together if a mobilization campaign were to succeed.

We may assume that all party officials from the informal leaders of the county court house clique to the chair of the national party committee strove for such mastery over their domain. Contemporary observer Ostrogorski attributed such authority to the urban machine: a hierarchy of relationships replicating itself like a set of Russian nesting dolls with each "[m]achine being in reality composed of a number of smaller and smaller Machines which form so many microcosms within it." He elaborated on the replication of organizational forms: "[T]he title and role of boss do not belong exclusively to the man who controls the Machine in the city or in the State: the leader is the local boss in his own district; the person in charge of the precinct is himself a little boss" (Ostrogorksi 1902: 184).

Ostrogorski concluded, that "their mutual relations are ruled by an iron discipline" (1902: 185), which, he might have added, is well-suited to the singular task of collecting votes. Among party professionals, this solution was probably widely admired and coveted, but rarely achieved. Few party operatives above the ward level could be accurately complimented as a "boss." And even bosses complained of a lack of ordinary discipline required to mount a successful campaign. Thomas Platt, the New York Republican leader of the 1890s who routinely cut deals with presidents as well as the Democratic Tammany Hall, lamented the absence of discipline:

During an experience of over fifty years in politics, I have learned that obedience to instructions and gratitude are about as scarce as snow in the dog-days [of summer]. In choosing my lieutenants and candidates, I invariably insisted upon the qualification that the man must know enough to "stand when hitched." The list of those who have ignored or defied this rule would fill a large volume. (Quoted in Gosnell 1923: 454)

History reveals serious coordination problems cropping up during campaigns at every level of party organization. They preoccupied all party leaders and frustrated most. Not only was their enforcement authority weak, they had no third agency – such as a judicial council – to appeal to for enforcing compliance. Indeed, only fifteen of the forty-five state Democratic parties and eighteen of the state Republican parties had any semblance of codified rules defining how local parties should conduct business (J.F. Reynolds 2006). Cooperation depended on party leaders' vigilance and power. During the heat of a campaign with funds sloshing across tiers of party subunits and to voters, party administrators had to keep as sharp an eye on fellow party members as on possible shenanigans from the other side.

Local Parties

Except for those New England states that relied on townships, counties provided the foundation for both government and party organization. County offices administered local and state laws, adjudicated civil and criminal cases, and administered state statutes, including conduct of elections. County parties were typically governed by county committees that presided over a local pyramid of responsibilities reaching down into neighborhoods. Perhaps Abraham Lincoln's instructions to a county committee in Box 2.2 were regarded as innovative in 1840, but within a couple of decades, his prescriptions described the organization of county parties throughout the nation. During the mid-nineteenth century state legislative districts were often drawn coterminous with county boundaries. As cities grew, state legislatures were far more inclined to award counties multiple seats rather than subdividing counties into new districts.

During the nineteenth century, among the nation's approximately 2,500 counties one can find descriptions of every imaginable form of party organization – from godfather-like autocrats summarily rotating incumbents across offices (such as John C. Calhoun in antebellum South Carolina) to adoption of rules for managing or coping with factional competition to anarchy (brawls, and in the Gold Rush western caucuses, knifings and even shoot-outs).

County party officials convened periodically to appoint delegates to the state convention, and they assembled biennially in district caucuses for the sole purpose of nominating a congressional candidate. In the absence of divisible goods to broker across the county organizations, a nomination decision frequently proved difficult. Some degenerated into protracted, raucous affairs with no county organization willing to withdraw its sponsored candidate in favor of one from another county. Missouri's ninth district Democrats cast more than 4,000 ballots over two conventions in 1886, and were set to repeat the episode in 1888 when the two largest county organizations finally agreed to rotate the office every four years (Clark 1920). Curiously, they did not discover this solution earlier; many others had (Kernell 1977). One study of Republican congressional renomination in 1866 concluded that thirty-seven incumbents abided their rotation agreement and retired; another seven were defeated in caucus when they reneged on their prior agreement (Powell 1973).

BOX 2.2. **Abraham Lincoln's Instructions to a Whig County Committee for the 1840 Presidential Election**

1st. Appoint one person to each county as captain, and take his pledge to perform promptly all the duties assigned to him.

Duties of the County Captain

1st. To procure from the poll-books a separate list for each Precinct of all the names of all those persons who voted the Whig ticket in August.
2nd. To appoint one person in each Precinct as Precinct Captain, and, by a personal interview with him, procure his pledge, to perform promptly all the duties assigned him.
3rd. To deliver to each Precinct Captain the list of names as above, belonging to his Precinct, and also a written list of his duties.

Duties of the Precinct Captain

1st. To divide the list of names delivered him by the county Captain, into Sections of ten who reside most convenient to each other.
2nd. To appoint one person of each Section as Section Captain, and by a personal interview with him, procure his pledge to perform promptly all the duties assigned him.
3rd. To deliver to each Section Captain the list of names belonging to his Section and also a written list of his duties.

Duties of the Section Captain

1st. To see each man of his Section face to face, and procure his pledge that he will for no consideration (impossibilities excepted) stay from the polls on the first Monday in November; and that he will record his vote as early on the day as possible.
2nd. To add to his Section the name of every person in his vicinity who did not vote with us in August, but who will vote with us in the fall, and take the same pledge of him, as from the others.
3rd. To *task* himself to procure at least such additional names to his Section.

From Basler (1953: volume 1, 180–181).

At one end of the local organizational continuum were those county organizations that were part of big city machines. Bosses atop a hierarchy solved local threats to collective action, but where control led to self-sufficiency, it sometimes became a fiefdom constituting a problem for state party officials. A local boss might be indifferent to politics beyond his jurisdiction, especially when local elections fell on a different date on the electoral calendar. They could mobilize (or demobilize) voters, depending on negotiated arrangements with state and national party leaders. The stronger the machine the more brazenly it could ignore the state and national organizations. "As the ballot was printed and distributed by the party boss," explained one analysis of elections before ballot reform, "there was no safe guarantee that he would not 'knife' or trade off a candidate in return for the opposition supporting another part of the ticket" (Fredman 1912: 28).[39] At the other end of the continuum, faction-riddled local organizations might be so enervated and impoverished – especially those that rarely captured office, depriving them patronage and money – the state party had little alternative to becoming directly involved in locally promoting the party ticket.

State Parties

Nineteenth-century state party organizations bear little resemblance to their modern counterparts. Indeed, modern state parties are mere shadows of those robust nineteenth and early twentieth-century organizations that reappear throughout this book. They may hold biennial conventions, but unlike those earlier gatherings, state laws in all but a half dozen or so states prohibit parties from nominating or even endorsing candidates in the primary election. Consequently, nineteenth-century conventions and their platforms received far more extensive coverage in the press, and their decisions were presumably more familiar to voters. Moreover, correspondents observed the decorum with which party factions engaged one another as an early indication of how smoothly and effectively the campaign would be conducted in the months ahead. Today, news coverage of state party meetings is virtually nonexistent, and voters learn nothing about their deliberations or decisions – deservedly so.

State parties helped elect tickets of state governors who had appointment authority and legislators who appropriated funds for state contracts; both served as financial larders for these ravenous organizations. Particularly, in large commercial states, such as Massachusetts, Pennsylvania and New York, political parties could tap large numbers of state patronage positions. Harold Gosnell's (1924) study of New York's Republican Party organization during the late 1880s offers a glimpse of the pattern of state and local party relations that matches the fragmentary information available for other state organizations during this era. With Tammany holding a firm grip over elections and patronage in New York City (except for the Custom's House), the Republican Party pacified the upstate, mostly rural counties. Occasionally, the party managed to mobilize sufficient turnout of these voters to withstand the massive numbers

---

[39] Perhaps one of the most consequential and famous instances of this occurred when New Yorker Grover Cleveland lost New York state by a little over 12,000 votes, which swung the Electoral College count from his reelection to defeat. *The New York Times* and Democrats around the country charged the Tammany organization with cutting a deal with Republicans to let Republican presidential nominee Benjamin Harrison win the city; in return Republicans handed out Harrison tickets loaded with Democratic candidates down ballot. In Tammany controlled districts, Cleveland ran over 11,000 votes behind the Democratic candidate for governor and swamped Republicans for local and state legislative offices (Freedman 1912).

BOX 2.3. The Organization of New York's State Republican Machine During the 1890s

Generally speaking, the office of the state committeeman in each one of the thirty-four congressional districts was a clearinghouse for all sorts of patronage. Thus, State Committeeman [William, "boss of Albany"] Barnes believed in "rotation in office," and any day the mayor of Albany might find himself in the postmastership of Albany or the state senator from Albany might land in the county clerkship. Barnes himself did not refuse an appointment as surveyor of customs.... The state committee, as a collegiate body, directed the entire process [of local, state and federal patronage] and sought Platt's advice upon questions of first importance. When state conventions assembled, this committee did not refuse to seat any delegate because he was only a local officer and not a state or federal employee; all office-holders alike were welcome. The delegates to the Republican State Convention in Saratoga in 1898 greeted the "old man" [Platt] with just as prolonged cheers as they greeted the hero of San Juan [Theodore Roosevelt].... They loved Platt... on the old principle, "Blessed be the hand that gives."

From Gosnell (1924: 260).

tallied by the regiments of Democratic voters Tammany marched to the polls. Yet they held a sizable base. By Gosnell's careful accounting, nearly 13,000 safe Republican elective offices assured the party a stable base of enthusiasts to challenge the next election. From the early 1880s through the turn of the century, Senator Thomas C. Platt presided over New York State's Republican Party.[40] From his Senate office he was able to direct thousands of federal appointments to the state that further sustained the party (see Box 2.3).

From this historical distance it is easy to lose sight of the sizable role state patronage and graft played in financing political parties' labor intensive mobilization campaigns. In part, the comparative prominence of federal patronage in the historical literature reflects the quality of the records available to historians.[41] The volume of federal patronage was certainly substantial;

[40] This period covers the years of Theodore Roosevelt's rise to power as a reformer. As they approached each other from polar ends of the political reform issue, they achieved a mutually beneficial *modus operandi* that depicts a less confrontational transition from the patronage regime than reformers and some historians have represented.

[41] It also reflects, we suspect, the web of political dependencies federal patronage required. Appointment of a 4th class postmaster might be fairly straightforward when the same party that occupied the White House controlled a congressional district. The member simply sent the nominee's name to the 4th class postmaster general, who added it to the list of the president's appointments. When the opposition party controlled the district, however, the process became more complicated and less certain. The state's senator from the president's party might weigh in, but in the absence of such intervention, nomination defaulted to the state's representative on the national party committee, who in turn consulted with the chair of the party committee for the congressional district in which the lowly postmaster was located.

it understandably galvanized state parties' attention during presidential campaigns – especially with the "federal crowd," appointees to post offices and other national government patronage appointees who attended their states' conventions and worked in the fall campaign.

Yet the admittedly sparse evidence available suggests that state coffers also provided generous government subsidies to the political parties. In his authoritative analysis of New York's party machine politics, Gosnell (1924) counted approximately 14,000 federal, state, and local patronage appointments in New York during the 1880s. Most occurred in the postal service, followed by the Customs House and Brooklyn naval shipyard. On the state government's ledger, an exhaustive accounting of patronage proved more difficult, but the numbers Gosnell managed to turn up were impressive. Of the 1,500 employees appointed to work on the state's canals, for example, only 200 satisfied even generous standards of suitability. Overall, about a third of the 8,000 New York state employees in 1900 were not protected by merit based appointment procedures. Contracts proved even more elusive for Gosnell's accounting, except that he noticed the state spent $1.5 million annually on legislative printing, an expenditure that exceeded the budgets for education, state mental institutions, and prisons combined!

In addition to the preeminent role of states in America's early federalism, the unit rule in Electoral College voting elevated statewide election victory as prized objectives of party competition. The unit rule allocates all of a state's electoral votes to the plurality winner. Wholly an invention of the states, there is no mention of it in the Constitution or federal statute. Virginia was one of the first states to recognize its strategic value in 1800 when, in order to boost Virginian Thomas Jefferson's election, it passed a law awarding all of its electoral votes to the plurality winner. Other states soon followed for much the same reason. No one, in principle, relished the possibility that the state's electoral vote would divide equally. Winning a plurality vote for its nationally victorious standard bearer placed the party at the front rank of patronage supplicants with the new administration.

Today, of course, the layers of organization vital to nineteenth-century party mobilization efforts have long been replaced by temporary organizations run by nimble entourages of consultants attached to the presidential campaigns (Polsby and Wildavsky 2000; Stromberg 2008). They are well suited for targeting voters with persuasive messages, but less well suited for the labor-intensive enterprise of ushering voters to the polls and monitoring their choices.

With the national party's coordination efforts sporadic and ineffective and local parties and local party organizations tempted at times to relax their efforts, state parties assumed primary responsibility for winning their state's presidential election. Given the critical value in winning the state plurality, state parties waged vigorous mobilization campaigns throughout the state – even in communities where the party might be generally unpopular. Winning control of the state capital and White House rewarded both state and local politicians with access to the reservoir of local patronage, which generally sufficed to energize a local minority party's mobilization efforts, as long as they might lead to success. The presence of an active state campaign reassured local party organizations – especially where they were destined to lose – that their efforts were being matched by other local organizations in their common pursuit of a state plurality.

National Party Organization

The state parties also selected and instructed delegates to the national convention. Reflecting the need to broker its northern and southern wings throughout its history, from 1828 through 1932 the Democratic Party maintained a two-thirds rule for nominating the presidential and vice presidential candidates. This rule, in effect, conferred a veto over the party's nomination to each region. The solution, the party convention system, provided a semblance of rationalize structure to an otherwise decentralized confederation of state and local parties. Arranged like a pyramid, county and congressional district conventions and caucuses selected nominees to run for a variety of local offices and chose delegates to attend the state convention. State conventions, in turn, nominated the party's statewide candidates, adopted platforms stating their position on issues and selected delegates to attend the national convention (Argersinger 1992). Although orchestrated by party insiders and at times rife with factional intrigue, the hugely attended national conventions – 18,000 at the 1880 Republican national convention in Chicago (Keller 1977) – served as instruments to promote the party's platform and generate enthusiasm for the upcoming campaign. Both inside and outside the assembly halls these party meetings became a form of political theater.

During the last half of the nineteenth century, both major political parties created national committees, headed by a national party chair, and campaign committees for each chamber of Congress (Kolodny 1998).[42] Although these offices may have given the appearance of centralization, in reality they sat atop a national party with closer kinship to a confederation. The critical national-level decisions of selecting a presidential candidate and adopting a party platform were prerogatives of state delegations at the party's quadrennial national convention. National party officials lacked authority to orchestrate these massive gatherings. Instead, their "main function was to advise not to supervise" (Dinkin 1989: 71).

Throughout the century the political parties frequently found it difficult to commit to common national policy. With state organizations, expressing

---

[42] Moreover, these chairmen also typically served as postmaster generals when their party occupied the White House (Fowler 1943), but rather than conferring much influence, the party chairman served as a clearinghouse for the appointments proposed by the state parties and members of Congress.

regional interests, differing significantly on national issues, the national party controlled too few resources to induce the state parties to unify behind a programmatic platform. As a result, parties' national platforms emphasized creed and sympathies and sublimated references to specific policy commitments. The difficulties this posed for waging a national campaign extended to nominations. Those politicians who championed some policy invariably found an unsympathetic response from fellow partisans from other parts of the country. As a result, delegates from the state parties could frequently agree only on dark horse candidates whose views were unknown, and hence inoffensive to some faction, or to candidates who enjoyed fame in some realm outside of politics. In the absence of authoritative central actors, national party leaders brokered state preferences in nominating a standard bearer and formulating a platform, but rarely attempted the next step to coordinate the individual efforts of state parties to win the election.

Conclusion

If the rationale for political parties lies in economy, they certainly fulfilled this essential function in America's nineteenth-century elections. Had parties been absent – say, had the "era of good feeling" persisted for another generation under the dominant Republican Party – one would be hard pressed to imagine how voters and candidates would have managed the profusion of elective state and local offices. In a world without meaningful party cues voters would have suffered from a cacophony of appeals, and so too candidates for all but the most important offices, from an inability to be heard.

The rapid expansion of suffrage in the late 1820s rendered election administration equally problematic. Voice voting was no longer manageable. The party ticket became an institutional acknowledgment of the state of American politics at the opening of the third party system in 1840. That the party ticket would be headed by the party's most visible figure is easy to appreciate. All this solved a formidable information problem for voters and communication problem for politicians. With a single sheet of names headed by a familiar figure, the voter possessed what he needed to elect officeholders for the panoply of offices in Washington, at the state capital, and at city hall. Single-member plurality districts further simplified choices by inducing two-party competition (Cox 1997).

By the 1840s, national two-party competition was already familiar and normal. Tracing its earlier development, McCormick (1982) explains that state politicians who might have little affinity for some distant party nonetheless recognized the need to coalesce behind a national standard bearer in order to avoid having voters judge them as irrelevant in the next election. Those who opposed the current government, whatever their reason, had sufficient cause to stand behind a common banner. By 1850 "strange bedfellows" had entered the nation's political lexicon (Safire 1978).

From the beginning presidents were focal points for voters in part because, then as now, the incumbent administration attracted controversy. Few today are aware of the polarized partisan rhetoric that swirled around John Quincy Adams's creation of a Mission to Panama, but in 1826 opponents equated it with a usurpation of constitutional authority. Limited to congressmen's circular letters and party-subsidized newspapers – think FOX News of this era – ordinary citizens were ready to expatiate at length about the goings on in Washington to a bemused de Tocqueville.

The presidential candidate heading a party ticket solved one set of problems wholesale, but it introduced another. How could this politician make a credible, compelling appeal to such a diverse electorate? Would not an issue stance designed to attract one region's voters repel voters in another region? War with Mexico, extension of slavery into the territories, tariff, currency and many other issues divided voters across regions. And still other issues – such as immigration and temperance – cleaved constituencies along ethnocultural lines. Toward the close of the century, the presidential administration's stances on labor strikes and regulation of railroads and industry tapped the increasingly sensitive nerve of economic class. Yet the party's nominee headed all of the states' party tickets.

Each one of the some 18,000 delegates attending the presidential nominating convention was (or should have been) concerned with three pivotal voters – those who decided the local pluralities, those who decided state pluralities, and those who would swing the majority of the Electoral College. Federal patronage holders (who in many states heavily populated state conventions) might well have paid closest attention to the preferences of the pivotal elector, while local politicos curried favor with the first. But all three pivots were tied together, via the party ticket, with the presidential nominee.

One tempting solution would be to manufacture a candidate whose appeal centered on each state's pivotal voter. The genuine Garfield could run in Ohio, the bimetallist Garfield throughout the West, the free trade Garfield in New York, the protectionist in Pennsylvania, and so on. Although some candidates (Winfield Scott's northern and southern posture toward Mexico comes to mind) may have yielded to this temptation, electoral dynamics doomed this as a dominant strategy. For one, each candidate faced an opponent well acquainted with the problem, who vigilantly monitored the other side's campaign for evidence of flip-flopping, contradiction or equivocation. Most communities of any size were served by one or two newspapers attached to the political parties. They were highly motivated to catch the opposition candidate and his spokespersons behaving duplicitously. In Chapter 3, we learn that the solution oddly involved muteness. At the convention, this strategy gave the candidate a chance to secure the votes of a simple majority of Republicans and two-thirds of Democratic delegates. In the general election, tickets headed by inoffensive candidates with vague if not inchoate views on the issues of the day gave the state parties a chance to fashion an appeal that gave them the best chance of winning plurality support.

Muzzling candidates may have solved the parties' problem, but it poses a serious issue for our theory. Recall we began our inquiry with an anomaly of small national popular vote swings generating office landslides in both Washington and the state capitals. We have so far described the electoral system based on party ballots extending presidential coattails into local and state elections and combined with districting strategies, converting coattail votes into victories. In order for these local processes to add up to nationally responsive elections, however, party fortunes must shift systematically across the states. Yet those nomination and general election strategies best suited to win elections deemphasized popularizing national causes. The efficiency with which the electoral system converted votes into seats meant that a political party's presidential candidate did not need to trounce his opponent in order to take over control of government, but some national movement of voter preferences did need to occur. Let us now consider what these national forces might be and how they could arise when the presidential candidates were determined to avoid taking risky positions.

3

National Forces in Presidential Elections

"Let him say not one single word about his principles, or his creed – let him say nothing – promise nothing."[1] These were the instructions campaign manager Nicholas Biddle gave to the handlers of Whig candidate William Henry Harrison in the 1840 presidential election. Silencing the nominee cleared the way for fabricating America's first log cabin campaign.[2] The orders were simple; the strategy worked and Harrison won. His success trained future candidates and their managers in the technique of image control. Even accomplished public speakers eager to mount the stump found themselves muzzled.

Abraham Lincoln had already established national credentials as a public speaker stemming from his debates with Democrat Senator Stephen A. Douglas during Illinois's 1858 state elections. Yet during his 1860 presidential campaign even Lincoln – this singularly talented thespian – complied with strict orders to "make no speeches, write no open letters" (Troy 1991: 61). Moreover, he rarely ventured beyond his Springfield, Illinois, home. Similarly, James Garfield, another accomplished campaigner, went mute on nomination. In selecting him the standard bearer, Republican delegations weighed his past campaigning as a credit to be rewarded, not an asset to be exploited. As had his predecessors, Garfield adhered to the strict order "to sit cross-legged and look wise until after the election" (Peskin 1978: 482).

Only those candidates clearly headed down a path to defeat failed to repose dutifully on the sidelines. Desperate circumstances prompted their desperate

---

[1] Quoted in Shepsle (1972).

[2] Harrison's beginnings were not modest. Born into a prominent political family, Harrison's father was a plantation planter who was both a signatory of the Declaration of Independence and governor of Virginia between 1781 and 1784. After his father's untimely death while away at the University of Pennsylvania, family connections with the then-current governor of Virginia eased his transition into the military, where he enjoyed a successful career.

efforts. But active campaigning never succeeded during this era. Democrat nominee Stephen A. Douglas campaigned tirelessly but futilely in his 1860 effort to repair Democratic Party's North-South coalition that the extension of slavery question had ripped apart.

[Douglas] embarked on a long cross-country tour, often speaking several times a day from railway platforms or hotel balconies, making a fervent plea for the Union.... Huge crowds...gathered to hear and see him...[but] opponents belittled this new departure of direct vote-seeking by a presidential candidate... "strolling around the country begging for votes like a town constable." (Dinkin 1989)

With the formation of a new Southern Democratic Party and nomination of Kentucky's James C. Breckinridge the break was irreparably sealed. Eight years later another Democrat, Horatio Seymour, traveled the same dismal path to defeat – this time losing to war hero Ulysses S. Grant. When news reporters queried Grant whether he, too, might campaign, the stone-faced general tersely replied, "No, I don't want to lose."[3]

James G. Blaine, a seasoned Washington politician, began his campaign conventionally by hiding from the press and refraining from public statements. Yet he monitored his campaign's success in the states and occasionally counseled stump speakers and others on rebuttals to the opposition's claims. During the fall as Republican canvasses confirmed voter enthusiasm drifting toward Democrat nominee Grover Cleveland in the swing states of Ohio and Indiana, Blaine could no longer resist the urge to take up his own cause. He launched a speaking tour of these states, waving the same "bloody shirt" that had staved off the Democrats' surge four years earlier in Hayes's slim victory. Once again, the more energetic candidate lost. Most contemporaries agreed he probably would have done no worse had he stayed home (Roseboom 1970).

Reclusive presidential candidates would not appear to make compelling focal points on which voters across the nation could pool their preferences and register the satisfaction with government performance. By temperament and ambition, we find that most candidates during this era – especially those with a decent chance of winning – closely followed the script party politicians had written for them. These candidates, after all, were the political types the state party leaders had sought when they nominated them and later conducted their campaigns and, once in office, proctored their performance. In the White House their diffident service to the congressional party did not sully their record when their party ran them for reelection.

---

[3] We do not know whether Grant was being facetious or stumbled into a fallacious inference. Given his demonstrated naiveté during his eight years in the White House, we do assume his answer probably did not grasp the real danger awaiting those presidents who ventured into the hustings while trying to conceal their views on sectionally contentious issues.

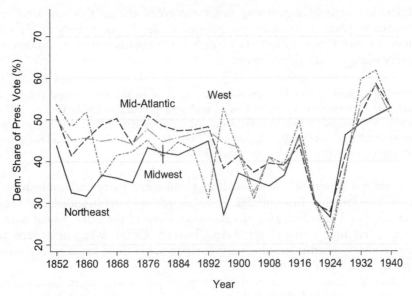

FIGURE 3.1. Regional Distribution of Presidential Vote, 1852–1940
Note: Percentaging based on total popular vote totals. States in regions: Northeast includes CT, ME, MA, NH, RI and VT; Mid-Atlantic includes NY, MD, NJ, PA and WV; Midwest includes IL, IN, MN, OH, and WI; West includes AZ, CA, CO, IA, MN, MO, MT, NE, NV, SD, ND, UT, NV, OR, and WY. OK and KY included with South and omitted from analysis.

Moreover, during the campaign, party leaders in the states diligently molded different, even discrepant, images of these candidates to appeal to their state's pivotal voter. To the degree they succeeded – and reclusive, noncommittal national campaigns stood out of their way – state campaigns undermined the status of presidential candidates as conduits through which national forces might systematically influence voting choices.

In this chapter we search for evidence of how presidential campaigns could generate swings in party fortunes, despite the forces pushing them to do nothing. One need not look hard to find evidence that national swings were in fact occurring throughout the nineteenth century. Consider the regional trends in popular voting in Figure 3.1. Clearly, during the first four decades of the twentieth century, the regional presidential votes are moving in tandem. Regional shifts in Democratic voting are more weakly correlated during the nineteenth century, but even here the regions by and large swung similarly. To see this more clearly, we have in Table 3.1 correlated each region's Democratic vote share with that of every other region and for the rest of the nation. Unsurprisingly, the statistical relationships are much weaker for nineteenth-century elections (correlations below the diagonal) than for twentieth-century elections. Yet with the exception of the West, partisan swings in presidential voting

TABLE 3.1. *Regional Correlations of Presidential Vote Shares (Percent Democratic), 1852–1940*

	Northeast	Mid-Atlantic	Midwest	West	National
Northeast	–	0.89	0.76	0.67	0.81
Mid-Atlantic	0.67	–	0.95	0.89	0.97
Midwest	0.63	0.58	–	0.98	0.99
West	−0.28	−0.14	0.33	–	0.97
National	0.52	0.83	0.72	0.42	–

Note: Figures below the diagonal are correlations for nineteenth-century presidential elections. Figures above the diagonal are correlations for twentieth-century presidential elections. The "National" totals purge the South and the region's vote with which the "National" vote is correlated.

shifted in the same direction across the regions. Moreover, every region's vote – including that of the West – is correlated with the vote for the rest of the nation.[4]

These relationships indicate that nineteenth-century politics provided ample raw material for the institutions manufacturing responsive elections to have fashioned widespread turnover in party control of government in Washington and across the country. What national issues, or indeed whether any issues at all, had a role in changing voter preferences, remains unclear. Perhaps these small swings in the popular vote nationally merely reveal that one party got the upper hand through some campaign machination for which nineteenth-century campaigns were notorious. Trumped-up charges of administration corruption – that is, beyond normal, expected levels – and rumors and innuendos of the opponent's malfeasance, incompetence and private foibles, such as allegations that bachelor Grover Cleveland had fathered a child, may have swayed voters' enthusiasm for a candidate across the regions. But there is good reason to suspect that more than transient campaign issues and shenanigans influenced voters.

In this chapter we examine four ways the presidential campaigns might have systematically shifted partisan preferences across the country. First, despite the candidates' studied blandness, most nominees began the campaign with a policy or political reputation. It might have reflected previous public support for a policy, such as a protective tariff, or simply expressed sympathy with some interest or constituency, such as volatile freight charges facing farmers. Second, despite these managers' best efforts, campaigns had a way of veering off script. How and how well candidates – flushed out of hiding – parried charges offered

---

[4] We adjusted the national totals to exclude the contribution of the region's vote with which it is correlated in the table. A more accurate label is "the other, non-Southern regions' popular vote." We repeated the analysis at the state level of presidential voting with very nearly the same results. The slope of the national presidential vote (sans the state being estimated) after 1900 was more than twice that before ballot reform, but both were statistically significant.

voters an opportunity to update their measure of the candidate. Personal attacks on a candidate virtually insist on a personal response. Contemporaries generally agreed that Grover Cleveland's above board, acknowledged out-of-wedlock patrimony effectively defused the potentially damaging issue for the remainder of the campaign. Third, incumbent presidents and their party entered a new campaign with a record to defend. Foremost among the criteria with which modern voters judge the current administration's performance is the state of the economy. Whether this was true during the nineteenth century is unclear. Certainly, presidents held fewer policy instruments for ameliorating hard times and restoring prosperity that might have either let incumbent presidents off the hook or placed them in an impossible position. Fourth, the state and national party conventions passed platforms in which they staked out positions on issues. Presidential candidates' state campaigns might have tried to disassociate the nominee from a locally unpopular national platform, but their success was always problematic. A candidate's unpopularity might have reflected deeper antipathy toward his party's policies. For the rest of this chapter, we assess each of these possible sources of systematic variance in presidential voting during the nineteenth century.

Candidate Reputation

In the modern era politicians who have forged national reputations from years of service in Congress or state governorship are frequently well positioned to win their party's presidential nomination and the election. This was not the case in the nineteenth century, when state delegations at the national convention viewed such credentials with circumspection. Experienced state-level politicians were presumed to be beholden to their state's and region's particular interests. In the spring of 1888, an all-star lineup of congressional Republicans gave the nod that they would welcome their party's nomination. Boosters for Senators John Sherman and William Allison vigorously championed their men on the convention floor, while Blaine's promoters worked discretely from the wings stirring up a draft movement. Instead, the convention chose Benjamin Harrison, a less seasoned politician and someone less associated with controversial policies that divided Republicans. His chief claim to the nomination appears to have been his lineage; his grandfather, William Henry Harrison, had served as the nation's ninth president four decades earlier.

Individuals who had achieved fame outside of politics made compelling candidates. The absence of regional and factional attachments rendered generals select grade presidential timber. President-makers recognized this from the very beginning of mass party politics in America. Consider one biographer's characterization of Andrew Jackson's campaign promises in the 1828 election: "As he subsequently defined it, his program was . . . conservative, leaning toward states' rights and the economics of laissez-faire, but so bland and inoffensive that those previously disposed to follow him could not seriously object to a single point" (Remini 1963: 73).

Both political parties recognized this logic and sought to enlist generals throughout the century. Republicans nominated political neophyte Ulysses S. Grant in 1868 and the Democrats nominated Winfield Hancock in 1880. Unlike established politicians, military men could more credibly support two, or even more, sides of issues that divided voters across the states and regions. Jackson's position on slavery was sufficiently malleable to assuage the concerns of both northern laborers and Southern slave owners and thus uniquely qualified him for the nomination (Aldrich 1995). Even those whose military careers fell short of heroic might still become legends with a little campaign burnishing. By the conclusion of the 1856 campaign, voters could be forgiven for believing that Republican nominee John C. Fremont (aka the Pathfinder) single-handedly opened the American West.

Given presidential candidates' long institutional coattails, war heroes and nondescript politicians offered perhaps the safest solution to America's peculiar democratic conundrum: winning this national office – prized for its control of thousands of patronage jobs throughout the country – while avoiding national issues likely to be divisive. Only by taking charge of the presidential campaign might state parties hope to fashion an attractive local appeal and navigate the candidacy between the shoals of national and state politics.

Despite the best efforts of the convention, most candidates entered campaigns with established personal and policy reputations, which voters found relevant to their choice. Unlike the cynical Madison Avenue executive in Frank Capra's "Meet John Doe," the parties did not so much fabricate candidates as recruit those who appealed to a broad cross-section of voters. Yet these candidates' policy preferences also needed to be certifiably consistent with those of their party. In 1864 Democrats sought not just any general who felt slighted by Lincoln, but one who was ready to end the war short of decisive victory. They found him in Lincoln's recently relieved general-in-chief of the Union Army, George B. McClellan.

Whenever the party nominated an established politician, his reputation constituted sticky information for voters that limited state parties' ability to remold the candidate's image to match the preferences of the state's pivotal voter. Abraham Lincoln followed his handlers' advice and confined himself to his home in Springfield, but the former Illinois congressman had already established his reputation as an opponent of slavery in the territories during his nationally monitored debates with Stephen A. Douglas two years earlier. Republicans hammered the Buchanan administration on economic issues and corruption (Dinkin 1989), while Democrats and compromise-searching Constitutional Unionists warned that the Republican Party's stand against any extension of slavery would doom the nation to division. Voters in 1860, we suspect, understood which of the candidates would firmly oppose extension

BOX 3.1. Presidential Campaigns as Purveyors of Issues

FIGURE BOX 3.1. Presidential Campaigns as Purveyors of Issues: Democratic Broadsides in 1864. *Source*: Special Collection Library, University of Chicago.

of slavery into the territories without Lincoln having to address the issue during the campaign. If they did not, all they had to do was read the broadsides Democrats were posting in Border States (see Box 3.1). After Lincoln's election, politicians from several Deep South states saw little reason to postpone secession. They were already well familiar with the president-elect's and incoming Republican Congress's position on the extension of slavery. Within weeks of Lincoln's inauguration the Civil War had begun.

Campaign Issues

Campaign issues can arise in a variety of ways and range in gravity from the trivial to threatening the future of the republic. Nineteenth-century political parties desperately sought to control the issue agenda by popularizing those matters that hammered wedges into the other party's fissures while minimizing exposure to such damage for themselves. Below we identify several ways issues found their way into national campaigns. We distinguish them in this fashion more for purposes of exposition than to reflect any differences in the kinds of issues they dealt with.

Acceptance Letters

About the only explicit policy statements most mid-nineteenth-century presidential candidates offered voters came from letters accepting their party's nomination. These open letters – little different than press releases – were delivered to the party headquarters usually about a month after the party convention. Historians' standard interpretation for this tardiness is that it allowed the delegates to leave town and cool their passions before the nominee made any declarations. They were no less managed and only a little more informative than the candidates' campaign statements. The candidates and their advisors crafted these acceptance letters to commit the candidate to as little as possible while endorsing the convention platform. All expressed love of country (which for postwar Democrats meant genuflecting before the American flag) and fealty to the national convention's platform. Occasionally, the nominee would seek to broaden the platform's appeal, which invariably involved adding a layer of ambiguity or equivocation. All of this required extensive vetting.

In the summer of 1864 with Confederate forces threatening Washington, President Lincoln's erstwhile commander, General George B. McClellan, accepted the Democratic Party's nomination on a platform to end the increasingly unpopular war. But Democrats at the convention had disagreed over whether peace overtures to the Confederates should commence immediately (the adopted plank) or await more convincing military success. With Democratic politicians from both sides importuning McClellan, he vacillated over several drafts of his acceptance letter. Finally, citing the sacrifices of "gallant comrades," McClellan spurned negotiations (as well as any talk of reparations for liberated slaves) with the South until after it quit the war (Roseboom 1970).

On advice from party leaders, Garfield accepted the Republican nomination in a letter vaguely endorsing civil service reform. Then, several sentences later, he reassured state party leaders that he would consult with them in all appointments. Confronted with this and other contradictory statements, Garfield averred that it was better "to run the risk of being stupid than to risk awakening unnecessary controversies" (Peskin 1978: 474). Perhaps a similar assessment guided Cleveland when he endorsed hard currency in his 1888 acceptance letter while acknowledging that this policy unnecessarily inflicted hardship on the West.

Toward century's end, presidential candidates became more forthcoming in stating their policy positions. Acceptance letters lengthened. Occasionally, the nominee demurred from embracing a platform provision or endorsed a more specific policy that deviated from the platform's brokered language (Korzi 2004).

Campaign Rhetoric

Beyond these obligatory early endorsements of the party platform, campaigns had a way of defeating handlers' best efforts and dredging up issues that the candidates were forced to address. Even minor gaffes that from our historical distance might appear too flimsy to matter could have provided voters with valuable information about these studiously ambiguous objects (Popkin 1991). During the 1884 campaign Republican candidate James G. Blaine failed to respond to a Presbyterian minister's benediction in which he portrayed the Democratic Party's program as little more than "rum, Romanism and rebellion." A Republican rally might have cheered this rhetorical flourish, and it would soon have been forgotten in the sea of rhetoric. But the audience in this instance happened to be a gathering of leaders of New York City's normally Democratic Irish community that Blaine hoped to woo to the Republican side. Compounding the problem immeasurably, Blaine stood nearby in plain sight unperturbed by the remarks, awaiting his turn at the podium. He later claimed that preoccupied with his own remarks, he was not listening to the minister's benediction. For the Irish Catholics in the auditorium, and soon after the story was picked up by newspapers nationally, for Irish everywhere, Blaine's failure to pounce on the minister's slander was all that mattered. For Irish and Catholics, the minister's catchy alliteration became a resonant campaign slogan. Blaine narrowly lost New York State by a measly 1,047 votes as New York City's heavily Irish precincts turned out as staunchly Democratic as ever. Even when they neutralized potentially galvanizing national issues and kept their presidential candidates hidden – although in this instance, not well enough – campaigns remained dynamic events, subject to shocks that refreshed signals to the electorate.[5]

National Issues That Attracted News Coverage

To suggest that national issues and events might systematically move votes toward a party assumes that national news and issues penetrated these state-managed campaigns. Again, we cannot confirm what voters knew and responded to in voting, but we can closely inspect the kinds of information they had readily available. By the 1880s the penny press, urban dailies whose revenue were based on sales and advertising, had largely replaced the party-subsidized press as the chief source of political news for most voters. During this era news was a growth industry. With circulations soaring, and by most any measure, newspapers' coverage of public affairs was becoming more comprehensive (Starr 2004). So it is not surprising that the Blaine fiasco was not confined to the upper Manhattan dinner party. More generally, national coverage signified the presence of a national campaign within sight of typical voters.

---

[5] We suspect, in fact, that the party ballot era elevated the salience and electoral consequence of national issues well beyond their substantive effects on the citizenry or the course of the nation.

This constrained the ability of state organizations to fashion a credible message targeting their local constituencies.

Albeit to a lesser extent, this constraint on the state-centered presidential campaign strategy had always been present. During the antebellum era, kindred partisan papers routinely exchanged stories, creating an early and partisan version of a wire service. Readers in one region soon learned what the candidates said elsewhere. A standard explanation of Democrat James K. Polk's victory over Whig Winfield Scott in 1844 finds the former having an easier time selling the "war with Mexico" issue to northern Democrats than did the latter in straddling the issue in an effort to preserve the fragile southern and northern bases of the Whig coalition.[6] Barely competitive in the South, southern Whigs lamely sought to match Democrats' pro-war rhetoric. Some northern Whigs sounded to Southerners suspiciously like abolitionists. Whig candidate Winfield Scott offered little reassurance, as he vacillated between hawkish and dovish blandishments.

Even though their positions were less established, nineteenth-century presidential candidates could face the same credibility issues that sometimes afflict modern candidates. Winfield Scott suffered charges of flip-flopping on the war with Mexico issue. With presidential candidates sitting on the sidelines, state party organizations enjoyed greater latitude in defining their candidate's image, but state campaigns were not wholly insulated from the campaigns in neighboring states and beyond. Unwelcomed national issues and party commitments could still knock a state campaign off message.

Perhaps elevating presidential candidates as focal points placed a premium on national political news beyond what one should expect in a nation of island communities governed by a weak national government. Yet candidates and the press appear to have been preoccupied by national events. If voters were, too, then national partisan swings in voting would come as little surprise. When asked on what issues he would wage his reelection campaign, Tennessee governor James K. Polk replied that he would not know the answer until the newly elected Whig president had appointed his cabinet (Sellers 1957). During presidential election years newspaper readers in Cleveland received more coverage about politics in Washington (Kernell 1986b) than about state and local politics combined. Table 3.2 displays the distribution of news stories that included references to policies or issues published in one of Cleveland, Ohio's daily newspapers during the presidential elections of 1840, 1860,

---

[6] The issue played better with the Democrats' constituency alignments, which allowed its party nominee, James K. Polk, to embrace a war platform without equivocation. Democrats in the South, a region that comprised a large share of the party's convention delegates as well its likely electoral majority enthusiastically endorsed "the liberation of Texas." Northern Democrats in New York and elsewhere tolerated the party's war-baiting politics as a way to win the election and achieve their priorities – tariff reduction and party control over the Eastern custom's houses and patronage (Holt 1999).

TABLE 3.2. *Nationalization of Political Issues During Select Presidential Election Years*

	1840	1860	1876
Governmental Level of Issue			
Local (%)	5	3	16
State (%)	20	12	11
National (%)	75	85	73
Total Column Inches	(186)	(2,635)	(1,697)
Share of National Coverage			
Slavery/Reconstruction (%)	0	69	14
Tariff (%)	0	1	3
Defense/Foreign Affairs (%)	9	9	8
Gov't Service/Patronage (%)	42	10	6
Scandal (%)	4	8	35
Rights (%)	0	2	6
National Affairs (%)	45	1	28

Note: "Government Service" included rivers and harbors, public lands, postal services, homesteading, veterans' benefits, roads, and general patronage. Among the prominent "Rights" issues were polygamy, naturalization, and suffrage. Finance is the largest component of "National Affairs; this category also includes pardons, territories, Indian relations, and capital administration.

Source: Kernell (1986a).

and 1876. Categorized according to the policy focus of the coverage, clearly stories about national issues dominated the city's newspapers during these presidential election years. In 1860, for example, 85 percent of political coverage focused on national issues with 69 percent of those stories covering the issue of slavery. With the potential secession of the South looming over the election, this national focus of news coverage in 1860 should not be too surprising. But one also finds national news dominating in the 1840 and 1876 election cycles. To the extent news coverage in Cleveland was similar to coverage elsewhere, one can imagine national issues cropping up throughout the campaigns.[7]

From Recluses to Campaigners

Toward the close of the nineteenth century even the viable candidates took tentative steps toward active campaigning. Benjamin Harrison was probably the first candidate to turn his front porch into a podium, but McKinley famously developed it as a campaign venue. He periodically summoned the press to his Canton, Ohio, porch to read a statement, and then promptly retreated

---

[7] Kernell (1986a) reports a similar concentration on national issues from the *Hartford Daily Courant*. In 1840, 97 percent of the news was national. This figure declined to 43 percent in 1860, where slavery was salient, and 66 percent in 1876.

into his house, leaving reporters' questions hanging unanswered. McKinley's front porch campaign mostly amounted to a public relations event. Railroad promotions transported more than 100,000 curious visitors to McKinley's home to see him and be briefly greeted by him (Keller 2007: 173).[8] Meanwhile, his underdog opponent, William Jennings Bryan, took his campaign to the people. Bryan logged more than 18,000 miles and delivered 569 speeches en route to lopsided defeat (Dinkin 1989).

Presidential elections changed dramatically early in the twentieth century. In 1910 Oregon adopted the first presidential primary; within two years eleven other states had instituted similar elections that obliged state delegates to the national convention to support the primary winner (Ware 2002). This lengthened the campaign season, giving controversial issues greater chance of emerging. By the 1920s all presidential aspirants found themselves campaigning across the country – first to demonstrate their electability in states' primary elections and several months later in the general election. Ironically, William Jennings Bryan's intensive campaigning had become the blueprint for twentieth-century candidates who found they could no longer retire to the wings during their campaigns.

Record in Office

Throughout most of the nineteenth century party politicians in Washington and the states treated presidential candidates as if they were merely the locomotive pulling the party train into Washington, whereupon they would decouple and retire to the White House to await the next election. This era's presidents had traditionally assumed diminutive roles as policymakers, except during national emergencies. That cabinet departments reported annually not to the chief executive but to the congressional committees apparently offended no one's sensibilities, including anyone in the White House (White 1958). Direct presidential efforts to influence legislation and administration were widely deemed inappropriate and unwelcomed. As late as 1888 John Sherman counseled the newly elected president Benjamin Harrison: "The president should touch elbows with Congress. He should have no policies distinct from his party; and this is better represented in Congress rather than in the Executive" (Socolofsky and Spetter 1987: 47). As one student of the era's presidential elections reasonably concluded (Troy 1991: 52): "Strong parties gorged on passive candidates and a weakened presidency."

Moreover, party politicians assumed (correctly in most instances) that when they were so fortunate as to elect an amateur, he would require their daily

---

[8] Although silent presidential appearances to review parades and the like were fairly common, rarely did they say anything – mostly when charges questioning their personal integrity or probity necessitated a response. During the 1884 campaign, Grover Cleveland acknowledged that he had fathered an illegitimate child and, for some time, had been supporting the mother.

TABLE 3.3. *Relative Proportion of Election and Institutional Coverage Given to the President and Congress*

	Election Articles			Institutional Articles		
	President	Congress	(# of Inches)	President	Congress	(# of Inches)
1820 (P)	88%	12%	(17)	0%	100%	(18)
1830 (C)	29%	71%	(58)	44%	56%	(88)
1835 (N)	98%	2%	(251)	66%	34%	(100)
1840 (P)	94%	6%	(501)	39%	61%	(23)
1845 (N)	18%	82%	(33)	11%	89%	(147)
1850 (C)	6%	94%	(174)	15%	85%	(1996)
1855 (N)	3%	97%	(131)	15%	85%	(246)
1860 (P)	95%	5%	(1665)	16%	84%	(655)
1870 (C)	11%	89%	(347)	20%	80%	(825)
1876 (P)	94%	6%	(1323)	17%	83%	(818)

Source: Kernell and Jacobson (1987: table 3). Coverage is measured in length (column inches) of news coverage. The news category for president also included any references to members of the president's cabinet. The labels "P," "C" and "N" next to the years refer to presidential election years, congressional election years, and nonelection years, respectively.

guidance in affairs of state, especially in the recondite business of filling the thousands of government patronage offices. In the White House, illustrious generals, men who had commanded others throughout their careers, were reduced to the government's "chief clerk" (Lincoln's phrase). When Republican leaders approached General William Sherman yet again in 1884 to allow his name to be entered for the presidential nomination at the Republican convention, the steadfastly uninterested general brushed off party politicians: "I remember well the experience of Generals Jackson, Harrison, Taylor, Grant, Hayes and Garfield...and am warned, not encouraged by their sad experiences. No, count me out...leave us old soldiers the peace we fought for and think we earned" (Brands 2010: 355).

For an indicator of the president's subordinate role in national policy, we return again to news coverage of politics in Washington in Cleveland's daily newspapers. Table 3.3 shows Congress dominating day-to-day coverage. As late as 1876 more than four-fifths of nonelection news about Congress and the presidency (including the cabinet secretaries) concerned the former. Only during presidential election years did these locomotives dominate the news, and then only for news related to the election.

Yet even before presidents became activist managers of the federal government, they made daily decisions that, for the most part, have receded into history as inconsequential, but appear to have been major public concerns to voters at the time. President Cleveland's 1888 campaign was burdened by his veto of a major veteran's pension bill, a decision not altogether surprising, as none of the Democratic Party's huge southern base was eligible for a pension anyway. This decision likely taxed his support throughout the Midwestern states in which Democrats normally began the campaigns as slight underdogs. His fate in many of these states was further sealed by a seemingly innocuous executive order returning captured Confederate battlefield flags. The uproar of veteran groups left Democrats quaking everywhere outside the South. Even the tin-eared Cleveland took notice. Belatedly, it occurred to him that he did not actually have the authority to return rebel banners and rescinded his order.[9] But serious damage had been done that left friends and advisors expressing concern for the president's personal safety, let alone his reelection prospects.

Arguably, the 1883 Pendleton Act in reaction to the assassination of President Garfield by a disgruntled job seeker launched the trend toward direct presidential involvement in administration and assumption of responsibility for its performance. It authorized presidents to issue executive orders expanding the civil service system as they deemed appropriate. Over the next several decades, every president found occasion to invoke this authority in an executive order. Civil service reform is emblematic of a more pervasive trend. From 1877 until 1900, Congress enacted twenty regulatory laws. During the next thirteen years, the number of such laws tripled (Johnson 2007). All delegated new appointment or administrative authority to the president.

The national policy agenda also included growing demands for an array of new and improved government services – mail delivery, pension homes for veterans and better road and water transportation systems. Not until the second decade of the twentieth century, however, did Congress begin to enact distributional policies at a pace comparable to regulatory policy. We can also see the emerging agenda of government services in Figure 3.2 in the steady growth of federal spending, particularly during the last quarter of the century when non-pension military spending consumed a relatively small and declining share of the budget.

A decade or so earlier, Congress had begun enacting policies that delegated supervisory responsibilities to the president, who for the most part had not sought them. The tension between the traditional and emerging roles of the national government – and hence the presidency – occurred graphically in 1887 when President Cleveland vetoed the Texas Seed Bill. This legislation undertook the modest purpose of helping financially strapped Texas farmers plant their next crop, but Democrat Cleveland vetoed the bill, targeting benefits to a firmly Democratic state, on the grounds that he could "find no warrant for such an appropriation in the Constitution; and I do not believe that the power and duty of the General Government ought to be extended to the relief of individual suffering.... Though the people support the Government, the Government should not support the people" (*Congressional Record* 1887).

---

[9] One Colorado group of politicos wrote to the White House: "As Democrats who supported you in the last Presidential Campaign, we are sorry to see that you are politically damned, and only seen as a representative of rebellion, a viper and an untrustworthy man" (Calhoun 2008: 38).

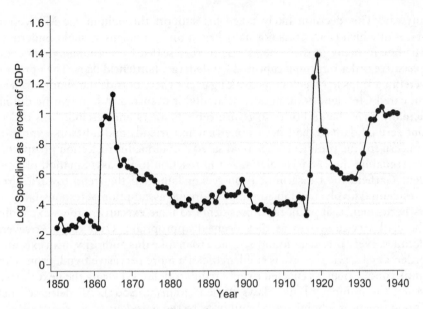

FIGURE 3.2. The Growth of Federal Spending, 1850–1940
Note: This figure displays federal spending as a percentage of GDP. The y-axis is in log scale. The figure was compiled by the authors from data retrieved from http://www .usgovernmentspending.com. The data on historical spending originally comes from *Historical Statistics of the United States, Colonial Times to 1970* (Washington, DC: U.S. Dept. of Commerce, Bureau of the Census, 1975). The data for historical GDP originally comes from Samuel H. Williamson, "What Was the U.S. GDP Then?" Measuring Worth, August 2013, retrieved from http://www.measuringworth.org/usgdp/.

The major growth spurt in services awaited the turn of the century, when two progressive presidents – Theodore Roosevelt and Woodrow Wilson – reversed the presidency's traditional reluctance to champion expansion of government services.

As the century came to a close, Senator Sherman's advice to Harrison that presidents were to be seen and not heard had already become antiquated. Incumbents were no longer discreetly parked in the locomotive barn awaiting the next election; they had records in the form of vetoes, executive orders and public statements to defend. As presidents' responsibilities and discretionary authority accumulated, fellow Washingtonians found themselves soliciting the president's views on issues in order to anticipate his reaction to their decisions. When during his first term Grover Cleveland failed to abide by patronage agreements among California's Democratic leaders, his independence represented little more than obstinacy to fellow politicians, and such assessments were probably correct (Williams 1973). Compare this to a contemporary observer's report of President McKinley's success in manipulating patronage a decade later.

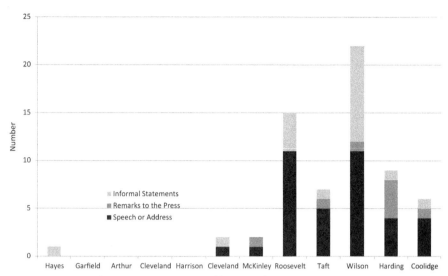

FIGURE 3.3. Presidents' Discretionary Public Speech
Source: Gamm and Smith (1998: 96)

He called an extra session of Congress in 1897, to revise the tariff legislation according to party promises ... [amid] great uncertainty as to the possibility of reaching an agreement in Congress. But the President made it clear to that body that there would be no new appointments made until the new tariff bill was passed. Thus, the Executive utilized the army of office-seekers besieging the members of Congress as a quasi-lobby for a legislative measure which he had determined to force through. (Macy 1912: 39)

This was one of the first occasions recorded in which this emerging class of "modern" presidents recognized they could flip their clerkship into leadership.

Presidents with Records to Defend
These new styled presidents were also quick to realize that taking public positions gave them an opportunity to set Congress's and other Washingtonians' agenda. Certainly, the trend in Figure 3.3 that counts instances of presidents' discretionary public speaking activity appears to bear this out. Benjamin Harrison may have been the last president to take Sherman's advice that presidents were to be seen and not heard. President William McKinley occasionally remarked in public on current issues before Congress, but the real change – one that was both widely heralded by the press and lambasted by conservatives in Congress – came with the arrival of Theodore Roosevelt in 1901. Roosevelt routinely held press conferences, announced his preferences on legislation, and occasionally delivered speeches seeking the public's support (Kernell 1986b). Every president since Roosevelt – including the taciturn Calvin "Silent Cal" Coolidge – has had more to say publicly about current issues than did any of their late nineteenth-century predecessors. News of these politicians taking

positions had become, in the words of Woodrow Wilson, "the atmosphere of politics" (Cater 1964).

This chronology suggests that at the opening of the twentieth century the modern type of presidents had arrived on the scene. As candidates they campaigned actively and promised solutions for an increasing variety of problems that voters had come to view as national. The emergence of federal regulations and services increasingly occupied the attention of Congress and the presidency. When presidents stood for reelection, they (and their party) had established records voters could assess in deciding whether they deserved another term. In this setting, one well familiar to the student of modern politics, we expect to find national forces flowing freely into presidential elections. Thus far we have considered only campaign politics as offering the kinds of information that might sway voters across the country to switch sides or, short of that, discourage one party's supporters from going to the polls while energizing their counterparts in the other party. Candidate reputation, campaign snafus, scandal, and missteps of presidents in office emphasize the politics of the moment.

Now, we turn to another class of potential determinants that set the issue agenda for all presidential elections – at least all modern elections. These are the state of the economy – more specifically, the current administration's economic performance – and the parties' issues appeals to attract the pivotal voter. Unlike modern elections, neither enjoys the compelling rationale for presidential voting in the nineteenth century. With the government controlling few levers of economic policy and a limited national domestic policy agenda offering few issues on which the candidates could bid for votes, we may find these ingredients of modern presidential elections having only faint, if any, impact on elections during the nineteenth century. Yet with this era's responsive elections magnifying popular vote swings, even weak economic or issue voting might have moved the popular vote needle and triggered a partisan flow of offices.

Economic Voting

After more than a half-century of research on modern presidential elections, political scientists (Sides and Vavreck 2013; Erikson and Wlezien 2012) still find themselves asking, "Do campaigns matter?" Candidate reputations, campaign occurrences, and incumbents' missteps in office may make the difference between winning and losing, but their impact must be assessed against the counterfactual of how different the result would have been had the campaign or the president acted differently. Frequently motivating this question are the long-standing, robust findings that modern presidential elections mainly turn on the incumbent administration party's economic performance.

Perhaps nineteenth-century voters also engaged in economic voting. If so, the administration's economic performance could generate the swings across states required to turn over party control of government. Moreover, economic voting offers a decision rule that befits the low informational environment of the era. All voters had to do was retrospectively evaluate their own or the nation's economic well-being as better off than when the current party administration took office. But whether this decision rule had any relevance for voters remains unclear. Perhaps voters began keying on the government's economic performance only when governments did. Or perhaps America's voters began holding the political parties and their presidential nominees accountable well before they were prepared to accept responsibility.[10] This would have had them voting the "rascals" out, even though the next class of "rascals" failed to offer any solution to the nation's economic ills.

Economic and social upheavals of the last quarter of the nineteenth century ended any lingering notion that a voter could safely ignore politics beyond town or even the state border. By the turn of the twentieth century America had been largely transformed into an integrated national economy. This meant economic problems had become national in scope, and increasingly, they called for national solutions. Early twentieth-century presidential candidates could no longer afford to be spectators to their campaigns. Some found themselves having to address issues they would have preferred to avoid; others – specifically, Theodore Roosevelt and Woodrow Wilson – bounded into the arena eager to manage the economy. The question for understanding the economy as a national force is, when did voters begin holding presidents responsible – Grant and Republicans during 1870s depression or Cleveland and the Democrats in 1894 or later still?

America's Economic Transformation

To answer this question, we first need to appreciate that the American economy underwent continuous transformation throughout the nineteenth century. After the Civil War the economy grew steadily, becoming more diversified and integrated. Well before Washington entered the realm of business regulatory policy or presidents began propounding national policy, the economy was dramatically expanding and integrating nationally from a set of regional, more or less self-contained markets.

Economic historians debate the chicken-egg question of the relationship between the remarkably swift development of a national railroad system during the last quarter of the nineteenth century and economic expansion, but the railroad holds a prominent place in every narrative. From 1880 to 1920 railway mileage increased by 175 percent. Contemporaries and historians agree that completion of the transcontinental railroad in 1869 and its subsequent, reticulated expansion throughout the nation provided quick movement of goods and labor (see Figure 3.4). Commerce weakened the forces of parochialism,

---

[10] This agrees with Burnham's argument (1965) that the political crisis brought on by the 1894 depression spawned serious third party movements, and in 1896 a critical realignment of the major party coalitions because the political parties were locked into patronage politics and incapable of addressing the economic crisis.

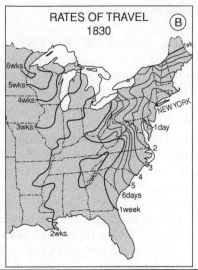

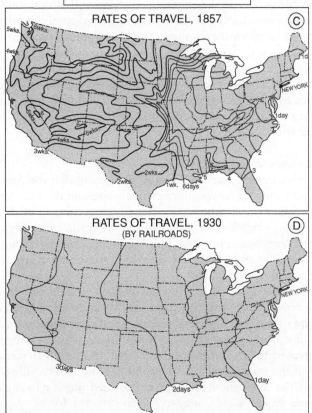

FIGURE 3.4. Railroad Travel Time to New York: 1830, 1857, and 1930
Source: Paulin (1932).

in large part by rendering such issues less relevant. Passenger, mail, and commercial shipping traffic increased sharply. The railroad opened national and international markets for western cash crop agriculture (principally, wheat, corn and hogs). It tied suppliers and markets to the large industrial centers. It allowed workers to easily relocate to new jobs (Easterlin 1958).

Regions that had once been relatively self-sufficient now became interdependent according to their comparative advantage in land, labor, abundant energy and access to transportation. The Northeast and Mid-Atlantic states shed agriculture, with the latter and the Midwest emerging as manufacturing centers. Expansion into the Great Plains turned the West into the nation's bread basket, supplying both the fast growing urban markets as well as export trade (see Figure 3.5). As the Midwest and West gained easier access to urban and export markets, their agricultural production grew dramatically. The regional specialization of these sectors can be more easily seen in Figure 3.6, which plots their relative contributions to the regions' productivity.

Integration ameliorated regional differences in wages. Americans migrated from rural poverty to cities with factories that paid higher wages. From 1880 to 1940 the average deviation of regional wages from the national average (see Table 3.4) nearly halved – from 46 percent to 25 percent. With rural migrants and the vast waves of immigrants directed toward eastern and Midwestern cities, the nation's urban population nearly doubled over a forty year period beginning in 1870.[11] By 1910 almost half of Americans lived in cities. The number of cities that exceeded 100,000 residents grew from 14 to 49. With urbanization came services. The per capita share of the gross national product (GNP) spent on public education more than doubled (Fishlow 1966).

All of these developments in production and markets spurred the emergence of a new kind of business enterprise – the multifunctional firm. In 1880, Western Union and Montgomery Ward were among the few large businesses to operate on a national scale. By 1900 the names of many integrated, multifunctional enterprises had become household words. They even surpassed the railroads in size and diversity of their operations and "as the focus for political and ideological controversy" (Chandler 1977: 288).[12] The modern firm exploited the nation's growing transportation and communications infrastructure and accelerated the development of an integrated national economy.

Regional economies increasingly became subunits of a national economy. With each decade, the prosperity of one region rested more heavily on the prosperity of all. As this national economy expanded and contracted, it increasingly changed voters' welfare everywhere. During the century following 1840 the

---

[11] The vast share of population growth came from two massive waves of immigration – first from the United Kingdom and northern Europe and beginning in the 1890s from southern and eastern Europe. World War I reduced immigration to a trickle, and in the 1920s anti-immigration laws virtually sealed the borders.

[12] Chandler (1977: 289) adds, "The decisions of its managers affected more businessmen, workers, consumers, and other Americans than did those of railroad executives."

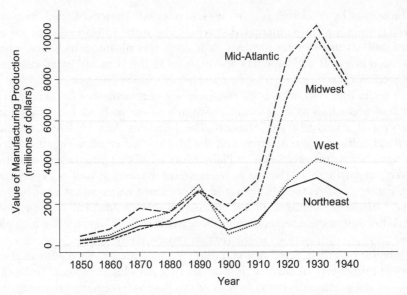

FIGURE 3.5a. Regional Differentiation of Manufacturing and Agriculture, 1850–1940: Regional Value of Manufacturing Production

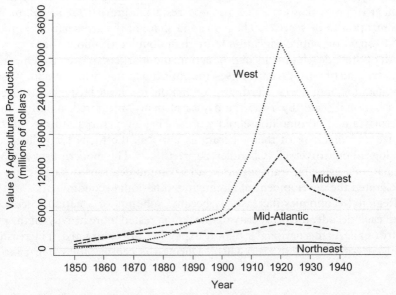

FIGURE 3.5b. Regional Value of Agricultural Production
Note: Values in constant dollars. *Source*: *Historical Statistics of the United States* (1975).

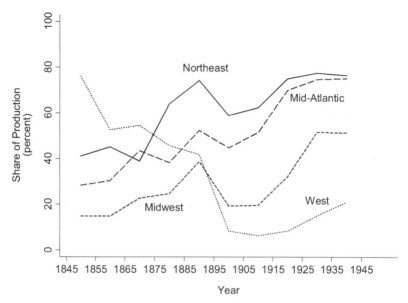

FIGURE 3.6. Manufacturing Share of Regional Production, 1850–1940
Note: Shares based on levels of productivity between manufacturing and agriculture presented in Figure 3.5. Values are drawn and interpolated from the decennial U.S. Census from 1840 to 1940.

TABLE 3.4 *Regional Income as Percent of National Income, 1880–1940*

	1880	1900	1920	1930	1940
United States	100	100	100	100	100
New England	141	134	124	129	121
Middle Atlantic	141	139	134	140	124
East North Central	102	106	108	111	112
West North Central	90	97	87	82	84
South Atlantic	45	45	59	56	69
East South Central	51	49	52	48	55
West South Central	60	61	72	61	70
Mountain	168	139	100	83	92
Pacific	204	163	135	130	138
Arithmetic mean deviation of regional per capita income from national level, percentage points	45.6	36.6	25.7	31.1	25.0

Source: Easterlin (1958: 315). The figures are per capita.

American economy grew steadily at roughly 5 percent per annum. While the nation's gross domestic product (GDP) grew steadily during the first half of this period (see Figure 3.7a), the year-to-year changes in GDP in Figure 3.7b identify a bumpier economic ride beginning in the 1880s, when Americans began experiencing severe recessions and depressions. There had been contractions in earlier years and some had persisted for long periods, as shown by the lengths of booms and busts in Figure 3.8.

But the recessions of the mid-1870s and 1880s paled next to the Panic of 1893. For the first time the nation's GDP shrank by 5 percent or more, leaving nearly a fifth of the labor force unemployed.[13] Clearly, near the end of the century the economy became more volatile, and we suspect, a more pressing political issue. Certainly, Americans during this era experienced the kinds of economic hardship that cause modern voters to turn out the administration party.

As noted earlier, the federal government had few policy instruments at its disposal. Almost all responses to economic downturns required legislative relief, for which classical economic theory offered few prescriptions and presidents had little influence. Nonetheless, from the early post–Civil War era on, deteriorating economic conditions appear to have triggered criticism of the administration's performance. High prices found critics calling for the administration to propose tariff reductions and even free trade. Tight credit renewed interest in inflating the currency by the unlimited coinage of silver.

Presidential elections during every contraction of the business cycle displayed in Figure 3.8 found the out of power party criticizing the administration's economic performance. In 1876 all pundits believed that Republican candidate Rutherford B. Hayes was doomed to defeat in light of the recession, compounded by the Grant administration's scandals. Directing campaigners privately from the sidelines, Hayes wrote fellow Ohioan James Garfield to take up the "bloody shirt" to distract voters from the economy: "Our strongest ground is the dread of a Solid South, rebel rule, etc.... It leads people away from 'hard times' which is our deadliest foe" (Hamilton 1895: 422).[14]

Although Republicans squeaked through a negotiated Electoral College victory despite a three percentage point deficit in the popular vote, those administration parties that presided over subsequent depressions – the Panic of 1893

---

[13] Some economic historians judge the 1890s double-dip depression to have been even more severe than the Great Depression. While the 1930s depression surpassed the 1890s downturn on most objective indicators, the population in the earlier era was significantly less wealthy and less able to cope with its severity. Moreover, government had fewer resources and responses available for stimulating the economy or ameliorating its adverse effects on the public (Higgs 1987).

[14] New York publisher Joseph Pulitzer rued the Republican campaign's success in deflecting economic issues. Exasperated, he wrote in the *World*, "'Hayes has never stolen.' Good God, has it come to this?" (Roseboom 1970: 241).

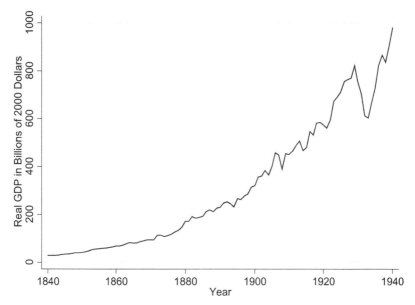

FIGURE 3.7 a. Real Gross Domestic Product, 1840–1940: GDP Constant Dollars

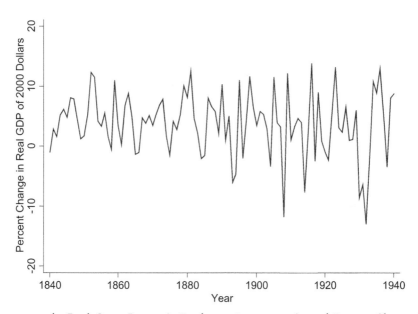

FIGURE 3.7 b. Real Gross Domestic Product, 1840–1940: Annual Percent Change in GDP

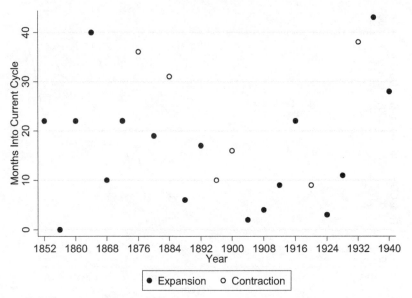

FIGURE 3.8 Duration of Business Cycles, 1852–1940
Source: retrieved from http://www.nber.org/cycles/cyclesmain.html. The figure displays
whether, and for how long, the economy was expanding or contracting at the time of a
presidential election. Hollow circles represent contractions while solid circles represent
expansion. The National Bureau of Economic Research (NBER) defines "expansion" as
the number of months of growth since the economy hit its lowest point. A *contraction*,
conversely, is the number of months that economic activity has receded since its last high
point. The thirty-six-month contraction for the 1876 election, for example, represents
a continuous decline in productivity since October 1873.

and the Great Depression – were trounced. Both depressions, in fact, sank the
presiding administration party's fortunes for the next decade or so. Democrats
lost 125 seats in the 1894 midterm House elections, as voters appear to have
blamed the Cleveland administration for the depression. The labor movement
mobilized discontent into major strikes (the most famous, the Pullman strike of
1894), from which emerged an incipient socialist party movement. Perhaps the
unprecedented depression took the nation into a new era of economic voting.
Or perhaps voters – as Hayes had advised two decades earlier – were already
accustomed to holding the government responsible for hard times. Tracking
vote swings during the 1870s and 1890s depressions Kleppner (1979: 366)
observed that his ethnoculturally defined constituency groupings behaved in a
way consistent with economic voting: "As a sense of 'hard time' was broadly
diffused among the mass public, voter groups responded... not to *polarize*
mass political behavior along class lines but to induce a general movement of
all voter groups in the same partisan direction."

The Econometrics of Economic Voting

Econometric research on economic voting has mostly ignored nineteenth-century elections (Kramer 1971). The few studies that do stretch time series back into the nineteenth century generally fail to separate nineteenth-century from twentieth-century relationships (Ferejohn and Calvert and 1984). Any significant relationships they report for economic voting could be based on behavior in the later era. One exception (Lynch 1999) that separates the analysis by century reports that for the period 1872 through 1912 the national presidential vote tracks changes in prices significantly but not growth in GNP. A 1 percent decline in prices (deflation) generated a roughly a 1.25 point reduction in the administration party's vote. This relationship accords fairly well with the historical record of presidential campaigns and third party movements during the last quarter of the nineteenth century. Prices of commodities and debt were episodically prominent issues throughout much of the second half of the nineteenth century. From 1867 until 1896, wholesale agricultural prices dropped by a third (Ratner, Soltow, and Sylla 1979). Inflating the currency was at times actively pursued by farmers and western mining interests and underwrote the meteoric rise of the Greenback Party in the late 1870s.

For our purposes, Lynch's time period poses a problem for assessing the impact of economic voting on nineteenth-century swings in presidential elections. His series begins late (1872) and continues into a significant period of the twentieth century (e.g., after 1940). In Table 3.5 we have reestimated the effects of the macroeconomy on voting separately for the last half of the nineteenth century (specifically, 1852 through the 1896 presidential election) and the first four decades of the twentieth century (1900 through the presidential election of 1940). In columns one through three, the dependent variable is the statewide Democratic share of the presidential vote. The first column presents results for the entire period, from 1840 through 1940. The next two columns separate the series into the nineteenth and twentieth centuries, respectively.

To measure the state of the national economy we use two variables that performed better than others in a preliminary analysis. The first – a standard measure of the business cycle – indicates whether the national economy was expanding or contracting (i.e., in recession) at the time of the election. Because one would expect vote shares to vary based not just on the simple presence of expansion or contraction, but also upon the time span of that growth or recession, we use the number of months the economy had been growing or contracting at the time of the election (e.g., de Bromhead, Eichengreen, O'Rourke 2013). Positive values indicate periods of growth, while negative values indicate periods of contraction.[15] To account for the partisanship of

---

[15] For example, on the eve of the 1876 presidential election the economy had been in contraction for thirty-six months. So this was coded in our dataset as −36.

TABLE 3.5. *State, Regional and National Presidential Voting as Function of Economy, 1852–1940*

OLS (with Fixed Effects)

DV = Democratic share of statewide presidential vote

Variables	State Vote			Regional Vote			National Vote		
	1852–1940	1852–1896	1900–1940	1852–1940	1852–1896	1900–1940	1852–1940	1852–1896	1900–1940
Lag State Dem. Vote (%)	0.40*** (0.03)	0.49*** (0.05)	0.24** (0.04)						
State 3rd Party Vote (%)	−0.35** (0.03)	−0.24*** (0.07)	−0.26* (0.04)						
Lag Regional Dem. Vote (%)				0.35*** (0.12)	0.46** (0.19)	0.04 (0.171)			
Regional 3rd Party Vote (%)				−0.25** (0.11)	−0.23** (0.11)	−0.11 (0.17)			
Lag National Dem. Vote (%)							0.28* (0.15)	−0.64 (0.53)	0.04 (0.17)
National 3rd Party Vote (%)							−0.21* (0.12)	−0.05 (0.14)	−0.03 (0.16)
Length of Business Cycle	0.18*** (0.02)	0.05** (0.02)	0.34*** (0.02)	0.19*** (0.05)	0.07*** (0.02)	0.41*** (0.10)	0.22*** (0.05)	0.11*** (0.04)	0.42*** (0.09)
Percent Change CPI	−0.34*** (0.05)	−0.05 (0.07)	−0.29*** (0.08)	−0.26** (0.15)	−0.01 (0.05)	−0.20 (0.30)	−0.23 (0.17)	−0.30 (0.22)	−0.13 (0.26)
Constant	27.22*** (1.30)	23.81*** (2.28)	31.13*** (1.54)	29.73*** (4.99)	24.34*** (8.07)	37.22*** (6.707)	34.21*** (7.25)	78.86*** (24.74)	39.71*** (7.52)
N	693	298	395	110	55	55	22	11	11
Adj. r²	0.48	0.25	0.61	0.50	0.22	0.71	0.62	0.58	0.80

$* \ p < 0.1, ** \ p < 0.05, *** \ p < 0.01$

Source for economic variables: NBER: retrieved from http://www.nber.org/cycles/cyclesmain.html and http://www.nber.org/cycles/cyclesmain.html and http://www.nber.org/databases/macrohistory/contents/.

the incumbent administration, we then multiplied the number of growing or contracting months by $+1$ for Democratic administrations and -1 for Republican administrations. The second economic variable, the annual percentage change in the Consumer Price Index, is similarly indexed against the administration party. To capture changes in the Democratic vote share, the model includes the statewide Democratic share of the vote in the prior presidential election.[16]

Column one of Table 3.5 presents the results for the whole series running from 1852 through 1940. Both the business cycle and changes in prices clearly influenced presidential voting. Of particular interest, however, are the results in the second and third columns, which separate the series into the nineteenth and twentieth centuries, respectively. The results for the nineteenth century show that the business cycle had a modest but significant impact on vote shares. According to these estimates, for every month of economic growth, or month of recession, statewide Democratic vote shares changed by 0.05 percentage points. The results for the twentieth century are much more robust. During the modern era every month of expansion or contraction changed Democratic vote shares by 0.34 percent.[17]

To further examine the impact of the economy on presidential voting, the successive columns in the table display results with the Democratic vote share aggregated at the regional and national levels. As with the state level vote, a similar pattern emerges: a modest role for the economy in the nineteenth century followed by a sharp uptick in the impact of economic voting in the twentieth century. Using the estimates from the national level models, the business cycle coefficient indicates that the thirty-eight months of contraction on the eve of the 1932 election cost the Republicans, nationally, nearly thirteen percentage points. Four years later, the economy's forty-three-month expansion during Franklin Delano Roosevelt's first term added about fifteen percentage points to his reelection vote. The Republican thirty-six-month recession in 1876, by contrast, cost Hayes about four percentage points.

Overall, we find that the macroeconomy played an increasing role in influencing presidential elections over this time period. Although the relationships for the nineteenth century's elections are comparatively modest, they do provide evidence of the presence of systematic national forces influencing voters' assessments of the presidential candidates and via lengthy coattails of all candidates on the ballot. Moreover, retrospective economic voting offers a model that befits the nineteenth-century's low information environment.

---

[16] To account for variation in state size, the estimates were weighted by the size of a state's congressional delegation.

[17] To test the differences in the coefficients across the pre- and post-1900 equations, we pooled the two time series together and interacted each coefficient with a pre-1900 dummy variable. For every coefficient, with the exception of the Consumer Price Index coefficients, the difference between the pre- and post-1900 coefficient was statistically significant at the 0.05 level.

Voters responded to the national economy and thereby gave politicians reason to pay attention to it. The downside, of course, is that there was not much this era's presidents could do. Mostly they tinkered with the tariff and spending and sought to distract voters with other issues. We turn now to another preeminent model of elections in two party systems – the median voter theorem – which also corresponds with important features of this era's presidential elections.

The Political Parties' Policy Commitments

We introduced the Westminster model in Chapter 2 as an electoral system that rewards with a disproportionate share of victories the political party that offers the most attractive program to the electorate. A well-configured national party platform in Britain or New Zealand might everywhere offer its homogeneous local constituencies a reasonably attractive policy promises. For a variety of reasons, America's nineteenth-century political parties fall well short of the requirements of the Westminster model. The historical period was not ripe for the emergence of political parties as purveyors of national policy. Even had circumstances been more favorable, America's parties faced a dilemma that made any national appeal risky. They needed to assemble pluralities in heterogeneous states and legislative districts. Voters' policy preferences were, for the most part, anchored in local, state, and regional interests. So too were the delegations the state parties sent to the national convention. With perhaps a few exceptions – such as the 1860 Republican convention and the 1896 Democratic convention – the national conventions did not contain majorities bent on promoting a policy more substantial that the standard statements of creed. Even were delegates so motivated, they confronted the problem of selling it to the nation. Even the most artfully crafted program would risk alienating more median voters across the states and legislative districts than it attracted. The same strategic problem that routinely silenced presidential contenders caused political parties to shy away from broadcasting programmatic appeals to the national electorate.

America's political parties were highly decentralized, freeing the state parties to pursue local pivotal voters with control over nominations and issuing separate party platforms. As voters around the country observed the national and their state campaigns, including signals emitted by these platforms, might they have learned information capable of systematically swinging party fortunes? Were a national convention to adopt a broadly unappealing platform, sufficient numbers of voters might have become alienated to drag down the party's turnout across the country and resulting in a vote swing toward the other party. Yet, we have already suggested that the diverse interests that the state parties sent to the national meeting probably precluded all but ambiguous homilies. And the state conventions were free with their platforms to repudiate odious messages and more generally reframe all national messages in the most favorable light.

Another consideration that we have thus far ignored in our discussion is that as state campaigns concentrated on mobilization they may have adopted platforms aimed more at energizing core supporters than at targeting a state's median voter. Spatial convergence of parties' platforms on divisive issues in a state would not only have been unnecessary, it might well have proved counterproductive. This suggests that we should find state party platforms separating on those issues that distinguish the political parties. And if they are separating, perhaps pressure to promote a consistent brand finds them separating on the same issues that divide the national parties.

One implication of such a strategy would be sharpening differences between partisans. Voters might become more steadfast, even fervent in their partisanship – a familiar claim of the ethnocultural historians, but one that our institutional explanation ignores. Second, if state mobilization campaigns centered their appeals on core voters, they might risk landing on the wrong side of an issue as circumstances changed. Grover Cleveland returned to the White House and Democrats took back control of Congress in 1892 on a promise to reduce the tariff. They pared back tariff rates only marginally, but their timing was terrible. Shortly thereafter the economy plunged into a deep depression that Republicans hammered in their midterm takeover of Congress and state governments and decisively, in the 1896 presidential election. In the next two sections, we examine national and state party platforms to learn the kinds of appeals they offered voters and determine whether they transmitted the kinds of messages that would have allowed voters to register their reactions to national politics in their support of the political parties. In mapping out the issue positions of national and state party platforms, we report evidence of separation on some issues (consistent with mobilization) and convergence on others (consistent with persuasion).

National Party Platforms

As long as one concentrates on party rhetoric at the national party conventions, party differences on important issues are not difficult to spot. Most Republicans favored a protective tariff, pensions for veterans, and a liberal homesteading policy. Most Democrats usually advocated lower tariff rates, opposed pensions as wasteful, and generally hesitated in endorsing expansion of homesteading.[18] As the nation approached the next century, the Republican Party had become associated with the party of efficiency and Democrats the party of economy.

That national party conventions consistently adopted a plank favoring a certain policy suggests to us that either party politicians promoted issues motivated by more than the opportunistic pursuit of patronage and graft or different politicians were at the helm – some preoccupied with patronage, others with policy. When the political parties differed on salient issues, even the positions

---

[18] We encountered a Republican broadside targeting recent German immigrants advertising simply: "Vote Republican – Get Farm."

of the most noncommittal candidate could be fixed with his acceptance letter's obligatory public endorsement of the party platform.

A systematic content analysis of these platforms and acceptance statements (Gerring 1998) turns up numerous differences between the two parties' rhetoric.[19] Moreover, adding credibility to party promises, many of these differences persisted over decades. Figure 3.9 presents the distribution of party rhetoric on several broad dimensions of national policy. Tariff and support for civil rights for African Americans divided the political parties consistently throughout the last quarter of the nineteenth century. The third variable – antibusiness sentiment – refers to a more diffuse object of opprobrium, which Democrats periodically summoned during hard economic times. Most elections, however, found both political parties endorsing American business. The party differences in all three figures follow historians' assessments of the issues separating the political parties.[20]

State Party Platforms

In running the presidential campaigns, the state parties were free to hide or trumpet planks in the national platform according to how well they squared with the preferences of their state's voters. Of course, we may assume that these party politicians embraced those inoffensive provisions of the national platform if only to project a consistent party brand. And the national party, coveting every state's electoral vote above all else, stated national policy goals to be as encompassing as possible without wholly diluting the party brand. Yet where a state's pivotal voter's preferences differed from those of the national median voter, the national and state parties might have found they favored different platform provisions.[21]

Consider the special appeal of the silver issue in the West as compared to the rest of the country in the 1880s and 1890s. Two large classes of voters in the West were ardent supporters of a bimetallism policy that would require the national government to restore silver as a basis for the currency. Debt-ridden farmers and ranchers sought an expansion of the currency and the reduction in interest rates that would follow. At the other end of the economic totem, were the miners who were producing prodigious amounts of silver and

---

[19] Many of the Gerring's variables concern style (preference or distaste for "statist" policies) and morality (Republicans' emphasis on family values). For the words that qualify for these variables and those presented in text, see Gerring (1998).

[20] Of course, historians frequently draw on these records as the source for ascribing party differences.

[21] Virtually all state parties convened before every election to nominate state officers and to adopt a platform on state and national issues. These "electioneering documents," as Key (1964: 421) referred to them, put the party on record for or against a particular policy and thereby created a kind of tacit, albeit weak, commitment. The party nominees pledged fealty to the platform – sometimes, as required, in writing. These policy statements were widely distributed to voters, excerpted in broadsides and cited by stump speakers.

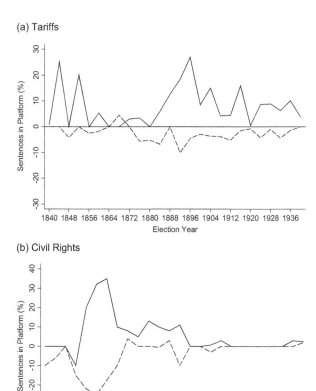

(a) Tariffs

(b) Civil Rights

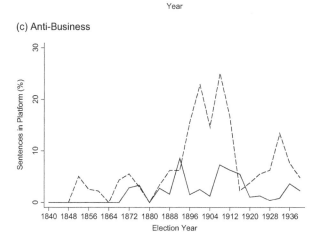

(c) Anti-Business

----- Democrat ——— Republican/Whig

FIGURE 3.9. (a) Major Party Platform References to Tariff; (b) Major Party Platform References to Civil Rights; (c) Antibusiness
Note: The top two panels display the percentage of positive statements (i.e., pro-tariff, pro-civil rights) minus the percentage of negative statements (i.e., anti-tariff, anti-civil rights). *Source:* Gerring (1998: 69, 77 and 110).

favored a policy that had the federal government purchase huge shipments of the metal and take it out of circulation into federal repositories. The political histories of this region suggest that politicians from both parties (and third party movements) found bimetallism irresistible. Politicians from the other regions, however, were mostly indifferent or hostile to the West's preference for silver.

If western Democratic and Republican politicians ignored their differing national parties' positions and matched each other, silver would remain a regional issue – incapable of systematically shifting party fortunes. If, however, one set of partisans brought the state platform into conformity with the national platform – even if it meant failing to take a position – the two state parties would separate on this major issue to local voters. On this particular issue, Republicans confronted a truly serious dilemma in that the national party stood foursquare for the gold standard. Did western Republicans toe the party line and oppose bimetallism or did they match the positions of their Democratic foes, whose national platform endorsed the silver industry's bimetallism proposal? This question can be asked for other issues, as well, some of which placed state Democrats at a disadvantage.

Many constituencies who wanted to change government policy launched their campaigns in these state party conventions' platform committees. According to Bensel (2000: 102), who tabulated the parties' policy stances in more than 2,000 state party platforms from the last quarter of the nineteenth century, "these planks were often bitterly contested... [and] frequently so intense that the losers bolted, forming their own organization, platform, and candidate list for the coming election period. There were dozens of such bolts in the late nineteenth century." Drafting these electioneering documents could be serious affairs.

The planks that generated the most intense politics concerned national policy. The same issues that dominated national platforms, Bensel (2000: 102) notes, also "dominated party competition at the state level where, in fact, few opportunities to shape national development existed... both minor and major parties in state after state, year after year, devoted most of their platform demands to issues associated with national economic development, often relegating local problems to a rather desultory, secondary role among partisans." These state platforms on national policy issues provide us a window for observing the mediating effects of state run presidential campaigns on national electoral forces.

Figure 3.10 displays the distribution of positions on various national policies taken by Democrats and Republicans at their state conventions. For each issue, the figure displays the percentage of state platforms that supported, opposed, or failed include a plank on that issue. For example, on the issue of federal supervision of elections in the South after the Civil War, 22 percent of Democratic planks explicitly opposed federal supervision, while 26 percent of Republican platforms supported supervision. The remainder, 78 percent

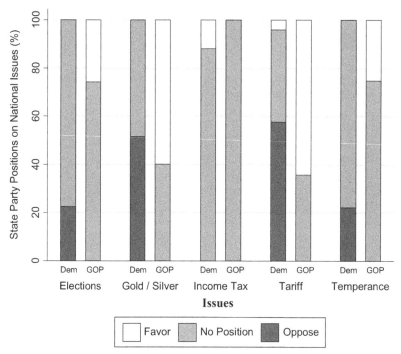

FIGURE 3.10. State Party Positions on Selected Issues, 1877–1900
Source: These estimates and those reported in following tables and figures are based on reanalysis of percentages and frequencies (N = 1446) compiled from tables 3.2 through 3.19 of Bensel (2000). The clear sections of bars indicate the percentage of state party platforms supporting a particular policy. The dark gray shaded areas indicate opposition and the grey shaded areas, the percentage of platforms with no plank on the issue. Southern states excluded from analysis. The issue labels on the *x*-axis refer to the following: "Elections" refer to planks on the intervention of the federal government into state elections; "Gold/Silver" refers to planks regarding the gold standard or the coinage of silver; "Income tax" refers to planks supporting a national income tax; "Tariff" refers to planks on the issue of tariff protection; and "Temperance" refers to planks concerning the regulation and/or prohibition of alcohol consumption.

and 74 percent of Democratic and Republican state platforms, respectively, failed to include a position either in support or opposition to federal election supervision. No Democratic platform endorsed federal supervision of elections nor did any Republican platform oppose it. About a quarter of Republican platforms favored temperance, while almost the same share of Democratic platforms opposed it. Again, about three-quarters of both parties' platforms ignored the issue. Of the five issues presented in Figure 3.10, only tariff and currency find a majority of the state parties taking opposite positions. These are the same two issues that found the national parties' platforms separating. Even here a small share of Democratic conventions adopted policies that contradicted their national party's position. (Eleven Democratic conventions endorsed the current tariff or opposed free trade.)

Second, although one finds sharp policy differences between the state parties, more than pure conformity to national party policy is present in the figure. As the percentage of platforms without a plank on particular issues attests, state parties were also very selective in deciding which issues to take an explicit stand on. As an example, 40 percent of state Democratic and 38 percent of Republican platforms failed to include a plank on tariff policy. We suspect that where public opinion within a state backed one party's views, the other party quietly ignored the issue rather than tout their national party's unpopular position. No platform opposed railroad regulation outright or pensions for Union veterans, which constituted the federal government's single largest domestic expenditure. Instead of expressing opposition, the parties' lack of enthusiasm for a proposed policy typically shows up in its absence from the platform. Bensel (2000: 169) reasons: "In those cases where a policy was unpopular with the electorate but otherwise essential to the programmatic design of the party's platform, a party often chose to silently suffer the damage caused by passive identification with that position rather than disrupt their coalition with an opportunistic and sometimes insincere renunciation." Appreciating their party's dependence on Irish Catholic support in the eastern states, Democrats everywhere refrained from endorsing anti-liquor laws even in states with large nativist populations and where prohibition parties were thriving. On the whole, we find that state party platforms did not balkanize the party label on prominent issues. At most, state parties' issue stances may have diluted the party brand by strategically deemphasizing some issues in favor of others.

Western Republicans were more likely than non-western Republicans to endorse the coinage of silver and less likely to endorse the gold standard (Bensel 2000). Nevertheless, the patterns of state party platforms suggests that voters across the nation essentially received the same Democratic and Republican appeals on core issues. Republican politicians favored continued supervision of elections in the South and Democrats were opposed; Democrats espoused some variant of bimetallism and Republicans (outside the West) supported the gold standard; Democrats opposed temperance and Republicans' supported it. On each of these issues the state parties followed their national parties.

Conclusion

The party ballot cast the presidential candidates as pivotal actors. And yet we have described presidential candidates as noncommittal recluses. How could these diminutive figures serve as focal points, if indeed they did, cuing voters on differences between the political parties on key issues in the election? Better serving responsiveness would have been presidential campaigns that had the candidates campaigning throughout the nation for a mandate to enact their policies. If presidential candidates had behaved more in keeping with their role as focal points, we would have a straightforward parliamentary-like account of issue-oriented voters responding to the candidates' and their parties' programs. Even when these candidates' policy preferences deviated from their party's platform, they would still have sent the national electorate a consistent signal that could have generated national partisan swings. These figures are missing in action in nineteenth century elections, at least in those elections involving viable competitors.

Some elections stood apart by sharply aligning the political parties with different positions on a highly salient issue during the presidential election. The clearest instances are the 1844 election that revolved around war with Mexico; 1860, which turned on the extension of slavery and the specter of disunion; and 1896, the nation's severest depression to date and an ideological appeal that for many voters represented a culture war. Though extreme, these cases demonstrate that – then as now – national policy could dominate campaigns and election outcomes. Although these elections do not require electoral machinery manufacturing responsiveness to explain their massive swings in party control, they contribute to our argument by displaying an electorate voting as if they were attentive to national issues. At least some voters – then as today – appear to have compared their own preferences with the stances of the candidates and voted accordingly.

Wherever we have looked, we have turned up evidence of modest national forces. Despite party managers' best efforts, campaign competition had a way of pulling issues to the foreground, as did the economy, and occasionally flushed presidential candidates out of their homes to clarify their positions on issues. And perhaps most impressively of all, state parties that ran the state presidential campaigns did not repudiate their national party's locally unpopular policies as they appealed to their state's median voter. Instead, they muted unpopular policy stances while touting those positions where they enjoyed an advantage over the other party. As a result, the thirty or so separate state party campaigns transmitted relatively consistent messages to voters. This both preserved the party brand, a collective good, and limited every party politician's exposure to costly contradiction.

4

House of Representatives Elections

Incumbents dominate modern congressional elections. Even when the public holds an unfavorable opinion about their political party, incumbents consistently tend to win reelection. Rather than depend on the vagaries of presidential coattails, modern congressional careers hinge on the ability to craft a home style (Fenno 1978) and cultivate a personal vote with constituents (e.g., Cain, Ferejohn, and Fiorina 1987; Carson, Engstrom, and Roberts 2007). To the extent national forces intrude into these elections, they do so through the anticipated reactions of potential candidates to enter or exit the congressional arena (Jacobson and Kernell 1983). The apparent separation of congressional elections from presidential outcomes can be seen in the contemporary frequency of divided party control of the presidency and the U.S. House. In only nine of sixteen presidential elections from 1948 through 2012 did the same party win both the presidency and the House.

By contrast nineteenth-century House elections appear to have more closely tracked presidential elections and national issues. From the rise of the Whig party in 1840 until the turn of the century, thirteen of the fifteen presidential elections found the party winning the presidency also taking or retaining control of the House. (One of these exceptions was 1876, when the Democrats won a majority of House seats as well as the popular vote majority for president. However, they lost the presidency in a contested Electoral College vote count.) When divided government did occur it was usually as a result of midterm elections (eight of the ten instances) when an unpopular administration became a burden for fellow partisans.

One can detect the basis for these dramatic episodes of party turnover in Washington in the aggregate connection between presidential voting and House seat shares during the nineteenth century. Consider the relationship shown in Figure 4.1, which plots the Democratic presidential vote and House seat shares for non-Southern states for the 100-year period from 1840 through 1940.

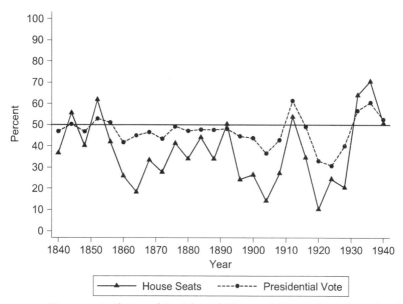

FIGURE 4.1. Democratic Shares of Presidential Vote and House Seats: Non-Southern States, 1840–1940
Note: The presidential vote percentage is the two-party percentage of the Democratic vote. Figure compiled by the authors from data in Rusk (2001).

Although congressional elections closely track presidential voting throughout this time period, nineteenth-century results appear to have been especially sensitive to slight shifts in presidential voting. To state this relationship more precisely we have estimated separate swing ratios before and after 1900 in Figure 4.1. As suspected, the swing ratio is a steep 3.83 percent for the nineteenth century compared to the significantly weaker ($p < 0.05$) and near-linear coefficient of 1.97 percent during the twentieth century.[1]

Because these coefficients are nonlinear (based on logistic transformations of House seats and presidential votes), their dissimilar effects can be better seen in the plotted relationships in Figure 4.2. As the Democratic vote outside the South crossed the 50 percent threshold, its share of congressional victories rose sharply. Added to its Southern seats, a narrow victory in the presidential election could give the Democrats control of the House of Representatives. Clearly, nineteenth-century congressional elections appear to have defied the Framers' script for preventing unified party control of the national government.

---

[1] In both periods the vote-seat relationship for the non-South shows a bias in favor of the Republicans. In the nineteenth-century bias is a small −2.37 percent, increasing to −8.17 percent after the turn of the century.

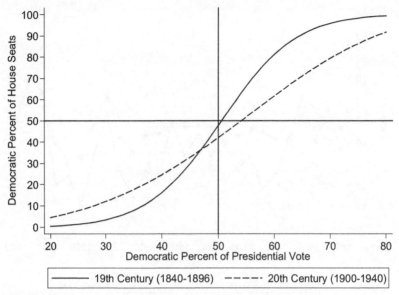

FIGURE 4.2. The Presidential Vote-House Seat Relationship: Non-Southern States, 1840–1940
Note: The vote-seat relationships are estimated using the non-Southern presidential vote and House seats from Figure 4.1.

Nineteenth-Century House Elections

In Chapter 2 we highlighted the importance of the party supplied ballot in inducing strong presidential coattails. Unless a voter undertook some extraordinary effort to split the ballot – such as tearing and submitting parts of different ballots, scratching off names, or pasting different candidate names over those of the party supplied ticket (Bensel 2004; Reynolds 1988) – in full view of party workers stationed at the polling place, coattail voting occurred by default. Party workers ushering voters to the polls could reliably count in their column even those citizens who expressed weak preferences.

Many students of electoral history (e.g., Ferejohn and Calvert 1984; Moos 1952; Rusk 1970) have previously noted the inherent coattail effects of the party ticket. But generally overlooked is the fact that not all party tickets could induce presidential coattails in House elections because states frequently held these elections on different dates. Until 1872, when federal law consolidated presidential and congressional elections (with minor exceptions), twenty non-Southern states at one time or another separated House and presidential election calendars by one to ten months.[2] In 1872, Congress attached a provision to the decennial Apportionment Act that required states to hold

---

[2] For an analysis of how separate calendars affected elections during the Civil War, see Carson, Jenkins, Rohde, and Souva (2001).

congressional elections on the first Tuesday after the first Monday in November. Some states were tardy in making the switch. Notably, Ohio continued to hold its congressional elections in October until 1886, Oregon until 1910, Vermont until 1914, and Maine until 1960. In 1845, Congress fixed the presidential election date we currently use, the first Tuesday after the first Monday in November.

The separation of congressional and presidential election dates, however, did not mean that non-November congressional elections were entirely insulated from the swirl of the national campaign (James 2007). In particular, the early state elections functioned as pseudo-public opinion polls, often indicating which way the electoral winds were blowing. Consequently these bell-weather states became the site of intense battles between the national parties. Each side poured money and patronage into them hoping to build momentum for the November presidential election. According to one historian, "Winning early, winning big, had a bandwagon effect. It could inspire party workers and tap the wallets of doubtful contributors for the general election. A big loss would tear the heart out of a campaign. The October states had done that to Democrats in 1868 and 1880" (Summers 2000: 257).

Recognizing their import, national leaders closely tracked the campaigns in these early states. During the 1864 election Abraham Lincoln camped out in the White House telegraph office awaiting news from the early states of Maine, Ohio, Pennsylvania, and Indiana (Waugh 1997: 332–346). Beyond their bandwagon impact, many of the early states contained large congressional delegations, and party politicians worked hard to swing the results in these states. An early loss might also spur a party to redouble their efforts. After losing big in Maine's September election in 1856, national Democratic leaders cajoled a group of Wall Street financiers into donating $50,000 to fund the October campaigns in Pennsylvania and Indiana. Illinois Senator Stephen Douglas sold some of his real estate to help finance the efforts in Pennsylvania (Nichols 1948: 47). With this money Democrats were able to send campaign literature into "every single home in Philadelphia" and naturalize "hundreds of foreigners" (Nichols 1948: 47). In addition, prominent Democratic politicians from around the country traveled to Pennsylvania giving stump speeches throughout the state. These efforts paid off. Democrats carried both Pennsylvania and Indiana, setting the table for James Buchanan's victory in November. In testing the effects of institutional arrangements on electoral responsiveness, it will therefore be important to distinguish those elections in Figure 4.3 where a consolidated party ballot was in place from those split ticket systems that arose from different electoral calendars.

Coattail voting represents only the first cog in the electoral machinery of manufacturing presidential votes into congressional seats. The potential impact of small swings in the national vote can be seen in Figure 4.4, which plots the distribution of the total Democratic vote in non-Southern House districts between 1840 and 1940. To better see changes over time in congressional competition, the figure divides the series into twenty-year periods. From the

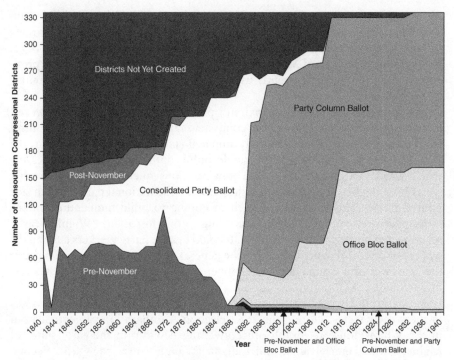

FIGURE 4.3. Ballot Format in Non-Southern Congressional Districts, 1840–1940
Note: We compiled this figure by combining information from Dubin (1998) (on dates
of elections) and Ludington (1911), Albright (1942), and Walker (1972) (on ballot
laws). In a number of instances, we confirmed the timing of congressional elections by
consulting various historical state Blue Books.

vantage point of today's uncompetitive congressional elections the numbers
in Figure 4.4 appear striking. The figure reveals that both parties remained
competitive throughout the non-South, with very few lopsided outcomes. For
most of the nineteenth century, the distribution of competition was distinctly
unimodal, with the large fraction of districts clumping near the 50 percent
mark. From 1882 to 1900, for instance, Democrats received between 45 percent
and 55 percent of the vote in 39 percent of House races. The large number of
close districts provided fertile ground for presidential coattails to translate into
large seat swings. Even a modest perturbation from the presidential campaign
could swing the outcome in numerous districts.

Close elections certainly reflected the tight partisan division of many state
electorates. But close elections were also a product of the strategic calculations
of partisan mapmakers in the states. At least since Elbridge Gerry's famous district map drawn in 1812, politicians have viewed districting as an opportunity
to influence future elections. Earlier we noted that Tufte's (1973) seminal analysis of electoral responsiveness showed strong swing ratios attending uniform

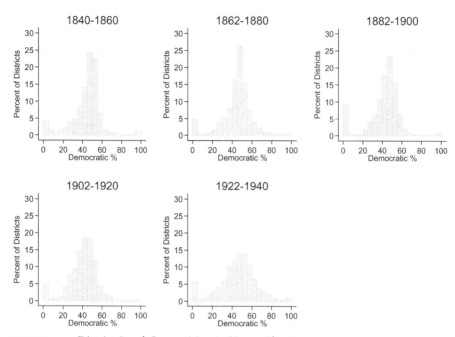

FIGURE 4.4. District-Level Competition in House Elections
Note: The *x*-axis is the Democratic share of the total vote within congressional districts. We compiled the figure from data presented in Dubin (1998).

swings in closely contested, narrowly decided national elections. Yet among the couple of dozen vote-seat relationships Tufte reports, the strongest swing ratios arose not in Westminster-style systems but in those nineteenth-century congressional elections held during presidential election years. Noting the sharp difference between swing ratios for nineteenth- and twentieth-century congressional elections, Tufte attributed the weakening relationship to the modern practice of bipartisan gerrymandering aimed at protecting incumbents of both parties. We accept his insight that district design matters but argue that it applies equally well in explaining the exceptional responsiveness of nineteenth-century elections. Politicians in this era dedicated themselves to congressional redistricting, sometimes to the exclusion of other legislative work. As party control of Ohio's state government flip-flopped repeatedly from 1878 to 1892, the legislature redistricted seven times. In one stretch, the state conducted six consecutive elections with six different districting plans (Argersinger 1992: 90; Engstrom 2006; Martis 1982).

Nineteenth-century politicians appear to have calculated political advantage differently than would their risk-averse twentieth-century counterparts, and in ways that rendered the era's congressional elections highly responsive to presidential outcomes. Partisan lawmakers during the earlier era were more inclined to construct gerrymanders in which "the dominant party magnifies

---

BOX 4.1. **The Federal Government Mandates Congressional Districts**

A number of states before the 1840s elected all of their House members in statewide at-large elections. This voting system was known as the "general ticket" (and is similar to how the vast majority of states currently select electors to the Electoral College). In this system voters possessed as many votes as there were seats to fill. As a result, a party winning a plurality of the statewide vote almost always swept the state congressional delegation. Congress banned the practice in 1842 when, as an amendment to the decennial Apportionment Bill, they mandated that all states use geographically contiguous, single-member districts. The decision to impose single-member districts was driven by partisan purposes. The new census had revealed that a number of states using the general ticket would be gaining seats in the new apportionment. These states also happened to lean Democratic. The Whig Party, however, held a majority of seats in the House and Senate. The Whigs calculated that they could pick up extra seats by forcing Democratic-leaning general ticket states to switch to single-member districts. With a few exceptions, the single-member district system for House elections has been in place ever since.

---

its popular vote by creating many districts it can reliably but narrowly carry" (Argersinger 1992: 75). Cain (1984) has termed these practices "efficient" gerrymanders because they waste few votes in a party's effort to maximize its seat share – that is, strengthen the swing ratio – by having each district mirror its favorable statewide vote.

To return to Ohio's instructive experience, each of the six districting plans effectively converted narrow statewide vote majorities for the controlling party into large seat bonuses to the House of Representatives. In 1886, Ohio Republicans could take special pride in their new district maps, which secured them fifteen of twenty-one seats (73 percent) with only 53 percent of the statewide vote (Engstrom 2006; 2013). In Maine, Republicans in 1884 crafted a gerrymander that allowed them to capture every single congressional district (four) for five straight elections despite an average district vote of only 54 percent. One of the beneficiaries of this gerrymander was Thomas Brackett Reed (R) – future Speaker of the House and creator of the transformative "Reed's Rules." Reed won reelection between 1884 and 1890 by an average margin of 2 percent.

The efficient gerrymander stands in contrast with the more familiar packing strategy of twentieth-century gerrymanders, in which out-party supporters are concentrated into one or a few districts while in-party supporters are distributed evenly throughout the rest of the state (Cain 1984; Cox and Katz 2002; Owen and Grofman 1988). This ensures a number of easy victories for the in-party while conceding a minimal number of districts to the out-party. It also yields flatter swing ratios.

Why would twentieth-century politicians prefer this alternative to efficient gerrymandering? One familiar argument (Tufte 1973) holds that during the twentieth century, increasingly careerist incumbents (Kernell 1977; Polsby

1968) in the House successfully importuned state legislatures to draw district boundaries insulating them from future challenges. Whether state politicians, some of whom might covet a seat in the House, would modify their districting preferences to accommodate these budding professionals remains unclear and conjectural (Cox and Katz 2002: 36).[3]

The answer might also reflect structural changes in electoral institutions that increased the risk of mistakes.[4] Districts with intentionally narrow majorities might in time become narrow minorities, opening the door for a disastrous sweep by the opposition. Efficient gerrymandering required accurate, up-to-date election forecasts, for which public voting monitored by legions of "district men" (Silbey 1991: 222) proved an essential asset both in identifying who to turn out and to prevent voters from reneging on prior commitments. Moreover, institutionally induced coattail voting meant that this era's politicians did not have to pay as close attention to some of the subtler aspects of voters' preferences, including strength and breadth of support down the ticket. An individual who a party canvasser scored as only marginally favoring James G. Blaine would be escorted to the voting place and safely counted in the Republican column for the House election. This rationale agrees with nineteenth-century electoral history that finds "politicians...able to predict outcomes with great accuracy," (Silbey 1991: 153) in large part because "the party structure ... provided them with a range and feel of information that the modern politician with... computers and survey data clearly does not have" (Marcus 1971: 10–14). Even in poor rural districts, party politicians developed sophisticated information-gathering machines. In the West Virginia panhandle, for example, reporters "found a regular district headquarters in constant touch with county leaders. A full corps of clerks and typists bustled about answering letters and evaluation reports from distant precincts. At the chairman's fingertips were tallies of the names, ages, occupations, politics, and color of every adult male in the Second District" (Summers 2004: 146).

The reformed ballot, in contrast, allowed variations in party loyalty and intensity of preferences to come into play and add an element of uncertainty to the outcome. Voters now privately chose among the parties' individual candidates and could even decide to quit voting as they moved down the ballot

---

[3] The increasing importance of seniority within the House (Katz and Sala 1996) might also have motivated state legislators to protect incumbents as a mechanism to direct federal funds and projects back to the state (McKelvey and Riezman 1992).

[4] Although we have already discounted the impact of a highly politicized, narrowly divided electorate nationally shifting its support from one party team to the next over a series of elections – thereby generating sizable swing ratios – one aspect of this argument that might still hold concerns the correlation between an election's swing ratio and closeness. This introduces the possibility that tight races outside the South up until 1896 account for the larger nineteenth-century swing ratios. We tested this alternative by substituting a dummy variable for the 1896 election in place of the date of a state's ballot reform. The resulting pre-post differences in the swing ratio are smaller than those reported in Table 4.2.

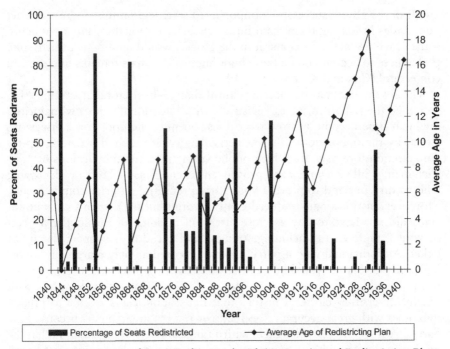

FIGURE 4.5. Percentage of Seats Redistricted and Average Age of Redistricting Plans, 1840–1940
Note: Figures calculated from the redistricting dates reported in Martis (1982). Congress failed to reapportion the House following the 1920 census, which helps to explain the comparative absence of redistricting during the 1920s.

into the region of unfamiliar names. Confronted with increased estimation error, partisan districters responded rationally (McDonald 1999; Owen and Grofman 1988) by covering targeted districts with extra partisans.

Finally, whether measured by the frequency of redistricting or the average age of existing boundaries, Figure 4.5 exhibits a clear trend away from the frequent fine-tuning of district boundaries that efficient gerrymanders require. Neglect could have arisen from the declining turnover in party control of state governments – itself possibly a result of shortening presidential coattails on state legislative elections after ballot reform – that had triggered redistricting events throughout the nineteenth century (Engstrom 2006; 2013).[5] Or it might simply be that because packing strategies involved surplus margins

[5] Yet another possibility, first noted by Burnham (1970), has party turnover declining in state legislatures after the realigning 1896 election sorted voters into safe Democratic and Republican districts. Consistent with this conjecture, a single party captured 23 percent of the state governments after presidential elections during the nineteenth century, compared to 16 percent from 1900 through 1940.

they required less maintenance. Whatever the cause, Figure 4.5 traces the steady decline in congressional districting after ballot reform at the same time swing ratios were turning less responsive (Brady and Grofman 1991; Tufte 1973).

Testing the Effects of Electoral Rules on State Outcomes

Control over the critical institutional ingredients in our model – ballot form, district lines, and, until the 1880s, election dates – resided with the states.[6] As a consequence, in any given election year one finds a number of institutional combinations in place across the nation. Although such variety across states cautions against inferences of institutional effects from national-level data, it represents a godsend for testing the mediating effects of this electoral machinery in a quasi-experimental setting.

Accordingly, we have pooled the relevant electoral and institutional variables for the thirty-seven non-Southern states for the years 1840–1940. Nineteen states entered the Union after 1840, giving us an unbalanced, time-series cross-sectional data structure.[7] Later in this chapter, we reaggregate these state-level relationships to assess whether they account for national trends in party control of the House of Representatives.

Coattail Voting and Ballot Form

To analyze the effect of presidential coattails and differing institutional regimes on House voting, we estimate the following equation:

$$\text{DHV}_{it} = a_i + b\text{DPV}_{it} + c(\text{DPV}_{it}{}^*\text{B}_{it}) + d\text{DPV}_{i(t-1)} + e(\text{DPV}_{i(t-1)}{}^*\text{B}_{it}) \quad (1)$$

The dependent variable, DHV_{it}, is the statewide Democratic percentage of the House vote for state i at time t, and the key treatment variable is the Democratic percentage of the state presidential vote (DPV_{it}). The presidential vote is then interacted with those state-level institutional variables hypothesized to mediate the impact of the coattail. The equation is estimated as a time-series cross-section model using Ordinary Least Squares (OLS) with panel corrected standard errors (Beck and Katz 1995). Because changes in institutional rules interest us more than do specific differences in a states' politics, we include state fixed effects to control for dissimilar partisan advantages across states.[8]

---

[6] The effects of other electoral laws, such as party registration, on the nineteenth-century electorate has been well documented elsewhere (see Keyssar 2000).

[7] Working with state-level seat shares also has the advantage over district-level analysis (for example, see Cox and Katz 1999; Cox and Katz 2002) of obviating the need to take into account that district apportionments did not occur in isolation from others within a state.

[8] Simply shifting the intercepts across states will fail to detect any state interactions with the parameters that interest us. We have also checked for the possibility of heterogeneity across states via the technique of cross-validation (Beck 2001). Specifically, we reran the model reported in Table 4.1, Column 2 but dropped one state at a time and examined the model's performance

Equation 1 frames two basic tests for the effects of the state Democratic presidential vote on its congressional vote share.[9] The first test identifies the direct effect of coattail voting on House elections both under the consolidated ballot, $b\text{DPV}_{it}$, and under various alternative ballot structures, $c(\text{DPV}_{it}*B_{it})$. If differences in state electoral laws mediate presidential coattails, then the coefficient for the stand-alone presidential vote term (here representing states with a consolidated party ballot) should be significantly stronger than when it is interacted with either off-November congressional elections or ballot reform. In Table 4.1 this is what we find. The consolidated party ballot generates a nearly one-to-one relationship between statewide votes for the two offices when both were present on the ticket. Separate election calendars cut the coattail effect approximately in half from 0.87 percent to 0.51 percent (Column 1). Ballot reform also trimmed presidential coattails, but contrary to our expectation, the office bloc form reduced the relationship no more than did the party column ballot. In Column 2 of Table 4.1 we have consolidated these reforms into a single Australian ballot variable. During the first four decades after the spread of ballot reform, the coattail effect lost about a quarter of its impact – from 0.86 percent to 0.64 percent.[10]

A second, indirect test of coattail effects is available by interacting the lagged congressional vote (i.e., the previous midterm vote) with the state's current electoral institutions. Where coattails are hypothesized to be strong, such as states with a consolidated party ballot, the lag effect should be weaker than in settings with an Australian ballot. This is precisely what we find in Table 4.1. Under the consolidated ballot regime, congressional elections did not track past results nearly as closely as they would after ballot reform. The combined weakening of the coattail and strengthening of the lag term presented House members with a much more stable electoral environment for contemplating a career in the House of Representatives. It is probably no coincidence that the

for the excluded state. Most of the mean absolute errors of these predictions fall within a narrow range of one to five percentage points. The estimates for Rhode Island, Kansas, Arizona, and Montana do not fit quite as well, with mean absolute errors above seven. These states are marked by small congressional delegations, suggesting that idiosyncrasies inherent in a single, statewide congressional race may alter the election dynamics prevailing elsewhere. Because we are more interested in the general structural properties of nineteenth-century election laws than with modeling the particulars of each states' politics, we have conservatively included these states in the analysis. A similar analysis to check for temporal heterogeneity was done by serially removing election years. The only election year that marginally stood out as an exception was (unsurprisingly) 1896, with a mean absolute error of 7.1 percentage points.

[9] We also include the lagged value of the statewide House vote to directly model the temporal dynamics (and eliminate serial correlation) (Beck and Katz 1996). Including a lagged dependent variable along with fixed effects, as we do, can lead to bias when T is small (Kvist 1995). Given that our average T is nearly twenty, however, any potential bias will very likely be small (Beck 2001). Nevertheless, as a check we ran our model without fixed effects and found almost no difference in the coefficients or standard errors.

[10] This result meshes with the findings of Carson and Roberts (2012), which show that the individual characteristics mattered more for election outcomes after implementation of the Australian ballot.

TABLE 4.1. *The Impact of Presidential Coattails on Congressional Voting in the States, 1844–1940*

OLS (with panel corrected standard errors)
D.V. = Percent Democratic of State's House Vote

Variable	(1)	(2)
Presidential Vote (% Dem.)	0.869***	0.861***
	(0.066)	(0.066)
Ballot Form		
Non-November Election	17.708***	16.542***
	(3.305)	(3.338)
Non-November Election ×	−0.359***	−0.345***
Presidential Vote	(0.086)	(0.088)
Party Column Ballot	12.579*	
	(6.889)	
Party Column Ballot ×	−0.248**	
Presidential Vote	(0.075)	
Office Bloc Ballot	9.552	
	(7.069)	
Office Bloc Ballot ×	−0.210**	
Presidential Vote	(0.079)	
Australian Ballot		0.835
		(2.922)
Australian Ballot ×		−0.223**
Presidential Vote		(0.074)
Political Setting		
Minor Party Vote	.404**	.412**
	(0.130)	(0.130)
Minor Party Vote ×	−0.010**	−0.010**
Democratic Presidential Vote	(0.003)	(0.003)
Lag of House Vote		
Lag of House Vote	0.138*	0.129**
(Previous Midterm)	(0.052)	(0.012)
Non-November Election ×	−0.017	−0.007
Lag Vote	(0.084)	(0.084)
Australian Ballot ×	0.167**	0.178**
Lag Vote	(0.073)	(0.073)
Constant	0.433	1.445
	(2.562)	(2.519)
R^2	0.781	0.779
N	733	733
# of Groups	37	37
Mean Obs. Per Group	19.81	19.81

* $p < 0.10$, ** $p < 0.05$, *** $p < 0.01$.
Note: State fixed effects are included in the estimation but not presented in the table. Panel corrected standard errors in parentheses.

proportion of non-Southern incumbents seeking reelection increased sharply during this period (Kernell 2003).

We also tested a number of control variables that capture important aspects of the broader political setting. With the Democratic vote for both House and president percentaged against a state's total popular vote, the coattail variables (i.e., the presidential vote and its interactions) may be diluted by the presence of third party candidates in the presidential or congressional races.[11] The positive relationship for the minor party presidential vote indicates that a state's Democratic congressional vote increases with the strength of minor party presidential candidates. This makes sense for a couple of reasons. First, throughout this period, minor party presidential candidates tended to draw votes at the expense of Republican or Whig candidates. And second, the model controls for the Democratic presidential vote, so that at a given Democratic vote share, the larger the minor party vote the smaller the residual share available to the Whig or Republican candidate. The significant, negative interaction between the minor party presidential vote and the Democratic vote, on the other hand, indicates that the stronger the minor party the weaker the pull of the coattail. Minor parties occasionally ran House candidates or fused their tickets with a major party's nominee. The net effect of the minor party terms in Column 2 reduces the Democratic House vote by one percentage point for each ten-point gain in the minor party vote.

Clearly, the findings indicate that the Australian ballot, whatever its form, weakened the link between presidential and congressional voting. One way to assess the cumulative, national impact of this reform is to ask the counterfactual question: How would the Democratic House vote have differed had ballot reform not occurred? In Figure 4.6 we simulate this for 1880 through 1940.[12] Beginning with the 1912 election, when presidential voting grew more volatile, the two series diverge from 1.4 percentage points on average prior to 1912 to more than 5 percentage points afterward. The 1932 election is instructive as an exception to this pattern. Here, the spread between the actual and simulated House votes shrinks to about three percentage points. Reprising Tufte's nationalization thesis, this finding suggests that a charismatic candidate promoting a national policy agenda could generate coattails nearly as long as those induced by consolidated ballots. Clearly though, normal nineteenth-century coattails became exceptional after ballot reform.

---

[11] In a separate analysis we tested and rejected other potential covariates, including a state's adoption of the nominating primary, a standard spatial autocorrelation term (i.e., contiguous states' election outcomes), national party realignment (Brady 1985; Kawato 1987), and state party realignment (Nardulli 1995).

[12] The hypothetical values for each state's post-reform years were calculated by passing the state's presidential vote through the consolidated ballot coefficients in Equation 1b and adding the state's fixed effects intercept. The weighted state totals were then summed to generate the national vote prediction.

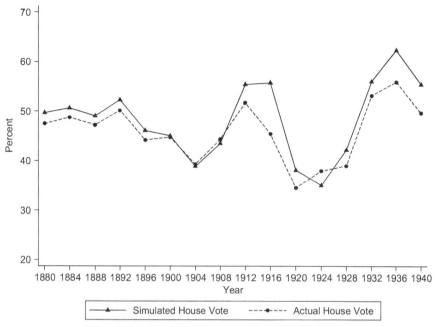

FIGURE 4.6. Actual and Simulated House Vote in Presidential Elections, 1880–1940
Note: We calculated the simulated House vote by passing the actual presidential vote through the parameters in Table 4.1, Column 2 assuming that the consolidated party ballot was in place for the entire time series.

Vote-Seat Conversion

Coattail voting represented only the first stage in the nineteenth-century man-ufacture of responsive elections. Vote shares must be transformed into compa-rable seat shares if presidential coattails were to contribute to unified govern-ments. Previously we argued that skilled mapmakers used sharp pencils to draw marginal yet winnable congressional districts. After ballot reform they adapted to their more uncertain environment by abandoning efficient gerrymanders in favor of a packing strategy. To test this proposition we estimate the following vote-seat relationships:

$$\text{DHS}_{it} = a\text{Partisan Bias}_{it} + b(\text{Partisan Bias}_{it}{}^{*}\text{B}_{it}) + c\text{DHV}_{it} + d(\text{DHV}_{it}{}^{*}\text{B}_{it}) \quad (2)$$

To distinguish efficient from packing strategies, consider the vote-seat relation-ship as comprised of two components – a swing ratio (captured by the coeffi-cients c and d) and partisan bias.[13] Recall from our discussion of Figure 4.2 that the former measures the sensitivity of legislative seat shares to changes in the vote. Bias refers simply to the intercept term, or as commonly stated the

---

[13] More specifically, we estimate the following standard vote-seat equation:

$$\ln(\text{DHS}_{it}/\text{1} - \text{DHS}_{it}) = \lambda + \rho\,(\ln(\text{DHV}_{it}/\text{1} - \text{DHV}_{it}))$$

party's expected seat share given 50 percent of the popular two-party vote. A positive 5 percent bias means that the state's Democratic candidates could expect to win 55 percent of the seats with 50 percent of the vote.

Following a technique introduced by Cox and Katz (2002), Equation 2 includes a number of interactive terms fashioned to compare the partisan effects of balloting plans drawn before and after ballot reform (B_{it}).[14] If, as we argue, ballot reform altered the redistricting strategies in ways that reduced the responsiveness of congressional elections, the swing ratios for the pre-reform era should be larger than those for the post-reform era. To test this we have classified all redistricting events according to the partisan control of the state legislature and governor (taking into account veto override provisions).[15] With each party holding a veto, redistricting will be less likely to occur under divided control of state government, but when lines were redrawn, these plans should take on a bipartisan cast that reflects each party's option to revert to the current apportionment.

In Table 4.2 we estimate bias and the swing ratio for each party regime presiding over redistricting. Because marginal changes in the vote near the 50 percent threshold have the largest impact on seat changes and weaken sharply toward a skewed two-party vote, the vote-seat function is conventionally represented as a logistic. Moreover, because there is a likely correlation across a state's districts in the probability of Democratic victory, we, like Cox and Katz, assume that seat shares follow an extended beta binomial distribution (King 1989; Palmquist 1998).[16]

where ρ is the swing ratio and λ taps partisan bias. To calibrate partisan bias at 50 percent of the vote, we pass λ through the following equation:

$$\exp[\lambda]/(\exp[\lambda] - 1) - 0.05.$$

This is standard procedure in the vote-seat literature (e.g., King and Browning 1987; Brady and Grofman 1991; Cox and Katz 2002).

[14] This classification, and indeed much of the rest of the analysis, follows the lead of Cox and Katz (2002) in formulating prior expectations about the bias and responsiveness of redistricting plans according to the political strategies of partisan state politicians. We depart significantly from their analytic approach, however, by not specifying the party that drew the reversion plan. This information is less relevant for bipartisan plans in the nineteenth century, as they occurred less frequently. We also suspect that the failure of reversionary variables in generating significant results reflects the faster decay rate of partisan advantages embedded in nineteenth-century partisan plans. Where Cox and Katz model redistricting strategies for regime periods of 18 and 6 years, respectively (1946 through 1970), we are working with a 100-year series with the same redistricting regime in place for an extended time period.

[15] In those states where the state constitution provided the governor with no veto (e.g., Ohio until 1912) or a veto that could be overridden by a simple majority (e.g., Missouri until 1874), we classified control according to party control of the legislative chambers.

[16] Using a simple binomial model would possibly lead to inefficient estimates and biased standard errors (King 1989: 119–121). Moreover, the extended beta-binomial model conditions on the number of seats in each state, thus taking into account any heteroskedasticity due to varying sizes of states' delegations (Cox and Katz 2002: 63).

TABLE 4.2. *The Conversion of Votes into Seats Under Different Districting Plans, 1840–1940*

Variable	Coefficient (Standard Error)
Swing Ratio	
Unified Government	4.64**
	(0.24)
Unified Government × Australian Ballot	−1.16**
	(0.29)
Divided Government	1.72**
	(0.52)
Divided Government × Australian Ballot	1.06*
	(0.62)
Partisan Bias	
Unified Democrat	3.34*
	(1.72)
Unified Democrat × Australian Ballot	3.89*
	(2.35)
Bipartisan	−2.60
	(3.57)
Bipartisan × Australian Ballot	−2.52
	(5.06)
Unified Republican	−6.41**
	(1.67)
Unified Republican × Australian Ballot	7.93**
	(2.37)
Minor Party Vote	0.036**
	(0.005)
λ	0.061**
	(0.008)
N	1206
Log-Likelihood	−6499.09

* $p < 0.10$, ** $p < 0.05$
Note: The parameter γ measures the correlation across districts (within a state) of the probability that the Democrats will capture the seat.

These relationships confirm that the partisan design of districts rendered the congressional outcomes highly responsive to vote changes before ballot reform and less so after.[17] The vote-seat conversion rates are, as hypothesized, significantly stronger for those redistricting plans passed in the party ticket era (swing ratio of 4.64 percent) than after reform (swing ratio of 3.48 percent).

[17] In separate analysis, we interacted the bias and responsiveness coefficients with a counter for the time since the last redistricting. Although we suspected that these interactions would mediate the effects of the redistricting regime, the interactions proved generally insignificant. Therefore, for parsimony we have opted to exclude them.

Similarly, districts drawn during divided control of the state government follow our prediction of weaker swing ratios than did their partisan counterparts.

The results for bias are presented in the lower half of Table 4.2. Because bias is directional (favoring one party over the other), we have split the bias coefficients under unified government according to the governing party that wrote the districting plan. During the era of the consolidated party ballot, unified Democratic plans produced a significant pro-Democratic bias of 3.34 percent and unified Whig/Republican plans an even greater pro-Whig/Republican bias of 6.41 percent. Unsurprisingly, plans passed during divided government display insignificant levels of bias.

According to these relationships, a statewide vote share of 50 percent yielded the Democrats anywhere from 47 percent to 56 percent of their state's delegation depending on the partisan origins of the current plan.[18] The post-reform results for bias are a little less straightforward. While bias for Democratic plans after reform increased to more than 7 percent, bias fell to nearly zero for Republican plans. This discrepancy possibly reflects the geography of the parties' strongholds. Democratic strength in the cities versus Republican dominance in many states' rural areas might have allowed legislators greater latitude in subdividing the more populous and Democratic urban counties where congressional districts had long abandoned the integrity of county boundaries that dictated rural districts in most states.

Nevertheless, the overall pattern of results in Table 4.2 remains consistent with our argument that strategic state legislators assiduously designed districts with narrow margins to maximize their parties' success. Moreover, following the adoption of ballot reform, these politicians generally changed the way they approached redistricting. They laid out district boundaries that generated more predictable and stable results – results less sensitive to the vagaries of presidential elections.

Do State-Level Relationships Explain National Party Control?

The statistical relationships uncovered thus far confirm the individual components of our model: first, nineteenth-century voters, keying on the presidential campaigns, cast coattail ballots for House elections to a significantly greater degree than did their post-reform counterparts; and second, these votes were generally distributed across districts in a manner that accentuated seat gains of the party winning the statewide plurality. The question before us now is whether, in fact, they combine to solve the puzzle of nineteenth-century responsiveness that motivated our inquiry.

There are a number of ways to sum the individual parts of the model and assess its overall performance. The standard approach looks to variance

---

[18] In addition, the estimate of gamma is positive and significant, indicating a correlation across districts within a state in the probability of a Democratic victory.

explained – in this instance to variance in a party's seat shares in the House of Representatives as a function of coattails and strategic gerrymandering. By this test our institutional variables perform quite well; specifically, the overall estimates based on combining Table 4.1 (Column 2) and Table 4.2 explain 88 percent of the variance in the actual Democratic seat shares for the House seats introduced in Figure 4.1. This compares to 66 percent of the variance explained by the lag term of seat shares for the non-Southern delegations in the previous Congress. So, knowing only the states' presidential vote gives us a significantly better guess as to the partisan composition of the next House of Representatives than does the makeup of the current House.

In Table 4.3 we report two additional tests that demonstrate the model's accuracy in generating individual point estimates of Democratic shares for state delegations and Democratic seat shares for individual congresses. Although we are principally interested in accounting for the highly responsive House elections of the nineteenth century and its subsequent decay in the twentieth century, the pervasive cross-sectional variation in institutional provisions offers another way to test the model's ability to reproduce particular partisan outcomes – in this instance, the party composition of individual states' congressional delegations. Again using the lag of the Democratic percentage as the benchmark for comparison, the first two columns of Table 4.3 show the predictive improvement of our model.[19] For most of the nineteenth century our institutional model performs much better. The difference in performance is especially notable during the 1844–1888 period, when the consolidated party ballot was common. Our model explains, on average, 90 percent of the variance in Democratic shares of state delegations, significantly better than the 81 percent ($p < 0.05$) accuracy for the lag benchmark. During the transition period between the party ticket and Australian ballot, the predictive accuracy of our model declines slightly, although on average it still outperforms the baseline. Once the Australian ballot is fully in place across the nation (1912–1940), however, our model offers no advantage over the lag term. But this null finding also corroborates our institutional story of a significant decoupling of presidential from congressional elections early in the twentieth century.

The second test in Table 4.3 allows us to assess the accuracy with which state electoral institutions can predict partisan changes in House party delegations from one Congress to the next. For this exercise we have simply summed the individual predicted seat shares employed for the first test, and compared the predicted changes in Democratic share in the last column of Table 4.3 with

---

[19] Specifically, we ran the following regression for each year: Democratic House Seats$_{it}$ = β_1 Predicted House Seats$_{it}$. To control for varying state sizes, we weighted each state by the size of their congressional delegation. The numbers reported in the first two columns of Table 4.3 represent the variance explained by each model for each year.

TABLE 4.3. *Variance Explained in the Partisan Composition of Non-Southern House Seats, 1844–1940*

| | | Variance Explained in State Democratic Congressional Delegations | | Error in Predicted Democratic Share of House Seats | | |
| | | Predicted Delegation by: | | Difference in Number from: | | |
	Year	Previous Election	Institutional Model	Actual # of Democratic Seats	Previous Congress	Institutional Model
Consolidated Ballot	1844	0.80	0.92	86	10	−10
	1848	0.81	0.91	67	3	−15
	1852	0.88	0.91	106	−14	−15
	1856	0.65	0.84	71	−34	−11
	1860	0.55	0.89	52	−1	12
	1864	0.72	0.83	35	40	21
	1868	0.90	0.90	62	−11	−6
	1872	0.83	0.93	61	14	10
	1876	0.94	0.95	89	33	13
	1880	0.88	0.93	76	10	10
	1884	0.93	0.93	106	16	6
	1888	0.83	0.86	96	10	8
	Average	0.81	0.90*	Mean Absolute Error	16.33	11.44**
Transition Period	1892	0.87	0.93	135	24	−12
	1896	0.55	0.80	66	−31	1
	1900	0.91	0.82	73	13	4
	1904	0.77	0.80	41	42	13
	1908	0.82	0.86	80	−5	−12
	Average	0.78	0.84	Mean Absolute Error	23	8.38*
Australian Ballot Years	1912	.86	.86	178	−39	−50
	1916	0.85	0.91	115	20	7
	1920	0.62	0.50	34	54	25
	1924	0.88	0.80	82	22	−25
	1928	0.89	0.87	68	25	8
	1932	0.73	0.91	213	−88	−45
	1936	0.96	0.93	235	−12	−1
	1940	0.93	0.99	168	−5	6
	Average	0.84	0.85	Mean Absolute Error	33.13	20.76*

* Difference is significant at 0.05.

Previous Election/Congress = Prediction of current Democratic share of the congressional delegation based on the number of seats Democrats held in the previous election.

Full Model = Prediction of current Democratic share of the congressional delegation generated using the coefficients from Table 4.1, Column 2 and then passing the predicted vote through the coefficients in Table 4.2.

the actual changes from the preceding Congress in column five. Once again our model, informed wholly by a state's presidential vote, outperforms predictions based on the lag term. Finally we return to where we began our investigation – the consistent occurrence of unified party control of the presidency and House of Representatives. At this stage, to assess the overall performance of the institutional model to account for actual party control of government, we need to simply add the South's large Democratic and small Republican delegations to the estimates in Table 4.3. When we do so, the model correctly predicts majority party control of the House in twenty-one out of the twenty-five presidential elections between 1844 and 1940. And in those instances where we end up on the wrong side of majority control (1848, 1880, 1888, and 1916), the estimates, nevertheless, come very close; the mean absolute error for these four elections is less than ten seats. In sum, whether measured by overall explanatory power or accuracy in estimating party shares of delegations across the states or in the House of Representatives, state electoral institutions had cumulative effects in shaping party control in Washington.

Conclusion

In the consolidated party ballot and efficient gerrymandering, nineteenth-century politicians opted for institutions that magnified slight swings in presidential preferences into pronounced shifts of fortunes in House elections. Minor shifts in party preferences reverberated to House elections via coattails and steep swing ratios. As these institutions were dismantled in the late nineteenth and early twentieth centuries congressional elections became less responsive. Here, in the details of state codes, one finds institutions manufacturing a level of electoral responsiveness that conventional theory reserved for highly nationalized, Westminster-styled electoral systems.

The implications extended well beyond the electoral arena. Following the introduction of ballot reform and less competitive congressional districts, modern executives entered office with clipped coattails – coattails that might have caused party members in the House to associate their own future success with that of their president. On entering office these new-styled presidents were greeted not by a beholden party team in control of the House but increasingly by insulated careerists, a majority of whom might belong to the opposition party bent on the president's failure.

Finally, the possibility that presidential elections – particularly those in the nineteenth century before ballot reform – sent strong partisan ripples into state legislatures is pregnant with implications for understanding the U.S. Senate. Until implementation of the Seventeenth Amendment in the 1914 election, state legislatures elected the state's U.S. senators. At the outset of this chapter, we observed the strong correlation between a party's success in winning the White House and its likelihood of winning control of Congress and unifying party control of government. The responsiveness of state legislative composition to presidential elections introduces the possibility that the nineteenth-century Senate – an institution the Framers designed to be insulated from popular passions – was, in fact, largely (perhaps equally) subject to the partisan tides of national politics. We subject this possibility to scrutiny in Chapter 5.

Appendix to Chapter 4: Data Sources

Election Results and Rules: The core source for both the statewide presidential and congressional vote is Rusk (2001) and Burnham, Clubb, and Flanigan (1972a, 1972b). The major difference between the two data sets lies in their political party codes. Burnham et al. codes as "major" those party candidates who ran solely under a major party label. Rusk expands this coding to those major party candidates who were also listed by another party (e.g., Whig-Free Soilers, Silver Republicans). When these data sources disagreed, we preferred Rusk's revision (see Rusk 2001: 199–202, for a fuller discussion). In a few instances, however, we differed from both Burnham et al. and Rusk. First, for the 1860 election, we combine the votes for Douglas and Breckinridge, within a state, into a single Democratic presidential vote. Second, for states that had no recorded Democratic presidential vote in 1892, we entered these candidates' Populist votes as a proxy for the statewide Democratic vote. These states are Kansas, North Dakota, Colorado, Idaho, and Wyoming. Third, we differ in coding the statewide congressional vote for Maryland in 1860 and Kentucky in 1860 and 1864, where we scored Sectional Democrats, Peace Democrats, and the Conservative Party as Democrats. We draw information on the timing and type of ballot reform from Ludington (1911), Albright (1942), and Walker (1972), and for election dates, Dubin (1998).

   Redistricting: Data on the timing of redistricting events come from Martis (1982). We exclude the few redistricting events that Martis classifies as "minor" (i.e., involving addition of new counties to existing congressional districts). Partisan control of redistricting was created by matching passage dates with party control of the state legislature and the party of the governor (Burnham 1985), taking into account various state veto provisions (i.e., requiring a legislative supermajority for a veto override) (Swindler 1973). We were also able in a number of instances to double-check Burnham's data against results printed in the *New York Tribune Almanac* and various historical state Blue Books. We found no discrepancies.

5

Senate Indirect and Direct Elections

During and immediately after the Civil War, the Republican Party dominated the national government, at times enjoying near supermajorities in the Congress. Despite their majority status, Republican leaders were nevertheless deeply concerned about the consequences Southern reentry into the Union would have on their electoral fortunes and policies. Republican leaders had ample reason to worry. Assuming that the Southern states would eventually come to support the Democratic Party, the readmittance of the South placed the Republican's electoral future, and postwar policies, in serious jeopardy.

So Republicans embarked on a strategy of admitting into statehood sparsely populated yet staunchly Republican territories. Because the Constitution guarantees each state two senators regardless of population, the admittance of scarcely populated pro-Republican territories promised a mechanism to secure Republican majorities in the Senate. In 1861, Kansas was admitted. By 1868, Nevada, Nebraska, and West Virginia were in the Union, and only a veto by Southerner Andrew Johnson kept Colorado out, but only for a few more years. These and subsequent state admissions proved critical in assuring the continuation of a Republican Senate. As a result, Republicans could veto the efforts of a Democratic-leaning House of Representatives to completely undo the policies it had established during the Civil War and early years of Reconstruction (Stewart and Weingast 1992).

Evidence of the pronounced effects of these new, sparsely populated states on party composition of the Senate can be seen in the success rates of Republicans from states admitted to the Union after 1860. From 1864 until the switch to direct elections in 1914, 75 percent of the senators these states sent to Washington were Republican. According to the calculations of Charles Stewart and Barry Weingast (1992), without the selective admittance of these states, nine of the next eleven congresses after 1876 would have found Democrats in control of the Senate instead of the two that actually occurred. Largely overlooked, however, is that the admissions strategy was not the only source of the anti-Democratic bias in Senate elections during this era. Even for non-Southern states that had entered the Union prior to 1860, Senate elections thoroughly favored Republicans. From 1864 to 1912, Republicans comprised 73 percent of the senators from these older states. The success of Republicans throughout all of the non-Southern states adds weight to the argument that elections in non-Southern state legislatures inherently favored Republicans, and therefore the main effect of direct election reform was to level the playing field for Democrats (e.g., King and Ellis 1996).

One might be tempted to conclude from the Republican dominance of Senate contests that the same level of pro-Republican bias occurred within state legislatures. Reports of the notoriously maldistricted, pro-Republican New England state legislatures during the late nineteenth century would seem to square with the Republican dominance of the Senate. Connecticut (Argensinger 1992; McSeveney 1972) offers an especially egregious instance where town-based representation managed repeatedly to frustrate the claims of popular Democratic pluralities (and even majorities) to control state government and with it the state's Senate delegation. Yet other state histories point to highly competitive state politics elsewhere, especially throughout the Midwest, in which political control of state governments swung with the ebb and flow of national elections. So the anecdotal record portrays heterogeneous state politics with some states responsive to national forces and others less so. The fact is that we know next to nothing about this era's state electoral politics and their subsequent impact on party control of the Senate. Any number of state characteristics from rotten boroughs to perfectly fair and highly responsive electoral arenas might have generated these aggregate relationships.

Pre-Reform and Post-Reform Senate Elections

In devising indirect Senate elections the Framers intentionally sought to create an institution insulated from transient, popular passions and capable of "cool" (Madison's phrasing) deliberation of policy. Certainly, indirect elections, along with the Senate's longer and staggered terms and its malapportioned seats, provide ample reason to suspect that this chamber's party ratios would have been much less responsive to national electoral forces than those for the House. Yet even in the Senate one can find traces of national forces in the form of presidential elections in the chamber's changing party composition. Between 1840 and 1914, the party winning the presidency also won or retained control of the Senate in seventeen out of the nineteen presidential elections. On four of the six occasions where an out-party won the White House and also sought to take away the Senate it succeeded. So perhaps this era's indirect Senate elections were not quite so insulated from short-term national forces as the Framers had intended and previous research appears to confirm.

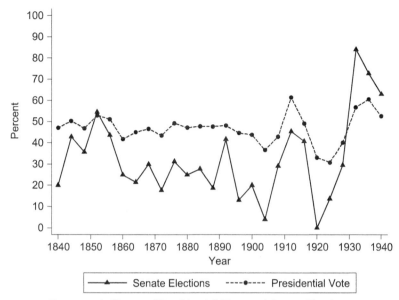

FIGURE 5.1. Democratic Shares of Presidential Vote and Senate Elections, 1840–1940
Note: The solid line displays the percentage of non-Southern Democratic victories in Senate elections during presidential election years.

Unsurprisingly, after implementation of the Seventeenth Amendment in 1914, the presidency-Senate connection strengthened significantly as party ratios in the Senate began to more tightly track the national presidential vote (Crook and Hibbing 1997). In the seven presidential elections from 1916 through 1940, the party that won the presidency also claimed victory in the Senate. As important as national party ratios in the Senate are for understanding the course of national policy during this era, they do not offer the only information for detecting the responsiveness of Senate elections to national forces. Only a third of Senate seats are contested during any election and therefore exposed to the effects of presidential coattails. We also must keep in mind that the Senate's party ratios included a large block of seats from the South that after the 1850s were impervious to national swings in party fortunes.

In Figure 5.1 we have plotted the Democratic share of the in-play Senate seats against the Democratic presidential vote. Certainly, the most prominent correspondence of these trends is the responsiveness of Senate elections to the presidential vote under direct elections. The effect of the Seventeenth Amendment in nationalizing Senate elections has been observed by others (Crook and Hibbing 1997; Wirls 1999), but none of the previously reported evidence offers the level of responsiveness displayed in Figure 5.1.

TABLE 5.1. *Responsiveness and Bias of*
Non-Southern Senate Elections under
Indirect and Direct Elections

Variable	Coefficients
Indirect Election Responsiveness	2.21*
	(0.57)
Indirect Election Bias	−16.81*
	(3.49)
Direct Election Responsiveness	3.25*
	(0.51)
Direct Election Bias	2.25
	(4.49)
N	515
Log-Likelihood	−283.86

* p < 0.05
Note: Standard errors in parentheses.

Two other patterns can be discerned in Figure 5.1 for indirect elections. First, as noted at the beginning of this chapter, throughout the nineteenth century Democrats ran much better for the presidency than reflected in their share of Senate seats. The second, less pronounced relationship in these indirect elections is that between presidential voting and Senate seat shares. Contrary to conventional wisdom, presidential coattails were present, at least for this large subset of non-Southern Senate elections. To see this better, we have calculated from the time-series data in Figure 5.1 the familiar vote-seat relationship (but bear in mind the vote here is the president's) separately for elections under direct and indirect election systems. The full contours and implications of the nonlinear relationships in Table 5.1 can be better appreciated in graph form in Figure 5.2. Both the bias and the presidential vote (responsiveness) coefficients are significantly related to the Democratic seat shares. The seventeen-point bias under indirect election is reproduced in the figure; when the Democratic presidential candidate won 50 percent of these states' votes his party managed to capture only 33 percent of the Senate seats up for grabs. It stands to reason that presidential voting would have a weaker impact on the Senate and would be more prone to bias under indirect elections. As national forces passed through bicameral, state legislative filters, their effects may have been attenuated by imperfect aggregation mechanisms and the interventions of strategic and highly partisan politicians.

An Institutional Model of Presidential Effects on Senate Elections

When nineteenth-century voters cast their ballots for president, what, if any, spillover effects did their presidential votes have on their preferred party's

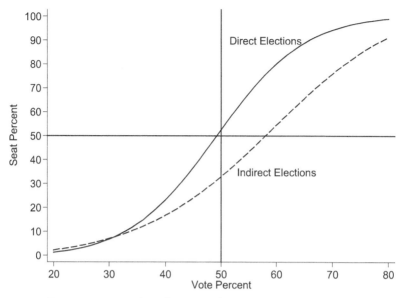

FIGURE 5.2. Democratic Presidential Vote and Senate Seat Curve under Indirect and Direct Elections
Note: The *x*-axis is the total non-Southern Democratic presidential vote share and the *y*-axis is non-Southern Democratic victories in Senate elections. The vote-seat curves are plots based on the estimates from Table 5.1.

chances of also capturing a Senate seat in the next legislative session? In answering this, one must consider the variety of political and institutional features of a state's electoral system that might facilitate or impede the transference of preferences for one office into representation in another. To identify those institutional mechanisms that might have pulled the fortunes of party politicians together (or apart) across offices, we need to separate the lengthy causal path of relationships that had presidential voting shape Senate elections. The path contained the three following steps:

1) Presidential Coattails: presidential vote → state legislative vote
2) Vote-Seat Conversion: state legislative vote → partisan composition of legislative chamber
3) Indirect Elections: party ratios of upper and lower chambers → Senate election

In order for presidential preferences to influence indirect Senate elections via coattails, it would help the voter to have the presidential and state legislative choices proximate to one another on the ballot, or better yet, to have a single choice – as in casting the party ticket or pulling the party column – decide both votes. Moreover, the institutional mechanisms that aggregate and distribute votes to offices may yield a vote-seat relationship that is highly fair and responsive or its opposite. Where legislative districts are seriously malapportioned and gerrymandered, any electoral connection between presidential voting and Senate elections might be broken regardless of the effort by voters to transfer their presidential preferences down the ticket. Finally, once a majority assumes control of the legislature for the next session, it must (in two-thirds of its sessions) perform one of the most important tasks of these nineteenth-century institutions – elect a senator. Divided party control of these bicameral legislatures would endanger any electoral connection even if the coattail mechanisms were in place and the vote-seat conversion were fair and responsive. Again, institutional rules govern outcomes. In the next section we test the first two stages of this process, estimating the impact of presidential voting on the partisan composition of state legislatures. Here we will provide an overview of the relationship between presidential voting and state legislative composition, in order to set the stage for examing the extended sequence of outcomes that linked presidential voting to Senate elections during the indirect election regime. In Chapter 6 we will fully unpack each step of the translation of presidential voting into state legislative seats.

The Presidential Vote – State Legislative Seats Relationship

Two potentially important features of the states' electoral systems that likely mediated presidential elections' impact on nineteenth-century state legislative elections, and by implication Senate elections, were the ballot structure and the electoral calendar. As we saw in Chapter 4, both had a substantial impact on congressional voting, and both institutions were certainly in play when it came to state legislative elections. As a result of ballot laws, the electoral fortunes of state legislative candidates, and by implication aspiring senators, were highly dependent on the success of the presidential standard bearer at the top of the ticket.

Another important feature of state elections that potentially affected the linkage between presidential and legislative elections was variation in state electoral calendars. States adopted numerous combinations of term lengths for the two chambers of their state legislatures. As a result, in some states all legislative seats were contested during presidential election years, while in others a half, third, or even none would be exposed to the electoral perturbations of the presidential election. In addition, some states held their legislative (and gubernatorial) elections at separate times from presidential elections. In some cases, state elections would be held months apart from the presidential contest. In testing for the effects of presidential voting we shall distinguish those state elections held simultaneously with the presidential election from those held on separate days.

Two other electoral institutions of special significance for Senate elections were the opportunities afforded voters in some states to express their candidate preferences for the Senate. Some states instituted nonbinding nomination primaries, which presumably guided, if not dictated, the choices of a party's caucuses in the two state legislative chambers. In 1901, Oregon went one step further, creating a straw Senate election that had voters select among competing candidates and sought to bind state legislators to follow the dictates of the vote in the state legislative election.[1] Prescriptive elections of this sort were soon adopted by thirteen other states and continued to be conducted until direct election. We suspect that the presence of senatorial candidates on the ballot shaped both coattail voting and the legislative elections. In the first instance it reminded voters of the broader implications of their state legislative vote, and in the second, informed legislators of the candidate choice that would meet with their constituents' approbation. If so, in those states where the Oregon plan was adopted, legislatures might have surrendered their partisan discretion and become merely Electoral Colleges registering popular preferences.

In Table 5.2 we test the impact of the state's presidential vote on the partisan distribution (percent Democratic in both instances) of the two chambers of the state legislature. In order to link these results to the next stage Senate elections we have limited the analysis to the era of indirect elections, 1840–1912. In both legislative settings the presidential vote appears to have been a major determinant of the state legislature's partisan makeup, and presumably, in turn, of Senate elections. All else equal, a 1 percent increment in the presidential vote increased Democratic seat shares by 0.86 percent and 0.63 percent in the lower and upper chambers, respectively.

To test for institutional mediation, we interacted the presidential vote with ballot structure, the timing of state legislative elections, and the presence of direct election reforms, and we have broken up the lag term to take into account the share of seats up for election and thereby exposed to potential coattail effects. We have also included intercept shifts for alternative ballot formats that must be taken into account in assessing the net mediating effects of ballot reform. The significant interactive coefficients in the hypothesized direction for both equations confirm the mediating role of electoral institutions. The structure of the Australian ballot reform appears to have had a substantial impact. In both chambers, the office bloc format significantly curtailed presidential coattails. Moreover, the party column coefficients are significant in both chambers. In all cases, ballot reform reduced the impact of presidential coattails on state legislative seat shares. The presence of a senatorial candidate on the ballot (Senate reform) also has a positive impact on presidential coattails. The interactions for non-November elections are in the hypothesized direction (negative), but not significant for either chamber.

The last four terms in the equations interact the share of seats up for reelection with the Democratic composition (percent) of the chamber prior to the

---

[1] Nebraska passed similar legislation in 1879, but it appeared to have very little effect. Haynes (1905: 142–143) reports that in Nebraska, until 1904, very few votes were actually cast for senatorial candidates.

TABLE 5.2. *The Impact of Presidential Vote on State Legislative Seats as a Function of Electoral Laws*

OLS with panel corrected standard errors
DV = Percent of Democratic Seats in State Legislature

Variable	Lower House Seats	Upper House Seats
Presidential Vote (% Dem)	0.86**	0.63**
	(0.16)	(0.12)
Ballot Form		
Non-November Election	13.78	10.58
	(8.73)	(8.48)
Non-November Election × Presidential Vote	−0.30	−0.26
	(0.19)	(0.18)
Office Bloc Ballot	22.76**	19.35**
	(8.03)	(5.72)
Office-Bloc Ballot × Presidential Vote	−0.55**	−0.48**
	(0.20)	(0.13)
Party Column Ballot	17.55**	17.51**
	(7.07)	(7.89)
Party Column Ballot × Presidential Vote	−0.28*	−0.35**
	(0.16)	(0.18)
Senate Reform	−25.81**	−16.60
	(12.92)	(10.09)
Senate Reform × Presidential Vote	0.98**	0.66**
	(0.36)	(0.26)
Lag of Legislative Seats		
Lag of Legislative Seats	0.54**	0.68**
	(0.05)	(0.06)
Lag of Legislative Seats × 1/2 up for reelection	0.17**	0.07
	(0.05)	(0.05)
Lag of Legislative Seats × 1/3 up for reelection		−0.08
		(0.07)
Lag of Legislative Seats × 1/4 up for reelection	0.28**	0.12**
	(0.13)	(0.06)
Constant	−23.19**	−23.14**
	(6.81)	(6.44)
N	488	484
R-Square	0.72	0.84

* $p < 0.10$, ** $p < 0.05$
Note: OLS estimates with panel corrected standard errors. State fixed effects were also estimated but not presented in the table.

election. The stand-alone lag term represents instances where all of the seats are in play. The results of the various lag terms indicate that the effect of presidential coattails varies with the number of legislative seats up for reelection. In the lower house, for instance, all of the interactions are positive and significant, indicating that the greater percentage of the legislative seats on the ballot the stronger the lag term. In the lower house, for example, this impact raises from only 0.54 percent when every seat is up for grabs to 0.82 percent when only a quarter of the legislature is up for election.

These findings show the partisan composition of state legislatures to be highly responsive to the kinds of short-run national forces that motivate and decide presidential elections. This is all the more impressive because, presumably, our inability here to separate coattails from the vote-seat function only serves to understate the underlying coattail effect. Moreover, each of the states' electoral institutions mediated the influence of presidential voting in the direction hypothesized. Ballot reform weakened but did not sever the connection, as did the electoral calendars of the legislatures. The presence of Senate candidates on the election ballot strengthened the association between presidential and state legislative voting.

Indirect Elections of Senators

Earlier we argued that the biased and less responsive (compared to direct election) presidential vote-Senate relationship under indirect election may not reflect comparable levels of bias and gerrymandered insulation in each of the states. The relationships reported in the previous section indicate much more responsive state legislative elections than we were led to suspect from the aggregate levels of bias and unresponsiveness under indirect elections. Of course, as we noted earlier, the national relationships could result statistically from simply the heterogeneous distribution of presidential and state legislative votes across the states instead of mirroring some average bias among them. In this section, we consider the legislative process of Senate elections as a potential source of bias.

State legislative election of a senator is akin to a single-member district, winner-take-all election in the electorate, but with two important differences. First, the electors are politicians and have more reason, and hence likelihood, of engaging in strategic voting; second, the election occurs simultaneously in two electorates (i.e., bicameral legislatures), both of which must separately give the winning candidate a majority. The incentives and opportunities for politicians to engage in strategic behavior should weaken the correlation between a chamber's party ratios and its probability of electing the senator. Instead, politicians within parties will sometimes find it in their interest to sell their votes for either personal gain or political rewards for their constituents. As vital as political parties were for nineteenth-century politicians, many states were rife with factional competition throughout the nineteenth and early twentieth centuries. Political parties were central organizing entities throughout this era, yet histories of senate elections (Hall 1936; Haynes 1906) are riddled with self-defeating, internecine struggles within party caucuses. In their detailed study of post–Civil War Senate elections, Wendy Schiller and Charles Stewart argued that, "Although it is true that virtually all U.S. senators from 1871 to 1913 were from the same party that controlled a majority of seats in the state legislature, state elections rarely settled anything more than the party of the senator. It rarely determined *which* same-party individual would go to Washington" (Schiller and Stewart 2007: 3).

Consider the Senate election of 1850 in Massachusetts. Lacking a solid majority in the state legislature, the Democrats forged a coalition government with members of the newly formed Free Soil Party. When it came to select a U.S. senator, however, the coalition reached an impasse. The Free Soil caucus put forward the well-known antislavery advocate Charles Sumner. Democrats, on the other hand, balked, "preferring a less radical anti-slavery leader" (Haynes 1906: 130). Sumner easily won victory in the upper house, but his candidacy ran into trouble in the other chamber. Here, Sumner outpolled the second place finisher 110 to 76, but with a number of scattered votes failed to reach the majority necessary to win the seat (Haynes 1906: 131). The result was a three-month deadlock. The impasse was finally broken after a number of townships in Massachusetts held a formal vote to instruct their state representatives to support Sumner. According to one of his biographers, the public pressure put Sumner over the top, securing his election (Haynes 1906: 133).

Next, we present suggestive, indirect evidence that the contingent effects of factional politics rewarded supermajorities with improved prospects of electing a senator. We can neither observe systematically nor control effectively for factional politics. Factional competition will manifest itself in Senate elections with an inability of the party caucus to reach consensus and enforce agreement on the party's nominee. Where present, a success will require a surplus of votes beyond the bare majority, a feature we can monitor in the analysis.

The second characteristic of indirect Senate elections that distinguishes it from single member district elections is bicameralism. The election of a senator requires the mutual agreement of constitutionally independent legislatures. We know that on occasion these legislatures could not agree on a candidate, even after prolonged negotiations and numerous votes. The concurrent bicameral selection of senators became especially problematic when party control was split within the legislature. The result, typically, was a loss of representation as the seat remained vacant. In California, factional splits within both the Democratic and Whig Parties prevented the selection of a senator in 1855. The Democrats were the larger party, but were rent with divisions over the issue of slavery, with the party dividing into pro-Northern and pro-Southern factions. This opened the door for the Whigs to step in and play kingmaker. But the Whigs were also divided on the issue of slavery and could not coordinate on a candidate, and the "badly divided legislature failed to elect a new United

---

BOX 5.1. **Regulating Senate Elections**

For nearly seventy-five years, Congress gave the states free reign to decide on the parliamentary procedures for choosing senators. As the nineteenth century wore on, however, deadlocks, corruption, and election challenges resulted. In some cases it became difficult for the U.S. Senate to decide which candidate was the rightful choice of a state legislature. In 1858, for instance, the Senate was confronted with two sets of senators from Indiana. The Democrats had selected two senators in 1857 (one was to fill a vacancy). A year later, Republicans regained a majority in the state legislature. They opted to select two new Republican senators, charging that the Democrats in the previous year had failed to follow Indiana state law for choosing senators. The Senate, controlled by Democrats, rejected the credentials of the Indiana Republicans and upheld the selection of the two Democratic senators from Indiana.

Such instances reached a head in late 1865 and early 1866. In 1865, New Jersey sent the Democrat John Stockton to the Senate. But a faction of disgruntled state legislators also submitted a memorial protesting Stockton's election. The memorial claimed that because Stockton was selected by a plurality of the legislature, rather than a majority, his selection should be nullified. After months of wrangling and recriminations on the Senate floor, the Republican-controlled Senate voted to remove Stockton from his seat. Although Stockton lost his Senate seat, a report he produced as part of his defense "established beyond question that senatorial election procedures in the United States represented a snarl of inconsistencies and mismanagement" (Byrd 1988: 392). Stockton's report, coupled with the time spent having to untangle election challenges from state legislatures, compelled the Congress to finally take action and lay down specific rules guiding Senate selection.

But a social choice devil lay in the details. By requiring a majority of all votes cast in joint assembly as opposed to a simple plurality, the new rules failed to reduce election deadlocks and likely exacerbated the difficulty of choosing a Senator. "Small factions could withhold their support for major party candidates until their various demands had been met" (Byrd 1988: 393). Between 1891 and 1905, for example, forty-five deadlocks occurred in twenty states (Byrd 1988: 393).

States senator" (Holt 1999: 858). On other occasions, if a legislature was unable to agree on a candidate, the governor might appoint someone to fill the vacancy. The validity of such appointments, however, was never fully resolved by Congress. Indeed, the decisions to seat these interim appointees were often simply decided by straight party-line votes within the Senate (Butler and Wolff 1995: xxv; Jenkins 2005).

In 1866, Congress had attempted to resolve these instances of bicameral gridlock, and ward off gubernatorial appointments with legislation regulating the election of senators (for more, see Box 5.1). The law stated that each chamber should first vote separately. If no candidate received an absolute majority in both houses separately, the two houses were to subsequently merge into one body and vote by joint ballot, the winner needing a majority for selection. The act also called for viva voce roll-call votes (i.e., no secret balloting) and created a timetable for voting. Voting was to begin the first Tuesday after the first meeting of the legislature, and there was to be at least one ballot taken every day until a candidate was finally selected (Haynes 1906).

Although the law's stated purpose was to resolve bicameral gridlock and regularize the election process, the historical literature suggests that deadlocks actually increased (Haynes 1906; Hall 1936; Schiller and Stewart 2004, 2007). The provision requiring a majority in both chambers or on joint ballot meant that determined factions could prevent the party caucus from unifying around a single candidate. The result was elections that sometimes stretched over months with upward of 100 ballots being conducted. Between 1891 and 1905, for instance, factional divisions led to fourteen states failing to elect a senator (Haynes 1906). In Delaware, the factional divisions within the majority Republican Party were so fierce that they failed to elect a senator in both 1899 and 1901, and as a result they were completely without Senate representation in the 58th Congress. In 1899, for example, the legislature in Delaware held 113 separate votes over 64 days, yet no candidate was able to break the 50 percent threshold (Haynes 1906: 38).

In all of the states in this analysis, the lower house was larger than the state senate, with a mean of 115 members (and a median of 100) compared to a mean number of 31 (and a median of 32) for the upper chamber. Presumably, for the majority of elections in our time series, legislative politicians incorporated this information in their separate Senate election decisions. Depending on the strength of candidate preferences in the lower chamber, its politicians would be less inclined to compromise with their Senate counterparts, knowing that they would probably prevail in joint votes.

Yet despite the complications arising from bicameral differences and factional in-fighting, one would expect that the most important factor in determining the outcomes of Senate elections would still be party control of the legislature. Where a single party had control of both legislative chambers we should expect they would almost always, barring self-defeating factional turmoil, elect a senator of their party. Table 5.3 displays the likelihood of electing a Democratic or Republican (or Whig) senator given various configurations of partisan control of state legislatures. When a single party controlled both chambers of the legislature, they elected a senator from their party in 97 percent (572 of 590) of the non-Southern elections from 1840 to 1912 (excluding vacancies).[2]

In Figure 5.3 we find that unified party control after the Civil War mostly meant unified Republican control of non-Southern state legislatures. Here,

---

[2] The cases of an opposition selection were therefore rare. In 1893, Kansas and North Dakota sent Democrats to the Senate despite substantial Republican majorities in the state legislature. According to Haynes, party discipline had become very weak, and cross-party coalitions formed in these instances (Haynes 1906: 92).

TABLE 5.3. *Party Control of State Legislatures and the Election of Senators*

	Partisan Control of Legislature		
	Unified Democrat	Divided	Unified Republican/Whig
Republican/Whig Senator Elected	7.3% (10)	43.8% (35)	97.9% (389)
Democratic Senator Elected	92.7% (127)	56.2% (45)	2.1% (8)

Note: Percentages are column percentages. Actual numbers are in parentheses.

then, might be a source of Republican structural advantage in winning disproportionate Senate elections at the aggregate level. From the Civil War until the end of the nineteenth century, the national Democratic Party remained surprisingly competitive outside the South, despite its "Copperhead" image that Republicans were quick to unfurl every four years for a long time after the war. Yet as Silbey (1977, 1991) observes in his post–Civil War history of the Democratic Party, the party's competitiveness rarely translated into victory. Even small but pervasive and persistent Republican majorities across the states could generate that party's disproportionate success in Figure 5.1.

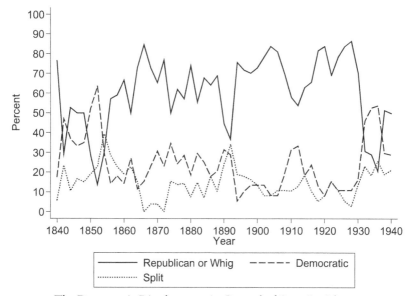

FIGURE 5.3. The Democratic Disadvantage in Control of State Legislatures
Note: This figure displays the percentages in party control of state legislatures at the end of every even-numbered year.

TABLE 5.4. *Percentage of Unified Partisan Control under Different State Legislative Configurations*

	Upper House		
Lower House	All up for Reelection	Half up for Reelection	One-Quarter up for Reelection
All up for Reelection	93% (138/148)	81% (201/246)	100% (9/9)
Half up for Reelection	–	96% (32/33)	88% (58/70)
One-Quarter up for Reelection	–	–	54% (6/11)

In Table 5.4 we see that states' legislative chambers generally followed different electoral calendars. Combined with the responsiveness of both chambers' partisan makeup to presidential elections, we may anticipate that for those states where all of both chambers' legislators stand for reelection during a presidential campaign, the likelihood of divided party control of the legislature will be much lower than where all of one chamber but not of the other are exposed to presidential coattails. The distribution of unified governments in Table 5.4 verifies the effects of institutional features on the prospects of bicameral legislatures to reach agreement on Senate elections. Limiting the analysis to presidential election years, those elections in which every member of both chambers stood for reelection yielded unified government 93 percent of the time. When a state's senate was not wholly elected in tandem with the lower chamber, the incidence of unified party control dropped to approximately 80 percent. Finally, in those few periods when no more than a quarter of either chamber was elected during the presidential election, the likelihood of a divided legislature was nearly as likely as unified party control.

Another feature of indirect Senate elections that may have altered the calculations of state legislators was the opportunity for voters to formally register their opinion for senatorial candidates. As noted in the previous section, some states created nonbinding primaries to select party nominees. In other states, such as Oregon in 1902, they went a step further and conducted balloting directly for Senate elections. Under this plan, state legislators were to function more like a pseudo-Electoral College, merely rubber-stamping the earlier choices of voters. Illustrating the punch of these partisan expressions, the Republican legislature of Oregon elected the Democratic candidate to the Senate after a majority of the state's voters favored the Democrat in the 1908 Senate election.

To test the effect of state legislative composition, along with environmental features that represent expressions of voter sentiment in their states, on the likelihood of electing a Democratic senator we estimate a logit equation with a Democratic victory as the dependent variable. We model this likelihood of

TABLE 5.5. *The Indirect Election of Senators, 1840–1912*
Logit estimates
DV = Election of a Democratic Senator

Variables	Coefficients (Standard Errors)	Magnitude of Effect	
		Change in X	Predicted Change in Prob. (C.I.)
Lower House Democratic Seat %	0.10**	45–55	0.22
	(0.02)		(0.14–0.28)
Upper House Democratic Seat %	0.05**	45–55	0.11
	(0.01)		(0.05–0.17)
Democratic Presidential Vote %	0.15*	45–55	0.31
	(0.04)		(0.17–0.46)
Presidential Election Year (Intercept)	−7.19**		
	(1.83)		
Preference Vote Winner	3.14**	0–1	0.44
	(1.56)		(0.09–0.64)
Constant	−9.48**		
	(1.22)		
N	590		
Log-Likelihood	−137.32		
Pseudo R-Square	0.63		

* p < 0.05, ** p < 0.01
Note: State fixed effects also estimated but not reported. Six states (fifty-one observations) dropped due to perfect prediction. The predicted probabilities are generated by holding the legislative values at 50 percent and the presidential Democratic percent at 50, and setting the preference vote winner to zero.

a Democratic victory as a function of the partisan composition of the state legislature and two measures of voter sentiment. These are the Democratic share of the state's presidential vote (along with an intercept for presidential election years) and a variable scored 1 for an Oregon-plan victory for the Democratic candidate for the Senate and −1 for a Republican victory. The results are presented in Table 5.5.

Unsurprisingly, the party composition of the legislature dominates the equations. As one would suspect from the joint election provision of the 1866 statute, party ratios in the lower chamber had a greater impact on the outcome.[3] The effect of the lower house, displayed in the predicted probabilities of the third column of Table 5.5, was twice the size of the upper chamber. Both of

---

[3] The difference in the lower and upper house coefficients remains about the same when the equation is estimated with only post-1866 elections. We do not have systematic information on the share of states that mandated joint sessions before passage of the 1866 law, but instances of these sessions do appear anecdotally in political almanacs and legislative histories.

TABLE 5.6. *The Effect of Joint Balloting on the Election of Senators in Divided Partisan Legislatures, 1840–1912*

Logit estimates
DV = Election of a Democratic Senator

Variables	Coefficients (Standard Errors)
Democratic Percent on Joint Ballot	0.12**
	(0.04)
Democratic Percent on Joint Ballot × Pre-1866 Dummy	−0.09*
	(0.05)
Pre-1866 Dummy (Intercept)	5.05*
	(2.16)
Statewide Democratic Presidential Vote %	0.08*
	(0.04)
Presidential Election Year (Intercept)	−4.01
	(2.25)
Constant	−5.64**
	(2.09)
N	590
Log-Likelihood	−137.32
Pseudo R-Square	0.63

* $p < 0.05$, ** $p < 0.01$

Note: We also included the preference vote winner as an independent variable, but this perfectly predicted the outcome so was dropped.

the variables tapping voter sentiment were positive and significant, suggesting that independent of the party makeup of the chambers, state legislators were attentive to the current political breezes as they elected the state's senator. An increase of 10 percent in the Democratic presidential vote, all else equal, increased the probability of a Democratic Senate victory by 0.31 percent.

To further assess the importance of institutional rules in guiding Senate elections, we next examine the impact of requiring states to merge into one body and elect senators on a joint ballot. Because the biggest impact of this provision would appear when each party controlled one chamber, and therefore could block the other's choice when voting separately, we narrow our focus only to instances of divided partisan control. Specifically, we estimate the probability of electing a Democratic senator, in divided legislatures, as a function of the joint combined number of Democrats in the state legislature. We also interact this with a dummy variable indicating whether or not the election was held before the 1866 law went into effect. In addition, as in the previous equation, we also included the state presidential vote and an Oregon plan winner variable.

The results are presented in Table 5.6. Not surprisingly, the combined percentage of Democrats in the legislature is positive and significant. Although once we interact this variable with elections held before 1866 the effect drops from 0.10 percent to 0.03 percent. Converting this into probabilities, the impact of the joint Democratic percentage increases by eight percentage points after 1866, indicating that the provision requiring joint balloting had a substantial impact on how senatorial elections were conducted.

Institutional Mediation under Direct Election

The Seventeenth Amendment brushed aside the role of state legislatures, and with it the complex set of coattail and vote-seat linkages that determined the impact of presidential voting on Senate elections. With statewide popular election of a senator, the formerly complex relation between votes and seats became a highly responsive, winner-take-all relationship. The only uncertainty concerned the impact of presidential voting on Senate voting. The literature suggests two possible sources of mitigation of presidential coattails in these post-1912 elections. First, the Senate gradually transformed into a body of career oriented politicians that were assiduous at holding onto their jobs regardless of national political conditions (Daynes 1971; Hall 1936). The ability of twentieth-century incumbents to withstand adverse national forces is well established in the congressional voting literature (Jacobson 2001). The second sources of mitigation were electoral institutions. Although many of the institutions we found mediating coattail effects in House and state elections – redistricting, differing electoral calendars, different legislative terms – are absent in direct Senate elections, there are still some electoral laws that might filter the effects of presidential voting on Senate voting (i.e., ballot structure).

In Table 5.7 we test the impact of presidential voting on Senate voting. Note that we are now using the Democratic percentage of the statewide Senate vote as the dependent variable. To test for institutional mediation, we interact presidential vote with differences in ballot structure. Recall that by 1914 all of the non-southern states had implemented the secret ballot, thus we only include the office bloc format, leaving the party column as the base category. We expect the office bloc interaction to significantly reduce the impact of coattail voting. Moreover, we included a variable indicating the presence of an incumbent senator on the ballot. We coded a Democratic incumbent as 1, a Republican incumbent as −1, and an open seat 0.

The results in Table 5.7 demonstrate the connection between presidential and direct voting for senator. A one percentage point increase in the presidential vote boosts the Senate vote by 0.46 percent. The incumbency variable is positive and significant, demonstrating a small vote boost (3 percent) when an incumbent is running.[4] Finally, the interaction between presidential vote and office bloc ballot is in the expected direction but not significant ($p < 0.13$).

---

[4] In a separate analysis (not shown), we also included a lagged dependent variable. This variable was not significant, and its inclusion did not alter the pattern of results we get here. In addition, including the lagged variable would cause us to lose all the first election immediately following the Seventeenth Amendment.

TABLE 5.7. *The Impact of the Presidential Vote on Senate Elections under Direct Elections*

OLS (with Fixed Effects)

DV = Democratic share of statewide Senate vote

Variable	Coefficients (Panel Corrected Standard Errors)
Presidential Vote	0.46**
	(0.08)
Incumbent Senator	3.04**
	(1.15)
Office Bloc Ballot	−7.635
	(6.803)
Pres. Vote × Office Bloc Ballot	−0.22
	(0.15)
Constant	26.10**
	(5.79)
R-Square	0.50
N	178

* $p < 0.10$, ** $p < 0.05$

Note: State fixed effects also estimated but not reported.

Presidential Voting and the Outcomes of Senate Elections

The statistical results demonstrate a strong connection between presidential voting and Senate outcomes. First, the presidential vote was strongly related to party ratios in the state legislatures during the era of indirect Senate elections. Second, these party ratios were – barring self-defeating factional fights – generally sufficient for a majority party to select a senator of their choosing. The question we now address is whether these individual relationships help explain both the puzzling responsiveness and anti-Democratic bias of nineteenth-century Senate elections. To what extent did voting for a party's state presidential candidate account for the partisan selection of senators within states and the overall party composition of the Senate in Washington?

To answer this question we have created an expected seat share for the Senate. For the period of indirect elections (1840–1914), the presidential vote is passed through the upper and lower house equations estimated in Table 5.2. This produces a predicted seat share for each state legislative chamber. Next, we use these seat shares to predict the outcomes of individual Senate elections. In doing this, however, we need to take into account the fact that Senate selection proceeded in two possible ways. We know that after 1866, if the two chambers could not agree on a candidate, they merged into a single unit and voted on a joint ballot. Before 1866, however, it was not always clear what procedure a state followed. Some states allowed for joint balloting, while others required concurrence from the separate chambers. Because we do not know which of these two types of selection occurred before 1866, in creating the predicted Senate election outcome we used the Democratic percentage on the joint ballot for the entire period between 1840 and 1914. Because the results earlier revealed that a simple majority on the joint ballot was almost always sufficient to elect a co-partisan, we expect that if the Democrats have a predicted majority on the joint ballot they will elect a Democratic senator, and vice versa for Republicans or Whigs.

The resulting estimates – again, based on the presidential vote and state electoral rules – correctly predict 84 percent of the Senate election outcomes. To fully appreciate the value of this model in accounting for state legislative elections, consider its predictive power to the conventional baseline – the lag term. Whether or not the Democrats held the Senate seat prior to the most recent election correctly predicts the partisan outcome 76 percent of the time.

Because direct elections collapsed the institutional selection into a single stage, predicting the likelihood of a Democratic senator after 1914 becomes more straightforward. Here, we simply pass the presidential vote through the equation estimated in Table 5.7. The resulting estimates correctly predict 70 percent of Senate outcomes after the passage of direct elections. Set against the baseline of the lag, which correctly predicts only 59 percent of outcomes, knowing the presidential vote provides a substantially better guess to the partisan outcome. In sum, the results demonstrate that the presidential vote as mediated by electoral institutions had cumulative effects in shaping party control of the U.S. Senate, both before and after indirect elections.

Conclusion: Senate Elections in American Political History

In designing the Senate, the Framers sought to create an institution insulated from transient public opinion. Staggered, six-year terms; statewide constituencies; and above all indirect election served this common purpose. The analysis presented here indicates that the Framers never wholly succeeded in their goal. By the 1840s mass mobilization of electorates behind party-nominated tickets meant that political recruitment for the state house as well as the White House tracked the party success in presidential elections. This list of party aligned offices, indirectly, included the Senate. Senate seats were highly prized offices because of their representation of the state's interest in making national policy, but no less because of their control of the federal patronage spigot through which flowed federal appointments, postmasters, jobs, and contracts to the state. Thus, the payoffs to capturing the state legislature, and with it a Senate seat, became key elements around which partisans rallied. As a consequence, unified party control of the national government was the norm.

Indirect election had its effects, but they assumed more the form of partisan bias rather than unresponsiveness. If the Democrats had a lock on the Southern seats, the Republicans had at least a distinct competitive advantage in the rest of the country. In part, this reflected the Republican Party's rotten borough strategy of carving out and admitting staunchly Republican states. The analysis here finds a Republican bias also embedded in the vote-seat relationships that determined the composition of state legislatures as well as in the joint agreement requirement that meant that the smaller, predominantly Republican upper chambers could block Democratic majorities in the lower chambers. The federal law of 1866 mandating joint sessions in the event of bicameral deadlock, however, opened the door to greater Democratic success, but this was not enough to bring Democratic seat shares into full equality with Republicans.

The Seventeenth Amendment cleared away this bias, while further increasing the responsiveness of Senate elections to national forces. After implementation of direct election in 1914, the bias disappeared and party control of the Senate more closely tracked presidential elections, a pattern that continues to the present-day Senate (Alford and Hibbing 2002; Erikson 2002). Voters are now able to bypass otherwise imperfectly responsive state legislatures. For this reason, one can argue that the passage of the Seventeenth Amendment was perhaps the single most important structural change to the Framers' original design. Senators became more attuned to state electorates and began to carve out the beginnings of a personal vote (Gailmard and Jenkins 2009). Indeed, in a twist that would perhaps surprise the Framers, the modern Senate has become the more electorally responsive chamber of Congress. The lack of competition in modern House elections, whether produced by redistricting, residential sorting, or the inherent advantages of incumbency, has significantly reduced the responsiveness of House elections to national political forces over the past thirty years.

6

State Legislative Elections

With the Constitution delegating election administration primarily to the states, state legislatures throughout the nineteenth and early twentieth centuries enjoyed ample opportunity to adapt election laws for partisan purposes. No elections from the White House down to the local collector of the deeds were exempt from at least occasional attempts at manipulation. Depending on their party's circumstances, they might design congressional districts that magnified slight vote gains into additional seats, or design districts that could withstand massive voter defections. Until 1913 these legislatures elected U.S. senators. Rarely did a party that controlled both chambers fail to elect its caucus's nominee. Yet when the chambers were divided, selecting anyone at all frequently proved nearly impossible. And toward the end of the nineteenth century, strategic legislators began tinkering with ballot formats and voting rules, invented nominating primaries for selecting the parties' state convention delegates, passed civil service laws, and reformed numerous other aspects of the electoral system.

Electoral history has long recognized that state legislators controlled election administration and might conceivably exploit this authority for political advantage. Only recently, however, have political scientists begun to inventory these legislatures' myriad activities in electoral administration and to assess whether these efforts yielded partisan electoral gains for offices throughout the federal system. Early evidence finds state legislatures to have been active and effective as partisan election administrators. Political strategy appears to have guided small and large institutional design decisions alike. Beyond districting, many state legislatures could adjust their electoral calendar, and in a few even their office's term lengths. They could also prescribe where and how party tickets were acquired and cast (Bensel 2004).

Only in the post-Reconstruction South did state legislatures succeed fully in manipulating election rules to attain hegemonic party control, and of course, their measures were extreme and abetted by violence. Nonetheless, we may suspect that politicians everywhere sought through more temperate legislation to attain the same happy equilibrium of perpetual victory. As we come to appreciate state legislatures' central role in regulating the electoral system, we find ourselves elevating to the forefront of explanation institutions about which we know next to nothing. America's nineteenth- and early twentieth-century state legislatures remain black boxes to systematic political science research.

In this chapter we turn our sights to this class of politicians. Specifically, we examine how these party politicians set the rules of their own election and how, as a result, they fared at the polls. How did the rules they created for all elections affect their own welfare? In particular, how did state electoral institutions mediate the relationship between presidential voting and state legislative outcomes? Moreover, with state legislators uniquely positioned to design their own districts, did they enlist different design principles than they followed in engineering electoral rules for other offices? More specifically, might these rational actors have served themselves when designing their own districts, while pursuing the party's collective welfare in designing riskier electoral rules for elections to the other offices?

Nineteenth-Century State Legislatures: Responsive or Insulated?

From the historical literature and contemporaneous accounts, two sharply different expectations are available concerning how the electoral connection shaped state electoral administration. We begin with a depiction of state legislatures so thoroughly corrupt and unresponsive one wonders how democracy in America managed to survive with these politicians running elections. It draws upon accounts of contemporary observers, mostly muckraking journalists and progressive reformers.[1] Historians of this era's politics, though loyally shedding the condemnatory rhetoric, fundamentally agree with critics on the facts. "The bosses were party professionals who knew their craft well, profited from it, and liked it," writes Yearley (1970: 125). He adds, "By the 1880s increasing numbers of politicians possessed business backgrounds or business affiliations.... They were professionals who worked full time to win elections and to retain power. Just this kind of man in New York, New Jersey, Pennsylvania, Ohio, and Illinois, for instance, occupied at least half of the seats in state legislatures" (Yearley 1970: 125).

Indeed, contemporaneous news coverage and reform commission exposés portray many legislators approaching election administration as a usufruct of office, available to the majority party to maintain its rightful hegemony

---

[1] Two systematic studies are available for nineteenth-century state legislative politics in Indiana (Vander Meer 1985), Wisconsin, Illinois, and Iowa (Campbell 1980). While both are mainly concerned with the cultural bases of representation and policy, they explore the central role of partisanship in guiding careers and legislation.

(Summers 2004). Less complimentary appraisals were commonplace. One participant complained in the late 1890s that it was "well-nigh impossible" to persuade "a man of serous knowledge on any subject" to serve. Most legislators in his assessment were "very poor men, with no reputation to maintain or political future to look after" (Teaford 2002: 14). Numerous other aspects of state legislative politics were portrayed as partisan cesspools. Senatorial elections were bought; candidates and state workers were assessed a portion of their salary (usually 5 percent) by party politicians (frequently, members of the legislature); special legislation was tailored to conferred franchises and sweetheart contracts to appreciative businesses; and numerous other imaginative schemes for extortion and pilfering were concocted to fill party coffers and enrich members.

A second discomforting historical fact that reinforces the negative image of this era's state legislatures is their poor record of redistricting state legislative seats to reflect changes in population. Legislative malapportionment was chronic, with its biases tending to accumulate. By the 1960s they would become infamous, forcing the Supreme Court to enter the political thicket in *Baker v. Carr* (1962) (Ansolabehere and Snyder 2008; Argersinger 2012). But even by the late nineteenth century, legislative malapportionment had already become a widespread issue and target of reform. With cities swelling, in part by draining population from surrounding communities, small biases in legislative representation grew ever larger. And as they did so, they increasingly defied solution. In Michigan, the Republican legislature confronted population based reapportionment squarely in the 1940s, but when they discovered that Detroit would be awarded many of the redistributed seats in the state senate the Republican majority reverted quickly to token concessions (Shull 1961).

In many states, constitutionally frozen districts had deteriorated into "a network of rotten boroughs" where state legislatures amounted to little more than government by small towns (Yearley 1970: 40). In Connecticut, the smallest 4 towns in the state, with a total population of 1,500, controlled half as many representatives in the lower house as did the 407,715 inhabitants of the 4 largest cities in 1900 (Yearley 1970). "In Vermont, 8 percent of the people controlled a majority of senate seats, in Rhode Island, less than 12 percent, in New Jersey, less than 20 percent" (Yearley 1970: 40). Nor were malapportioned districts limited to the East Coast. Michigan's apportionment of the state senate in 1885 left the largest district with 84,600 people, while the smallest had more than half as much with only 31,617 people (Argersinger 1989: 67).

We now turn to a more salutary story. The electoral rules and results of their policies for other offices lead us to suspect that elections to these legislatures may have been fairly responsive to their electoral environment. These legislatures, after all, fashioned election laws that yielded reasonably democratic outcomes for other offices that appear to have reflected the changing moods and preferences of the electorate. The partisan composition of state congressional delegations closely tracked the state's presidential vote (see Chapter 4).

More revealing still, U.S. Senate elections in these legislatures similarly followed the partisan division of the state's recent presidential vote (see Chapter 5). The stronger the Democratic presidential candidate's performance in November, the better were the Democratic U.S. Senate candidate's chances months later in the legislative election. Although certainly not transforming votes as efficiently as the Electoral College, there is some reason to suspect that these nineteenth-century legislatures, nonetheless, responded impressively to short-term changes in the partisan political environment.

Some evidence for the responsiveness of partisan legislatures to presidential voting can be found in Figures 6.1a and 6.1b. These figures plot the percentage of legislative chambers where the Democratic Party had majority control of the chamber. The figure also plots the Democratic share of the non-Southern presidential vote. For both lower and upper chambers one finds a fairly strong correspondence between presidential voting and legislative outcomes. Although the Democrats were a distinct minority for most of this era, their fortunes appear to track changes in national electoral forces in the form of presidential voting. We can further see this by estimating the vote-seat relationship between presidential voting and partisan control of state legislatures. Between 1840 and 1900, the swing ratio between the presidential vote and Democratic control of lower houses was 6.55 percent. To visualize this relationship, Figures 6.2a and 6.2b trace out the relationship between the presidential vote and party control of state legislatures such a swing ratio implies. In lower houses, near the 50 percent vote threshold, the estimates indicate that a 1 percentage point increase in the Democratic presidential vote produced a 6.55 percentage point increase in the number of lower chambers controlled by the Democrats. After 1900, the swing ratio for lower houses dropped to 2.65 percentage points. The same pattern appears in upper houses. The estimated swing ratios were 6.43 percentage points and 1.78 percentage points before and after 1900, respectively. In estimating these relationships one also finds a substantial amount of pro-Republican bias in both lower and upper chambers. Even when Democrats cracked the 50 percent threshold in their presidential vote share, it rarely gave them a majority of state legislatures. Nevertheless, the patterns in Figures 6.1 and 6.2 suggest that partisan control of state legislatures in the nineteenth century closely tracked movements in the presidential vote, although this rarely led to the Democrats capturing a majority of state legislative chambers.

In sum, the characterization of nineteenth-century state legislatures as populated with corruptible representatives of rotten boroughs is difficult to square with the highly responsive elections they superintended. Can these portrayals be reconciled? We suggested one possibility: these rational politicians engineered elections to allow them to free ride while elsewhere fashioning responsive elections that better pursued their political party's collective interest. The critical evidence for verifying the insulation of state legislative elections and testing this strategic rationale is to be found in the dynamics of this era's state legislative elections.

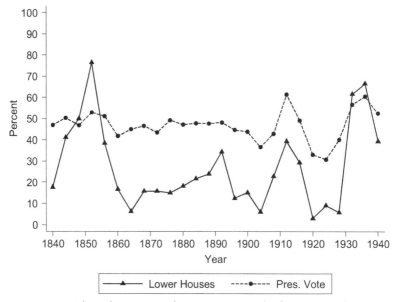

FIGURE 6.1a. Presidential Voting and Partisan Control of State Legislatures, 1840–1940: Lower Houses

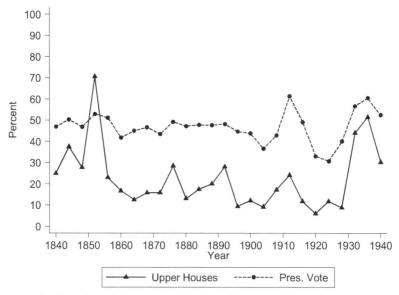

FIGURE 6.1b. Presidential Voting and Partisan Control of State Legislatures, 1840–1940: Upper Houses

Note: This figure displays the Democratic percent of the presidential vote in non-Southern states and the percent of legislative chambers where the Democrats had majority control. The latter only includes those states where legislatures held elections during a presidential election year.

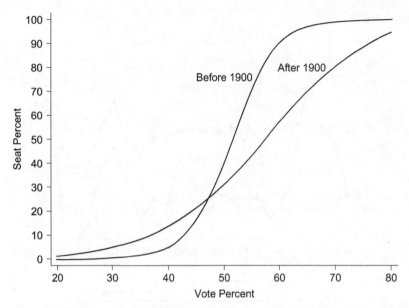

FIGURE 6.2a. The Responsiveness of Partisan Control of State Legislatures to the Presidential Vote, before and after 1900: Lower Houses

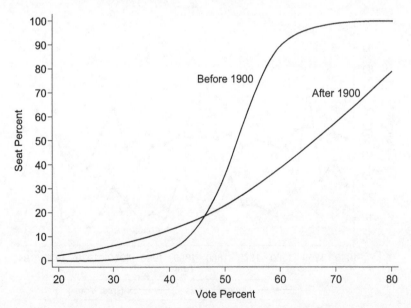

FIGURE 6.2b. The Responsiveness of Partisan Control of State Legislatures to the Presidential Vote, before and after 1900: Upper Houses
Note: The figure plots the estimated vote-seat relationship between the presidential vote and party control of state legislative chambers. The *x*-axis is the Democratic percent of the vote in non-Southern states. The *y*-axis is the percent of non-Southern state legislatures where Democrats were in the majority.

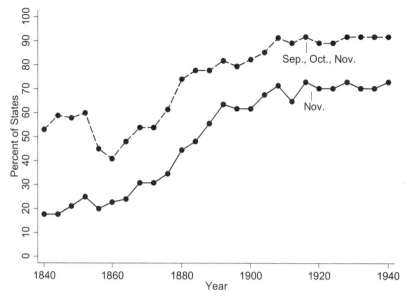

FIGURE 6.3. State Legislative Calendars

Mediating Institutions in State Legislative Elections

Our analysis of state legislative elections follows the model developed earlier in this book to track the effects of state-defined electoral rules on congressional elections. It consists of two stages: coattail voting and the vote-seat conversion.

Presidential Coattails and State Legislative Voting

As we have seen in the preceding chapters, the party ballot used throughout the nineteenth century produced a strong coattail connection between presidential and congressional outcomes. There is ample reason that such a connection also existed for candidates further down the ballot, in particular state representatives and state senators. As shown in the sample ballots in Figure 2.2 from Chapter 2, presidential and vice presidential candidates appeared at the top of the ballot, with state legislative candidates falling toward the lower end of the ticket.[2]

The impact of the party ticket on coattail voting presumes that state legislative candidates were elected at the same time as presidents. The percentage of state legislative elections held simultaneous with the presidential election, displayed in Figure 6.3, increased over the course of the nineteenth century. Much like House elections, before the Civil War a large number of states held their legislative elections in months other than November. Figure 6.3 reveals

---

[2] For a time, a few states apparently required that ballots be separated by office. In such instances, the voter bundled several or more ballots, facilitating split ticket voting (Bensel 2004).

that most of these off-November elections occurred in September or October. So, although not always simultaneous with the presidential election, these state legislative elections were wrapped up in the presidential campaign season. Moreover, as more states converged on the November election both the benefits and the perils of the ticket system grew in importance.

The ticket system tied to the success of the party's standard bearer the electoral fortunes of these state legislative candidates further down the ballot. By consolidating national, state, and local elections on a single ballot, state parties solved a collective dilemma of having to mobilize votes for a multitude of dispersed local campaigns. Yet in consolidating the ballot and concentrating their energies on the presidential or gubernatorial contest, these politicians created another potentially serious collective action problem – free riding. With the head-of-ticket's success conferring a public good to all candidates, state party organizations had to ward off the temptation of state legislative candidates to both shirk their campaign effort and discreetly reposition themselves to accommodate potential bolters or other unhappy segments of their local constituency.

Party leaders counteracted free riding among state legislative candidates in several ways. In some states, coveted legislative nominations came with levies. In late nineteenth-century New York State, Senate candidates had to pony up $50,000 or more to the ticket's campaign fund (Yearley 1970), a suspiciously large sum that lends certitude to charges of legislative corruption. Alternatively, nominations might go to candidates who had already demonstrated loyal party service and could safely be counted on to work actively for the ticket. To make sure no lower ticket candidates would deviate from a uniform appeal, the recently formed Illinois Whig Party in 1840 forced all of its state legislative candidates to sign a loyalty oath to the party's national ticket and platform (Leonard 2002: 217).

To the degree these and other selective incentives succeeded, the parties entered the campaign vigorously, transmitting the clear and simple message – namely, elect the head of ticket. State legislative candidates were among the chief beneficiaries of the ticket system. As shown in Figure 6.4, however, not all party tickets extended the president's coattails to state legislative candidates. Absence from a presidential ticket might reflect a different electoral calendar. Whether ticket separation reflected state law or simply the division of nominating and campaign responsibilities within the state party organization remains unclear (Bensel 2004). In modeling the effects of coattail voting on state legislative elections we shall keep in mind its essential value, but problematic occurrence, for down-ticket races.

The passage of ballot reform dramatically altered the campaign strategies of state legislative candidates – especially those who shifted abruptly from a consolidated party ticket to the office bloc ballot without a party box. These candidates faced an even more serious problem of vote splitting and voter fatigue. Though they no longer needed to worry about vote leakage from bogus tickets or pasters surreptitiously attached over their name, candidates now faced a

DEMOCRATIC TICKET.

For Electors of President and Vice-President.

CHARLES R. INGERSOLL,
LOREN P. WALDO.
RICHARD W. H. JARVIS,
HENRY G. HUBBARD,
CHAUNCEY F. CLEVELAND,
DARIUS N. COUCH.

For State Officers.

FOR GOVERNOR,
JAMES E. ENGLISH.
FOR LIEUTENANT-GOVERNOR,
CHARLES M. POND.
FOR SECRETARY OF STATE,
STEPHEN S. BLAKE.
FOR TREASURER,
MERRICK A. MARCY.
FOR COMPTROLLER,
CHARLES R. FAGAN.

For Member of Congress.
JAMES PHELPS.
For Sheriff,
ARTHUR B. HART.
For Judge of Probate,

Daniel W Stevens

FIGURE 6.4. Truncated Ballot: Connecticut, 1876

certain and potentially more formidable source of defection – an ambitious opponent's direct appeals to their constituency. Mobilization no longer sufficed; candidates bore individual responsibility for attracting a voter's support.

The benefits of the consolidated party ballot dissipated on another front, as well. Where a party box was unavailable or independent-minded voters decided to weigh candidates' merits individually, down-ticket races faced a potentially serious problem of roll-off. As they descended the ballot into the region of less familiar names and less consequential offices, some voters would quit voting as they lost interest and confidence in their selections. Working cumulatively, split ticket voting and roll-off could combine to decouple candidates from their standard bearer and render state legislative elections highly unresponsive to national or even statewide forces. To test the possibility that roll-off rendered coattails irrelevant, we have inspected numerous states' turnout trends for state legislative elections in comparison with head-of-ticket elections.

The evidence contained in the several states' time series reported in Figures 6.5, 6.6, and 6.7 suggests that roll-off was not so great as to prevent coattail voting.[3] For example, Figure 6.5 presents turnout figures for the Connecticut state senate along with turnout for the head of the ticket (either the presidential or gubernatorial candidate). The figure shows that the number of votes cast for each office closely tracked each other. Even after ballot reform, which in Connecticut meant a party column ballot with a party box, roll-off increased but rarely accounted for more than a 5 percent drop-off. The roll-off numbers for Kansas and Massachusetts, presented in Figures 6.6 and 6.7, respectively, tell a similar story. In both cases there was some, but minimal, roll-off prior to ballot reform. Following the adoption of the Australian ballot roll-off increased. The increase was most pronounced in Massachusetts, which had opted for the office bloc format of the new ballot. Overall, the time series of these states suggest that while roll-off occurred, it was not substantial enough to deter coattail voting for state legislative candidates.

The Conversion of Votes into Seats
In Chapter 4, we found that prior to ballot reform, when elections followed more predictable mobilization strategies, state legislatures carefully designed

---

[3] States' election rules pose some serious barriers to the seemingly simple issue of comparing turnout for presidential or gubernatorial elections with state legislative elections. One problem, particularly for the upper chambers, is staggered (and to a lesser degree, floaterial) elections. This requires that one identify turnout for the head-of-ticket offices for those districts with a legislative election; district-level figures are rarely published in the standard sources. Another problem is the pervasive use of multimember districts. One cannot simply sum the legislative votes because some constituencies select numerous members for a given legislative chamber. Aside from the revealing qualities of the states and chambers reported in these figures, for each these thorny election rules do not apply. Data for the eligible electorate for these figures were found in Burnham, Clubb, and Flanigan (1972b).

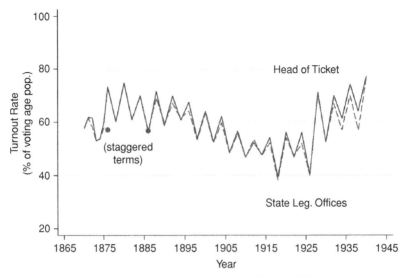

FIGURE 6.5a. Turnout in Connecticut Elections for Head of Ticket and State Upper House, 1865–1940: Turnout Rates

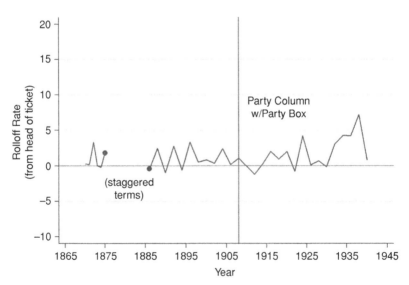

FIGURE 6.5b. Turnout in Connecticut Elections for Head of Ticket and State Upper House, 1865–1940: Roll-Off Rates

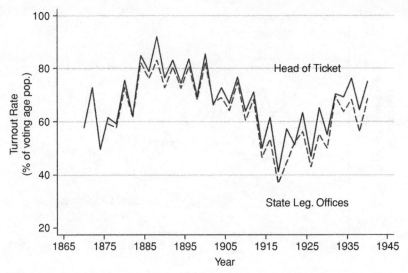

FIGURE 6.6a. Turnout in Massachusetts Elections for State Upper House, 1865–1940: Turnout Rates

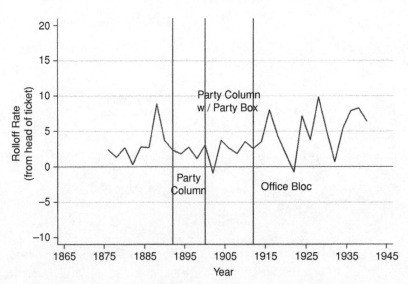

FIGURE 6.6b. Turnout in Massachusetts Elections for State Upper House, 1865–1940: Roll-Off Rates

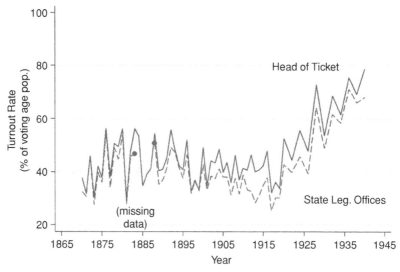

FIGURE 6.7a. Turnout in Kansas Elections for State Lower House, 1865–1940: Turnout Rates

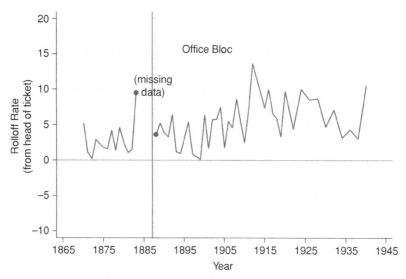

FIGURE 6.7b. Turnout in Kansas Elections for State Lower House, 1865–1940: Roll-Off Rates

and frequently updated efficient gerrymanders in laying out congressional districts. After ballot reform, when voting became secret and the coattail less certain, majority party legislators switched to a packing gerrymander strategy. This alternative ensured a number of easy victories in the face of uncertainty for the in-party, while conceding some districts to the out-party (Cain 1985). Because a greater change in votes is necessary to flip partisan control of packed districts, this strategy yielded smaller swing ratios in House elections than compared to those produced by efficient gerrymanders.

Did state legislators enlist similar strategies in designing their own seats as they did in congressional districts? One historian of nineteenth-century state party politics has concluded they did:

Cheating the enemy of its due could be done in different ways. In some places the dominant party gave itself the largest possible number of potential seats by devising districts with just enough of a margin for its side to make victory feasible. In others, the dominant party fixed boundaries to banish as many of the opposition as practical into one district, the better to make all the other districts safe. (Summers 2004: 128–129)

Probably all single-party-dominated state legislatures aspired to enlist one form of gerrymander or another, but compelling considerations may also have been present to deter seat-maximizing policies. For one, we may suspect that these low-rung politicians nurtured the same reelection aspirations as did their more successful counterparts in higher office. If so, efficient gerrymandering could seriously undermine their understandable desire for easy reelection. Each would be tempted to carve out for himself the safest district possible and let his colleagues provide the party's collective good in their marginal districts. In Indiana during the 1885 state legislative session, the majority Democrats fought just as much with each other as they did with Republicans over the issue of reapportionment. According to Argersinger, "Numerous Democratic legislators also introduced their own bills, drafted to advance particular personal or local interests, often with little attention paid to assuring equal district populations. Intraparty conflict over apportionment soon bogged down the legislature and even prompted some optimistic Republicans to imagine exploiting Democratic differences to shape the final bill" (Argersinger 2012: 35).

Also, in many states, legislators faced serious constitutional constraints in drawing districts. Box 6.1 presents a sample of the kinds of redistricting dicta that pervaded state constitutions. The most common of these provisions limited the number of representatives available to a county, guaranteed representation to every county, fixed the size of the legislature at some small number, prohibited the division or combination of counties, and automatically expanded representation (and with it the size of the chamber) whenever a county's population crossed some threshold.[4] Many of these same constitutions admonished legislatures to follow population-based representation, but given the explicit constraints listed, these provisions amounted to little more than homilies that members could liberally interpret and safely ignore (Key 1932).

---

[4] By specific constitutional provision, Arizona apportions its senate by counties, and Louisiana apportions its representatives by parishes. Eleven other states accomplish the same results for the senate and twenty-three for the lower chamber by allotting at least one member to a political subdivision-county, town, or parish. These provisions invariably result in overrepresentation of

BOX 6.1. **Samples of State Constitutional Redistricting Provisions**

California (1879). Art 4, Sec 6. Beginning with census of 1880, every ten years apportionment will occur at the first session after the census. Districts are to be created in "as near equal population as may be." (1926) Art 4, Sec 6 Amend 163 "in the formation of senatorial districts no county or city and county shall contain more than one senatorial district, and the counties of small population shall be grouped in districts of not to exceed three counties in any one senatorial district."

Illinois (1848). Art 3 Sec 6: The house has 75 members, the senate 25. After "one million souls" reside in the state, five members shall be added to the house and five members for every additional five hundred thousand until the total number of representatives equals 100. Thereafter, the number of representatives will not change. Apportionment to be determined by the number of white inhabitants. Furthermore, "in all future apportionments, where more than one county shall be thrown into a representative district, all representatives to which said counties may be entitled shall be elected by the entire district." (1870) Art 4 Sec 6: one senator per district. However, "counties containing not less than the ratio and 3/4ths" are entitled two senators, "and to one additional senator for each number of inhabitants equal to the ratio contained by such counties in excess of twice the number of said ratio."

Indiana and **Nevada**. No constitutional rules provided until modern era.

Iowa (1857). Art 3.02, Sec 35, Amend 13 (1904) Allocation of representatives shall be done by dividing the population of the state by the number of districts. Each county is entitled to at least 1 rep. Each county having a ratio of more than 3/5 is entitled to an additional rep (as long as they are among the nine counties having the largest population).

Maine (1821 in force until 1931). Art 4, Sec 2.02. Beginning in 1821, senate districts to be apportioned by the legislature according to the number of inhabitants and "conform, as near as may be, to county lines." The number of senators shall not exceed 20 at the first apportionment, but may increase until they reach 31. Art 4, Sec 2 Sets number of representatives based on census and provides an upper limit of 200. Provides that every 5–10 years (as decided by the legislature), reapportionment will occur based on a census. When the number of representatives reaches over 200, the state can vote to decide whether to increase the number of representatives.

New Jersey (1841). Art 4 Sec 3, reapportionment of representatives to the counties will occur after every census as equally as can be according to the number of

(*continued*)

the least populated areas. A few states discriminate more directly by denying the more populous districts their proportionate share of legislators. This is done in various ways: in one state by a system which requires a substantial increase above the ratio for each succeeding legislator; in six others each county is assured a member, but the fractions of a ratio are placed so high that additional membership is denied the highly populated districts; three states have fixed a maximum number of seats in their constitution (by assuring each county at least one seat; few seats are left for distribution to the larger districts upon a population basis); five states have limited the maximum number of legislators any district may have, irrespective of population (Harvey 1952).

inhabitants. Each county is entitled to at least one member and the total number of reps cannot exceed 60.

New York (1894). Art 3 Sec 4, the legislature will redraw senatorial lines after every census such that each district contain as equal as can be a proportional number of inhabitants excluding aliens. Districts should be contiguous and compact. No county can have more than 4 senators unless it has a full ratio (50/population excluding aliens). No county can have more than one third of all senators. There will always be 50 senators unless a county has three or more at the time of apportionment and is entitled to another senator. The size of the senate will increase to that extent. Art 3 Sec 5, the legislature will apportion the 150 representatives among the counties based on the population excluding aliens after every census. The legislature can further divide counties into assembly districts such that every district have similar number of inhabitants.

Source: Wallis (2006)

One common method for reconciling the integrity of counties with some semblance of population-based representation involved periodic addition of seats to counties (and expansion of the legislature) with multimember districts. By the 1930s Detroit voters were electing dozens of representatives.[5] The combination of single and multimember districts of various sizes across a state might show up in estimates for both the stages of our model. A vote for president would generate as many coattail votes as there were legislative candidates on the ballot. Similarly, a single-vote plurality for a party's ticket could, in multimember districts, generate multiple single-vote victories.

Testing the Effects of Electoral Rules on Coattails and Vote-Seat Conversion

Two serious data requirements challenged our ability to test coattail and vote-seat relationships in state legislative elections. The first barrier to this study was the shocking absence of state election returns. Nowhere (except for Stuart Rice's partial compilation of New Jersey assembly elections) have statewide election returns been compiled for this historical period. To overcome this historical gap, we gathered state legislative election results from as many states, and for as many elections, as possible. Most of these elections were recovered from states' legislative manuals (commonly called Blue Books) or secretary of state election reports where, invariably, returns are reported for individual districts and frequently without the candidates' party affiliations.[6] Where necessary

---

[5] With multimember districts in place, Illinois launched its experiment in cumulative voting in 1870, in which voters had the option of casting more than one vote for an individual candidate (Mott 1927).

[6] Party information was recovered successfully for all states, except some years in Massachusetts, from biographical directories, published party caucus lists, and newspapers.

and convenient, the original primary sources were consulted, generally to fill in small gaps in the data series. Although other states' election results exist in some poorly accessible form – such as microfilm of the original, barely legible handwritten county vote reports without party labels – the elections employed here constitute a nearly complete set of state legislative election returns from readily available sources.[7]

The second daunting data problem arose in identifying state legislative redistricting events. Unlike U.S. House elections, redistricting state legislatures can be an ambiguous and frequently obscure activity. Beyond general redistricting laws, many other constitutional and statutory provisions automatically altered the composition of legislatures during this era (Advisory Commission on Intergovernmental Relations 1962; Bone 1952; Dubin 2007; Jewell 1955; Reock and Shank 1966). Typically, seats were added when counties crossed a specified population figure. Constitutional conventions might change the basis of representation or dramatically shrink or enlarge the size of the legislatures. Both events generally triggered major changes in district boundaries. In Appendix Table A.2, we display two reasonable definitions: a general redistricting law and a sudden change in the legislature's size by 20 percent or more.

For analyzing the mediating electoral effects of institutional variables – election calendars, ballot form, and district lines – the numerous combinations of state laws, both cross-sectionally and temporally, represent a research windfall. Tables A.1 and A.2 in the Appendix display the full array of combinations of the relevant laws, some of which – such as redistricting – differ between a state's upper and lower chambers as well as across states and over time. For this analysis, we have pooled the relevant electoral and institutional variables for twenty-seven non-Southern states for the years 1865 through 1940. This seventy-five-year period spans the important changes in the institutional environment and provides sufficient observations at the beginning and end of the series to estimate the stable effects of the pre- and post-reform electoral regimes. With seven of these states entering the Union after 1865 and the series for all states missing elections, we shall be estimating an unbalanced, time-series cross-sectional data structure pairing 1,201 upper or lower chamber elections with presidential elections.[8]

---

[7] To the best of our knowledge, historical statewide state legislative votes have been examined only once before. Stuart Rice employed New Jersey assembly races from 1877 through 1924 to explain time-series analysis. In a note, he reported the difficulty of obtaining such data: "In some issues of the New Jersey *Legislative Manual*, the required data is given in summary form. More frequently it was necessary to compile it laboriously from the detailed tables of votes for the individual candidates. Travel to several New Jersey cities was necessary to compile the data" (Rice 1928: 283).

[8] Working with state-level seat shares also has the advantage over district-level analysis (for example, see Cox and Katz 2002) in obviating the need to take into account that district apportionments did not occur in isolation from others within a state.

Coattail Voting and Ballot Form

If state legislative elections respond to the broader campaign environment, the Democratic vote shares should track the statewide Democratic head-of-ticket percentages – that is, for the presidential candidate. Moreover, if the consolidated party ballot boosted coattail voting in these elections, as it has been shown to do elsewhere, the coattail should weaken after ballot reform. These hypotheses are largely supported by the distributions of the states' individual OLS coattail slopes in Figures 6.8a and 6.8b. For each state, we estimated a regression model with the Democratic share of the state legislative vote as the dependent variable and the Democratic share of the state presidential vote as the independent variable. Figures 6.8a and 6.8b present the distribution of these state-by-state coattail slopes. The figures show that during the pre-reform era the Democratic legislative vote shares for both the upper and lower chambers appear to have been highly responsive to presidential voting. On average, they even exceed a 1:1 ratio, an anomaly consistent with extensive use of multimember districts in most states. As predicted, presidential coattails weaken sharply after the introduction of ballot reform. Because the systematic effects of institutional rules hold more interest than do specific states' politics, we have pooled these data into cross-sectional (state), time-series (year) data format and estimated the overall impact of presidential voting on state legislative voting.[9] The dependent variable is the Democratic share of the statewide legislative vote. Five different ballot regimes were identified that could induce varying levels of coattail voting. In addition to the pre-reform consolidated party ballot, the reform ballots combined either the office bloc or party column format with or without a party box option. Clearly, the party supplied ballot should generate the strongest coattail relationships. Beyond this our expectations are not so clear-cut. The party column should yield a stronger coattail connection than the office bloc; certainly, decoupling the ticket was the purpose behind reformers' ardent promotion of the latter form. Although voters' early use of the party box option remains understudied, one may reasonably suspect that its presence (frequently accompanied by a prominent image of the party mascot, such as the Democratic rooster) would repair the ticket's coattail effect.

The relationships in Table 6.1 allow us to test these hypotheses. In a preliminary analysis (not shown), the office bloc/party column distinction failed to generate significantly different relationships (although generally the strengths of the coefficients ranked according to the model's predictions). Consequently, Table 6.1 estimates three different ballot regimes: pre-reform ticket, ballot reform with party box, and ballot reform without party box for each

---

[9] For purposes of presentation, the reported equations omit each state's intercept shift, which is estimated in the model.

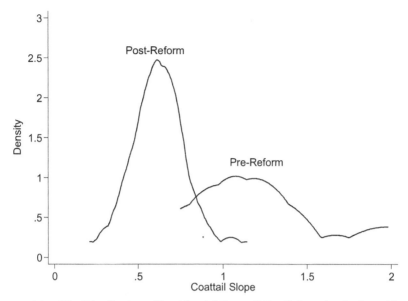

FIGURE 6.8a. The Distribution of Presidential Coattail Coefficients for the States' Legislative Elections, 1865–1940: Lower Houses

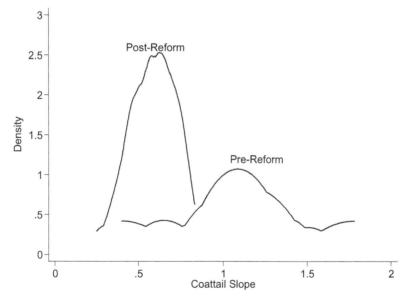

FIGURE 6.8b. The Distribution of Presidential Coattail Coefficients for the States' Legislative Elections, 1865–1940: Upper Houses

Note: The plots represent kernel density distribution of separate OLS estimates for the following equation:

$$\text{Dem. Legislative Vote}_{it} = a_i + b\text{Dem. Pres. Vote}_{it}.$$

The relationships were estimated separately for each state's pre- and post-ballot reform years. Only state series with a minimum of six observations during each period were included in the analysis.

TABLE 6.1. *The Impact of Presidential Coattails on State Legislative Voting*

Legislative Chamber	Lower	Upper
Presidential Vote	0.792***	1.066***
	(0.214)	(0.195)
Ballot Form		
Australian Ballot	9.627	−5.544
	(10.852)	(8.692)
Australian Ballot × Presidential Vote	−0.384*	−0.724***
	(0.219)	(0.213)
Party Box	−15.666***	−10.317***
	(2.995)	(3.202)
Party Box × Presidential Vote	0.320***	0.289***
	(0.064)	(0.068)
Political Setting		
Minor Party Vote	0.295**	0.077
	(0.142)	(0.242)
Minor Party Vote × Presidential Vote	−0.0002	0.007
	(0.004)	(0.007)
Lag Terms		
Lag Dem. Two-Party Share	0.242	−0.318
	(0.260)	(0.216)
Australian Ballot × Dem. Two-Party Share	0.152	0.667***
	(0.260)	(0.229)
Constant	0.576**	15.653*
	(10.592)	(7.232)
R^2	0.800	0.739
N	290	284
# Groups	26	25
Mean Obs. per Group	11.154	11.360

* $p < 0.10$, ** $p < 0.05$, *** $p < 0.01$

Note: State fixed effects are included in the estimation but not presented in the table. Panel corrected standard errors in parentheses.

chamber's legislative elections. Table 6.1 also includes lag terms and information about minor party competition in the election.

If differences in state electoral laws mediate presidential coattails, the coefficient for the stand-alone presidential vote term (representing elections under a consolidated party ballot) should be significantly stronger than those for the ballot interaction terms. In Table 6.1 this pattern holds. The presidential candidate was clearly a more potent draw for his party's legislative candidates during the pre-reform era than after. Yet some reformed ballot configurations weakened coattails more than did others. The presence of a party box almost restores the party ticket for presidential elections.

The two pairs of control variables provide additional information about the implications of the alteration of ballot regimes on these elections. We include the lagged value of the statewide chamber vote (whether annual, biennial, or quadrennial) to directly model the temporal dynamics and eliminate serial correlation (Beck and Katz 1996).[10] The lag terms also offer a second, indirect test of coattail effects. Where coattails are strong, such as states with a consolidated party ballot, the lag effect should be weaker than in settings where these beyond-the-district forces were abrupt or weak. This is precisely what we find in Table 6.1 in the positive coefficient for the interaction of the ballot dummy variable with the lag term. Under the consolidated ballot regime, legislative elections did not track their past results as closely as they would after ballot reform.

With the Democratic presidential and legislative votes percentaged against a state's total popular vote, the coattail variables may be diluted by the presence of third party candidates in either or both contests. The positive relationship for the minor party presidential vote indicates that a state's Democratic congressional vote increases with the strength of minor party presidential candidates. This makes sense for a couple of reasons. First, throughout this period, minor party presidential candidates tended to draw votes at the expense of Republican candidates. Second, in controlling for the Democratic presidential vote, the larger the minor party vote the smaller the residual share available to the Republican candidate.

Overall, voting in state legislative elections for this seventy-five-year period appears to have been far from insulated from short-term national and statewide forces. Nonetheless, after ballot reform presidential coattails weakened sharply in the absence of a party box. Given the distance down the ticket these offices resided, a 0.5 percent slope during presidential campaigns indicates that voting remained impressively tied to national elections. This figure corresponds closely, in part, with the strength of presidential coattails on congressional voting during the post-reform era found in Chapter 4. Under both ballot regimes state legislative voting appears to have benefited from the same national forces that shaped elections for offices higher up the office structure.

Vote-Seat Conversion

Coattail voting represents only the first cog in the institutional machinery manufacturing presidential votes into legislative seats. Vote shares must be transformed into comparable seat shares if partisan control of state legislatures is to reflect a state's presidential or gubernatorial election. In designing congressional districts, nineteenth-century legislators were skilled mapmakers. They carefully designed marginal yet winnable congressional districts during the consolidated party ballot era. As circumstances dictated a change in rational strategy, they just as effectively installed packing gerrymanders (see Chapter 3).

---

[10] Including a lagged dependent variable along with fixed effects as we do can lead to bias when T is small (Kvist 1995). Given that our average T is eleven, however, any potential bias will likely be small (Beck 2001).

Anecdotal evidence presented earlier suggests that legislators pursued similar schemes in designing their own state legislative districts. Perhaps so, but we noted that working against this strategy were a compelling desire to free ride and serious constitutional constraints, both largely absent in redistricting House seats. Appendix Table A.2 reports a large number of redistricting events either in the form of general redistricting legislation or in a sizable expansion of the legislature. Whether all this activity amounted to strategic gerrymandering remains to be seen.

To begin our examination of the vote-seat relationship in the state legislatures, Figures 6.9a and 6.9b display the states' separate swing ratios.[11] Because marginal changes in the vote have the largest impact on seat changes as vote shares approach the 50 percent threshold, and taper off sharply as the vote shares extend toward lopsided vote distributions, the vote-seat function is conventionally represented as a logistic (Tufte 1975). Several features of the distributions in Figures 6.9a and 6.9b are worth noting. First, despite the conventional wisdom that the smaller upper chambers were more seriously malapportioned than the lower chambers, the distributions closely resemble each other during both the pre- and post-reform eras.[12] Second, both chambers' vote-seat swing ratios become less responsive after reform. This is unsurprising, but in neither instance are the shifts substantial enough to suggest a major change in districting strategy from efficient to packing gerrymanders. The circumstantial evidence, instead, supports a gradual process of elections becoming less responsive throughout the twentieth-century segment of our time series. When the state series are divided for pre- and post-1900, slightly greater spread occurs in the distributions. The smallest median swing ratios appear when the calculations are confined to the last two decades of our series.

In order to investigate the effects of ballot reform and the biases introduced by party control over the redistricting process, Table 6.2 aggregates all vote-seat pairs for each chamber's elections.[13] Earlier, we defined the vote-seat relationship as comprised of two components – a swing ratio and partisan bias (Tufte 1975). A highly responsive plan will display a large swing ratio

---

[11] We have calculated the swing ratios for each state for which we have six or more elections for both the pre- and post-reform time periods. More specifically, we estimated the following standard vote-seat equation:

$$\ln(DHS_{it}/1 - DHS_{it}) = \lambda + \rho(\ln(DHV_{it}/1 - DHV_{it}))$$

where ρ is the swing ratio and λ is partisan bias.

[12] For the 27 states in this analysis, the average sizes of the lower and upper chambers were 104 and 32, respectively, in 1890. By 1940, these means had increased to 125 and 37.

[13] Because a correlation likely arises in the probability of Democratic victory across a state's districts, we assume that seat shares follow an extended beta-binomial distribution (Palmquist 1998; G. King 1989). Using a simple binomial model would possibly lead to inefficient estimates and biased standard errors (G. King 1989: 119–121). Moreover, the extended beta-binomial model conditions on the number of seats in each state, thus taking into account any heteroskedasticity due to varying sizes of states' delegations (Cox and Katz 2002: 63).

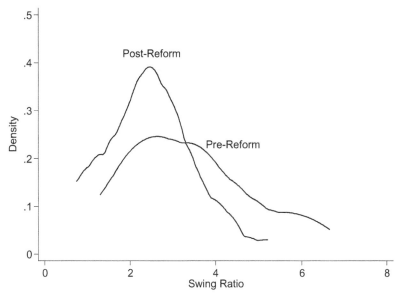

FIGURE 6.9a. The Distribution of Swing Ratios for the States' Legislative Elections, 1865–1940: Lower Houses

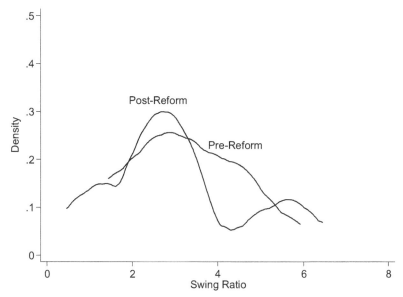

FIGURE 6.9b. The Distribution of Swing Ratios for the States' Legislative Elections, 1865–1940: Upper Houses
Note: The plots represent kernel density distribution of separate swing-ratio estimates for each state. The relationships were estimated separately for each state's pre- and post-ballot reform years. Only state series with a minimum of six observations during the period were included in the analysis.

TABLE 6.2. *The Conversion of State Legislative Votes into Seats, 1865–1940*

	Lower House All Years	Lower House Presidential Election Years	Upper House All Years	Upper House Presidential Election Years
Swing Ratio				
Unified Government	2.71*	3.57*	2.69*	3.57*
Pre-Reform	(0.42)	(0.67)	(0.34)	(0.63)
Unified Government	1.99*	2.12*	2.19*	2.44*
Post-Reform	(0.10)	(0.15)	(0.12)	(0.19)
Divided Government	3.77*	2.62*	3.03*	1.81*
Pre-Reform	(0.52)	(0.73)	(0.44)	(0.48)
Divided Government	2.31*	2.67*	2.99*	3.81*
Post-Reform	(0.12)	(0.18)	(0.17)	(0.27)
Partisan Bias				
Unified Democrat	0.08	−0.09	0.09	−0.24*
Pre-Reform	(0.05)	(0.10)	(0.06)	(0.12)
Unified Democrat	0.03*	0.01	0.03*	0.01
Post-Reform	(0.01)	(0.03)	(0.01)	(0.03)
Divided Pre-Reform	−0.02	−0.13*	−0.07*	−0.19*
	(0.02)	(0.05)	(0.02)	(0.04)
Divided Post-Reform	−0.06*	−0.06*	−0.05*	−0.03*
	(0.01)	(0.01)	(0.01)	(0.01)
Unified Republican	−0.07*	−0.05	−12*	−0.10*
Pre-Reform	(0.02)	(0.04)	(0.02)	(0.04)
Unified Republican	−0.08*	−0.06*	−0.09*	−0.06*
Post-Reform	(0.01)	(0.02)	(0.01)	(0.02)
γ	0.07*	0.07*	0.06*	0.06*
	(0.01)	(0.007)	(0.01)	(0.01)
N	712	300	791	323
Log-Likelihood	−48214.93	−20708.67	−11098.17	−4220.01

* $p < 0.05$

Note: The parameter γ measures the correlation across districts (within a state) of the probability that the Democrats will capture the seat. The bias coefficients have been converted to their Democratic seat shares.

coefficient such that a slight plurality of the popular vote will generate a disproportionate share of seats gains. An extreme form of this is a winner-take-all election, which in fact might approximate countywide elections comprised of multimember seats. Bias refers simply to a party's expected seat share given 50 percent of the popular two-party vote. A positive five percentage point bias means that the state's Democratic candidates could expect to win 55 percent of the seats with 50 percent of the vote.

If ballot reform altered the strategic purposes of redistricting state legislative seats, as they did for House boundaries, the swing ratios for the pre-reform era should be significantly larger than those occurring during the post-reform era. Table 6.2 provides estimates of swing ratios and partisan bias for redistricting plans that were passed before or after a state's initial ballot reform. All of the swing ratio terms post-reform are smaller than for their comparable pre-reform plans, but only one (i.e., for the lower chamber during divided government) represents a significant reduction in responsiveness. For example, the swing ratio in lower chambers for plans passed by unified governments was 2.71 pre-reform and 1.99 after ballot reform. Similarly, in upper chambers the swing ratios were 2.69 and 2.19 before and after reform, respectively. Interestingly, the results become even sharper when we confine the analysis to just presidential election years. Columns two and four of the table present the estimates of this restricted sample. Here we find even sharper swing ratios before reform and a more precipitous decline in swing ratios after reform. In lower chambers the swing ratio before reform was a substantial 3.57 and dropped to 2.12 after reform. In upper chambers the swing ratio was 3.57 before and only 2.44 after.

To better comprehend the relationships that these nonlinear coefficients describe, Figures 6.10a–d trace out the estimates for plans passed by Republican state governments (these comprise the largest category of district maps). The figures reveal that nineteenth-century state legislative elections did indeed respond to marginal changes in the preferences of the constituents in the districts. And the responsiveness of state legislative elections picked up substantially during years when presidential candidates were at the top of the ticket. During the twentieth century these relationships weakened, yet none of these slopes approximates the flat-line electoral insulation conjured up by muckraking journalism's representations of these politicians' cynical indifference to the electorate.

Another test for detecting strategic purpose compares the strengths of the swing ratio coefficients between divided and unified government at the time the plan was enacted. Table 6.2 also includes interactive terms identifying which party, if either, controlled state government at the time of adoption of the current redistricting plan.[14] With each party holding a veto, redistricting was less likely to occur under divided party control of state government. But when divided governments did redraw district boundaries – including automatic expansions of seats after a census according to state constitutional prescription – these plans should have taken a decidedly bipartisan cast, preserving the current partisan division of seats. These hypothesized differences were confirmed for congressional districting during this era in Chapter 4. Comparing

---

[14] In those states where the state constitution provided the governor with no veto (e.g., Ohio until 1912) or a veto that could be overridden by a simple majority (e.g., Missouri until 1874), we ignored the governor's partisanship in classifying party control for a districting event.

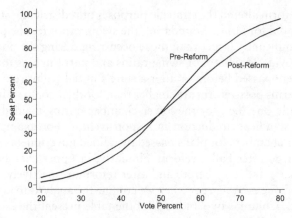

FIGURE 6.10a. Vote-Seat Translation Before and After Ballot Reform for Republican District Plans: Lower Houses, All Years

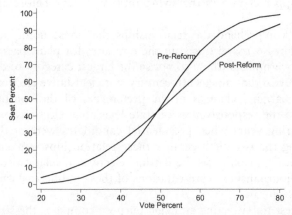

FIGURE 6.10b. Vote-Seat Translation Before and After Ballot Reform for Republican District Plans: Lower Houses, Presidential Election Years

the divided to the unified swing ratios in Table 6.2, one finds no substantial difference in swing ratios between divided and unified state governments. In both chambers, and for both ballot regimes, redistricting plans adopted during divided governments prove marginally more responsive than those devised with a single party in control of the process.

The results for bias are presented in the lower half of Table 6.2. Because bias is directional (favoring one party over the other), we have split the bias coefficients for districting under unified Democratic and Republican regimes. Here we find clear evidence of partisan districting. During the era of the consolidated party ballot, unified Republican plans produced a significant pro-Republican bias of eight and nine percentage points for the lower and upper chambers,

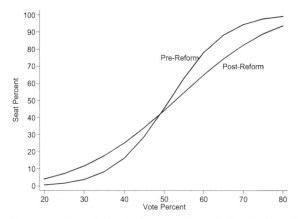

FIGURE 6.10c. Vote-Seat Translation Before and After Ballot Reform for Republican District Plans: Upper, All Years

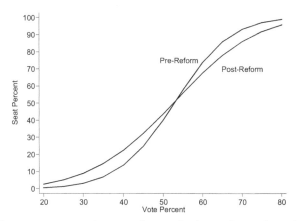

FIGURE 6.10d. Vote-Seat Translation Before and After Ballot Reform for Republican District Plans: Upper, Presidential Election Years
Note: These figures plot the estimated vote-seat relationship between the Democratic state legislative vote and Democratic seats won in state legislative elections. The figure displays the relationship only for redistricting plans passed by Republicans. The *x*-axis is the Democratic percent of the state legislative vote and the *y*-axis is the percent of seats won by the Democrats.

respectively. Democratic plans, however, failed to produce significant levels of partisan bias. Nevertheless, one finds significant differences in partisan bias across the Republican and Democratic plans. With one exception, these biases weaken during the post-reform era. Unsurprisingly, plans passed during divided government display weaker partisan bias, although Republicans did enjoy an advantage under bipartisan plans.

Combined Coattail and Vote-Seat Effects

Both stages of the model portray much the same image of responsive state legislative elections during the nineteenth century, becoming significantly less responsive for the twentieth. We see the resemblance in strong coattail voting weakening after ballot reform, except where the party box option is available. This sequence is repeated in the weakening swing ratios after party reform. Yet both mechanisms remain significant determinants of party control of state legislatures during the later period.

With both components significantly and independently shaping elections throughout both ballot regime eras, we turn now to assess their combined effects. To what extent did voting for a party's state presidential candidate account for the partisan division of the next session of the state legislature? To answer this question we created an expected seat share by passing the state's presidential vote through the equation estimated in Table 6.1, and in turn the predicted legislative vote share through the vote-seat equation in Table 6.2. The resulting estimates – again, based on the presidential vote – explain 75 percent and 64 percent of the variance of the actual party breakdowns in the lower and upper chambers, respectively.[15] To fully appreciate the value of this model in accounting for state legislative elections, consider its predictive power to the conventional baseline – the lag term. The Democratic Party share of seats in the chamber just prior to the most recent election explains 56 percent and 52 percent of the variance for the lower and upper chambers, respectively.[16]

One can further see the match between statewide presidential voting outcomes and party control of state legislatures in Tables 6.3 and 6.4. The tables show the proportion of instances in which the party winning the statewide presidential vote also won control of either the lower house (Table 6.3) or the upper house (Table 6.4). Turning to the lower houses first, between 1840 and 1900 the party winning the statewide presidential vote captured majority control of lower assemblies 87 percent of the time. One can also see during this period the substantial advantage Republicans (and Whigs) had at the legislative level. Of the fifty-three instances of split outcomes, the majority (thirty-nine) were cases where the Democrats won the statewide vote but Republicans captured majority control of the state assembly. After 1900, the percentages of overall matches substantially declined; the percentage of cases where the presidential winner failed to match state legislative outcomes grew to 21 percent. Moreover,

---

[15] These R-square values summarize OLS estimates using a fixed effects model with panel corrected standard errors.

[16] This exercise can be stretched one step further by taking change scores of the variables. The quantity of interest now becomes the capacity of the model to predict changes in the Democratic composition of the chamber from one presidential election to the next. Changes in the estimated Democratic shares explain 21 percent and 11 percent of the variance in the actual changes in legislative composition of the lower and upper chambers as compared to 5 percent and 16 percent by changes in the lag terms. This upper chamber prediction is the only instance where the past composition performs better than the two-stage model.

TABLE 6.3. *Statewide Presidential Vote and Party Control of State Legislative Lower Houses*

1840–1900

Party Control of Lower House	Party Winning Statewide Presidential Vote	
	Democrats	Republican/Whigs
Democrats	0.70 (91)	0.05 (14)
Republicans/Whigs	0.30 (31)	0.95 (256)
Total Same Party	0.87 (428)	
Total Different Parties	0.13 (53)	

1904–1940

Party Control of Lower House	Party Winning Statewide Presidential Vote	
	Democrats	Republicans
Democrats	0.62 (96)	0.09 (19)
Republicans	0.38 (60)	0.91 (190)
Total Same Party	0.78 (286)	
Total Different Parties	0.21 (79)	

Note: The cells display column proportions. The raw numbers are in parentheses.

TABLE 6.4. *Statewide Presidential Vote and Party Control of State Legislative Upper Houses*

1840–1900

Party Control of Upper House	Party Winning Statewide Presidential Vote	
	Democrats	Republican/Whigs
Democrats	0.60 (78)	0.06 (15)
Republicans/Whigs	0.40 (52)	0.94 (255)
Total Same Party	0.83 (333)	
Total Different Parties	0.17 (67)	

1904–1940

Party Control of Upper House	Party Winning Statewide Presidential Vote	
	Democrats	Republicans
Democrats	0.45 (71)	0.10 (20)
Republicans	0.55 (85)	0.90 (189)
Total Same Party	0.71 (260)	
Total Different Parties	0.29 (105)	

Note: The cells display column proportions. The raw numbers are in parentheses.

most of this growth occurred at the expense of Democrats. Of the seventy-nine instances of split outcomes, sixty were cases where Democrats won the state vote but failed to garner a majority in the lower chamber.

A similar pattern can be seen in upper chambers (Table 6.4). Again, we find a discernible difference between the two periods. Between 1840 and 1900 the percentage of presidential vote-majority control matches was 83 percent. After 1900, the percentage dropped to 71 percent. Also interesting to note is the substantial anti-Democratic bias of upper chambers across this entire period. In both centuries, Democrats had a much more difficult time translating presidential victories into control of state senates. In the nineteenth century, when Democratic presidential candidates carried a state, their party only won the state senate 60 percent of the time. By comparison Republicans (or Whigs) jointly won both contests 94 percent of the time. After 1900, the Democratic deficit grew even larger. Even when Democrats won the presidential vote they carried state senates only 45 percent of the time.

The substantial anti-Democratic bias found in these tables likely reflects the districting regimes in place in many upper chambers. Consider the example of Connecticut. The Connecticut state constitution provided that each county would receive at least one state senator regardless of population. With rural populations favoring Republicans, the deck was stacked against the Democrats to take control of the state senate. Notably, in the elections of 1884, 1888, and 1892, the Democrats carried the state presidential vote but failed to win control of the Connecticut state senate in each case. Thus, while the share of seats tracked the direction of presidential voting there was enough bias built into the system to prevent Democrats from crossing the 50 percent threshold in the state senate.

Conclusion

The two-stage model of coattails and swing ratios incorporates the principle institutions mediating elections: ballot form, election calendar, and districting. At both stages state legislative elections reflect the effects of these institutions. Coattails weakened when presidential candidates were absent and when ballot reform replaced the party ticket. As expected, the presence of party boxes strengthened coattail voting to near its pre-reform levels. The transfer of votes to seats proved on balance to be more responsive than the rotten boroughs label would suggest, but significantly less responsive than the swing ratios reported for congressional elections. After ballot reform and continuing over the early twentieth century, party shares of seats became less responsive to vote shares.

Whether weaker swing ratios for state legislative than congressional elections during both ballot regimes reflect rent-seeking or free-riding behavior is difficult to judge with these relationships. The results are consistent with these legislators' compelling incentive to occupy a safe seat that is not present when districting Congress. Yet the differences are not dramatic or conclusive. They might well reflect the design constraints implanted in state constitutions; even disinterested districters would have had a hard time achieving the level of vote-seat responsiveness drawn into congressional district boundaries. One difficulty in assessing the source of the legislatures' weaker vote-seat relationships lies in the fact that strict adherence to some provisions over others (and resistance to reform) corresponded to the self-interest of the party and region that controlled districting or, generally sufficient, held a veto over any revision. Their confining effects are apparent in the inability of Democrats to win control of many states' governments despite success in the state's presidential votes. Even with significant coattails and relatively responsive swing ratios, Democrats failed abjectly in many states to win majorities of both chambers of the legislature. As a result, control over redistricting eluded these politicians until the 1960s when an outside actor, the U.S. Supreme Court, intervened.

7

Gubernatorial Elections

In September 1862 – a week after the Battle of Antietam – governors from thirteen Union states convened in Altoona, Pennsylvania. The purpose of this unusual summit meeting was to discuss troop quotas, war strategy, and the impact an emancipation proclamation might have on the commitment of Border States to the Union (Hesseltine 1948: 249–272). This summit, dubbed the Loyal War Governors Conference, affirmed the support of these state governors to both the war effort and a potential emancipation proclamation. After the conference, the delegation traveled to Washington, DC, to meet with President Lincoln and relay the outcome of the conference deliberations. The meeting with Lincoln included a heated exchange in which some members of the gubernatorial delegation voiced their displeasure with the war effort and General George B. McClellan in particular. In the weeks following the War Governors Conference, President Lincoln both removed McClellan from command of the Army of the Potomac and issued the Emancipation Proclamation.

To modern readers the Loyal War Governors Conference might appear rather remarkable. It is difficult to imagine modern state governors convening in the hopes of influencing national military policy. Although somewhat extraordinary even in the context of the nineteenth century, the Loyal War Governors Conference illustrates the importance governors had during this era. Because the Federal Army was, to a large extent, dependent on local volunteers and state troops, state governors were lynchpins in the war effort (Hesseltine 1948). For this reason, Lincoln and the Republican Party were justifiably concerned with winning or maintaining control of governors' mansions across the country in the 1864 election. Charges of Republican fraud, in particular Lincoln's decisions to let select troop regiments return to their home states to vote, were leveled by Democrats at the time. These charges continue to dog Lincoln and the Republicans in the historical literature. Whatever the merits of the Republican efforts, their work paid off. Not only did Lincoln win reelection in 1864, but the Republican Party won all twenty of the governorships up for reelection. In every state carried by Lincoln, the Republicans won the gubernatorial election.

Nowhere was the linkage between presidential and gubernatorial outcomes more powerfully displayed than in New York State. Due to its substantial population, New York supplied a significant proportion of the Union Army's troops. The requisition of troops from New York State was not without controversy, however. New York City, notably, had been the site of violent draft riots in 1863. Although the incumbent Democratic governor, Horatio Seymour, was by all accounts loyal to the Union, Republicans hoped to take back the governorship and put New York back into the Republican column. Notably, Seymour did not attend the Loyal War Governors Conference. Nor did New York sign the document produced at the meeting. In a virtual dead heat, Seymour was defeated by the Republican candidate Reuben Fenton. Fenton won by less than 8,000 votes out of 730,000 cast. Even more remarkable, this razor-thin margin almost perfectly mirrored the vote division between Lincoln and McClellan in New York. Lincoln defeated McClellan by less than 7,000 votes (Rusk 2001: 180).

Thus, at the beginning of 1865 all but one state in the Union had a Republican governor; New Jersey was the only state that still had a Democratic governor. New Jersey held its gubernatorial elections on three-year cycles, and was not slated to hold its next election until 1865. As a result, the state elections had been insulated from Lincoln's coattails and the Republican tide in 1864.[1] Nor was this pervasiveness unique to the 1864 election. The tight link between presidential and gubernatorial outcomes in 1864 could be found throughout the nineteenth century.

In helping design electoral rules, dispensing state patronage, and providing coattails to state legislators – who would go on to draw congressional districts and elect U.S. senators – governors played a critical role in state and national party fortunes. Despite this significance, very little is known about nineteenth-century gubernatorial elections. Once we begin to look behind the curtain, however, we find a rich tapestry of electoral situations and political personalities. Almost no two states were alike when it came to electing governors. Variations in electoral calendars, term lengths, term limits, majority versus plurality vote requirements, and, of course, ballot structure all marked gubernatorial elections during this era.

In this chapter, we focus on the unique role of governors in the nineteenth-century party system. Specifically, we ask, were gubernatorial elections responsive to national forces? Or did governors use the statewide visibility of their office to carve out personal electoral niches? Finally, did governors become more or less susceptible to national forces over time?

---

[1] Lincoln lost New Jersey to McClellan.

Governors in the Nineteenth Century: Political Ciphers or Party Leaders?

The framers of the original state constitutions, reacting against their negative experience under colonial governorships, placed the locus of constitutional authority in the state legislatures (Lipson 1939; Nevins 1924). Short gubernatorial terms, bans on succession, frequent elections, and weak or nonexistent veto powers were all part of the attempt to reign in state executives. In Maryland, for example, the original constitution stipulated that the governor could serve for only a single three-year term. Many subsequent state constitutions followed this lead. Under Indiana's revised constitution of 1851, the governor served one four-year term, and his veto could be overridden by a simple legislative majority.

Despite these formal constraints, governors emerged throughout the nineteenth century as key figures in many states' party apparatus. Although certainly not policy leaders like modern state executives, the governor's office was a crucial piece of the overall nineteenth-century party system. With almost all of the states by 1832 adopting a winner-take-all rule for the selection of presidential electors, there were strong incentives for local and national party organizations to coordinate their efforts statewide (Aldrich 1995; McCormick 1967). As the most visible statewide office, governors emerged as pivotal players in the presidential game (McCormick 1982). In fact, for most of the nineteenth and early twentieth centuries, the governorship attracted some of the era's most skilled politicians. The governor's mansion was a stepping-stone to the White House. Along with former war heroes, governors from the Electoral College swing states served as the farm team for presidential nominees (e.g., Grover Cleveland, Rutherford Hayes, William McKinley, Samuel Tilden).

Moreover, gubernatorial candidates were compelled by circumstance to become experienced campaigners. While presidential nominees typically waged front porch campaigns, gubernatorial candidates often took up the brunt of campaigning on behalf of both themselves and the state ticket. State political histories are rife with stories of candidates barnstorming across the state giving stump speeches and rallying the party faithful. In Missouri, the Democratic candidate for governor in 1888 – David Rowland Francis – crisscrossed the state, visiting each of Missouri's 114 counties (Barnes 2001: 61). During his run for the governorship of New York, Theodore Roosevelt led one of the country's first whistle-stop campaigns, traversing the state by train. In the last six days of the campaign he delivered a staggering 102 speeches (Grondahl 2004: 297).

During the 1851 Maryland Constitutional Convention, delegates debated whether to combine the dates for gubernatorial and presidential elections. One rationale given for keeping state and national elections separate was the campaign burden gubernatorial candidates would face. As one delegate put it, "He wished to see a man selected as candidate for Governor without making it necessary for him to traverse the State. If connected with national politics, he would be selected to give strength to the electoral ticket by his powers of oratory" (Mr. Spencer, vol. 2, p. 205, *Debates and Proceedings of the Maryland Reform Convention to Revise the State Constitution, 1851*).

Incumbent governors also at times provided important support to the presidential campaign. In 1860, with the relatively unknown Lincoln at the top of the ticket, the mobilization efforts of Republican governors in a number of swing states aided Lincoln's eventual victory (Hesseltine 1948). Governors also wielded influence over elections through their status as chief executive. In many states, governors oversaw the administration of electoral laws. In some cases, this afforded governors the opportunity to selectively interpret electoral statutes, bending the meaning of an electoral rule to favor their party (Summers 2004: 107–125).[2] For example, in New Hampshire the governor was responsible for certifying electoral returns. In the 1876 election, the Democratic governor threw out the returns for a number of Republican state senate candidates, thereby ensuring Democratic control of the state senate. According to the *New York Times*:

Under the law it is the duty of the Governor to summon such persons as appear to have been elected Senators, but the Republicans claim that under the law the Governor has no right to go beyond the certified returns. Gov. Weston and his Council did do it, however, and in the Fourth District proceeded to elect the Democrat by throwing out votes enough cast for other candidates on various flimsy pretexts to give him a majority. (*New York Times*, March 9, 1876)

Governors not only enforced the existing laws; many were forceful legislative leaders. One can find a number of instances in which governors used their bully pulpit to advocate electoral reform; sometimes out of a genuine interest in cleaning up elections and in other cases for barely hidden partisan motives. Robert La Follette's championing of progressive reforms in Wisconsin, such as the direct primary, is one of the better-known examples of the former. In New Jersey, the governor was one of the first politicians to call for ballot reform. In his annual message to the state legislature, Governor Robert S. Green "recommended that a secret, official ballot be adopted as the best means of ending buying and intimidation" (McCormick 1953: 174). In Missouri, the Democratic Governor Joseph Folk led a movement to adopt the direct election of U.S. senators.

Beyond the power to lead public opinion, the power of the governor in the legislative realm increasingly grew during the nineteenth century, usually at the expense of the state legislature. The early state constitutions made the governor little more than a bystander to the legislative process (Kallenbach 1966). Weak or nonexistent veto powers gave early governors little leverage

---

[2] In addition, as noted in Chapter 4, governors in a number of cases selected U.S. senators when the state legislature deadlocked.

or say in constructing public policy. Yet by 1860 nearly every governor had some form of an executive veto, and by 1900 most governors had a strong veto on par with the U.S. president (i.e., requiring two-thirds of both legislative chambers to override) (Prescott 1950). And in some cases governors' veto powers actually outstripped the national executive. For example, in the years following the Civil War, a number of states gave the governor a line-item veto over appropriations legislation.

Finally, control over patronage, state contracts, and appointive positions, such as oil inspector or railroad inspector, put a premium on capturing the governor's chair. The patronage handed out by the governor fed the party's mobilization efforts. For example, so potent was Governor Samuel Tilden's monopoly over New York patronage that it was nicknamed Uncle Sammy's Barrel. In 1876, his strategic allocation of the patronage barrel helped push New York's electoral votes into the Democratic column (i.e., Tilden's) (Summers 2000: 28).

National Forces and Gubernatorial Elections

There is good reason, therefore, to suspect that governors were essential components in the nineteenth-century party apparatus. Yet much like state legislative elections, we know next to nothing about the dynamics influencing this era's gubernatorial elections. The modern literature argues that contemporary governors are mostly insulated from national political tides. Although governors have always been held responsible for the ups and downs of state economies, the impact of national forces weakened over the latter half of the twentieth century (Chubb 1988). Denationalization is often blamed on the trend of moving gubernatorial elections to non-presidential election years (e.g., Burnham 1970). This trend has been further reinforced by the emergence of governors as formidable politicians who are adept at skirting blame for national issues (Chubb 1988; Key 1964). Overall, the main thrust of the modern literature is that state and local conditions are the predominant factors in gubernatorial elections (e.g., Chubb 1988; Tompkins 1984; Turret 1971; Carsey and Wright 1998).[3]

Although not usually stated explicitly, these findings imply that nineteenth-century governors were much more susceptible to national political forces than their modern counterparts. This research, however, has rarely pushed back beyond 1900, hence what can be said systematically is speculative.

Despite the formal constraints placed on governors, there is evidence that these elections were not wholly insulated from national political forces. Between 1840 and 1940, the party winning the presidency also held a majority

---

[3] This is not to say that national conditions play no role. Carsey and Wright (1998), for example, have found that in recent elections presidential approval and national economic conditions correlate with voter's evaluation of gubernatorial candidates.

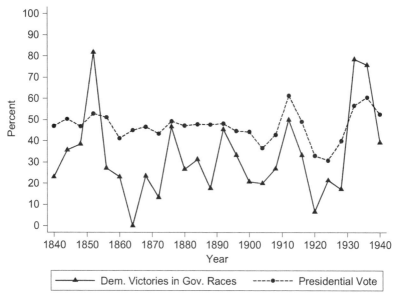

FIGURE 7.1. Presidential Vote and Gubernatorial Election Victories in Non-Southern States, 1840–1940

of non-Southern governorships in nineteen out of twenty-six elections (73 percent) (not including two ties). By comparison, from 1944 to 2000, only eight out of fourteen presidential elections (57 percent) found the president's party winning a majority of the state governorships. To see this connection more clearly, Figure 7.1 plots, for non-Southern states, the Democratic share of the in-play gubernatorial seats against the Democratic presidential vote. Gubernatorial victories appear to track presidential voting, with small shifts in the vote sometimes producing large swings in governorships. This suggests that just as presidential coattails contributed to unified control of the presidency and Congress, so, too, might they have affected the partisan distribution of gubernatorial elections.

Figure 7.1 also demonstrates, however, that the connection between the two series was not one to one; a fair amount of residual variation remains. With electoral laws varying considerably across states, exposing some governors to coattails and insulating others, it stands to reason that the impact of presidential elections would differ according to the institutional configuration of state election rules.

We argue that presidential elections served to nationalize gubernatorial elections, but subject to the mediating role of electoral institutions. Where gubernatorial nominees found themselves running on the same ticket with presidential candidates, state elections responded closely to national forces. In other states, the separation of the electoral calendar weakened the influence of national forces on gubernatorial voting. Finally, the adoption of ballot reform loosened the bond between gubernatorial and presidential candidates, making governors responsible for their individual fates.

Mediating Institutions in Gubernatorial Elections

The analysis of gubernatorial elections follows the model of presidential coattails developed in previous chapters. Because districting is obviously not relevant for governors, the model has a single stage: coattail voting and its mediation by state electoral institutions. The particular institutions mediating presidential coattails in gubernatorial elections are, in some cases, similar to the other offices we have examined (i.e., ballot laws, calendars) and in other instances distinct (i.e., term limits, term lengths, plurality versus majority rules).

In earlier chapters we have laid out the effects of the consolidated party ballot. Here it is important to note that nineteenth-century tickets almost always listed gubernatorial candidates directly below the presidential nominee. Because the consolidated ballot produced coattail voting almost by default, governors likely played second fiddle to the standard bearer at the top of the ticket. Yet in both off years and states with non-November elections governors typically served at the head of the ticket. Figure 7.2 presents a typical example. Other state and local candidates appear further down the ballot. The prominence of the governor's race in off-year elections raised the importance of nominating a strong candidate who attracted the support of party factions in the state and who could serve as a focal point for the campaign.

In the second half of the twentieth century, the pattern had been to move gubernatorial elections to non-presidential years, but the nineteenth-century trend was the reverse. Figure 7.3 shows that the general drift was a synchronizing of presidential and gubernatorial elections. At the beginning of the century, many states held state elections separately from the November presidential elections, but by the end of the century a majority of states had consolidated state and federal elections onto the same day in November. In 1852, only four states were synchronized; by 1896, twenty-one states had consolidated their electoral calendar.

The consequences of synchronizing electoral calendars were not lost on political observers. Prior to the 1876 election, Connecticut amended its constitution to move state elections from March to November. The *New York Times* reported that switching the state election to November would not change the presidential vote, but the state vote would be considerably altered from previous patterns.[4] Republicans expected the stimulus of the presidential campaign

---

[4] In some states, moving electoral dates to November may have increased turnout for a more mundane reason. In New Hampshire, it was expected that moving from March to November would boost turnout because weather conditions would be better. The *New York Times* reported

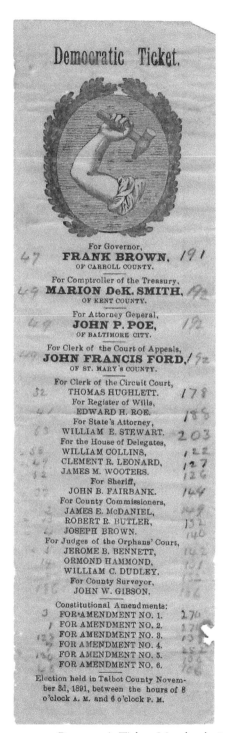

FIGURE 7.2. Democratic Ticket, Maryland 1891

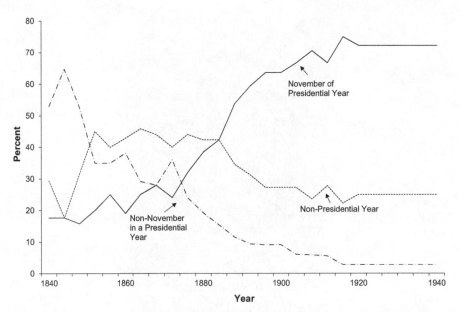

FIGURE 7.3. Gubernatorial Election Dates

to aid state candidates. Because Republican turnout was typically stronger in presidential elections, linkage was expected to aid state-level candidates[5] (*New York Times*, October 28, 1876).

Though same-day elections strengthened coattails, the adoption of the Australian ballot worked in the opposite direction. The widespread implementation of ballot reform partially freed governors from the vagaries of presidential elections. One direct consequence was that gubernatorial candidates could carve out their own personal electoral fortunes. In the 1904 election in Missouri (after ballot reform), the popular Democratic candidate Joseph Folk ran well ahead of the overall party ticket, easily winning, while Republicans captured all of the other state offices. Once in office popular governors may have used the freedom of the new ballot to cultivate a personal vote. After barely winning in 1928, Franklin Roosevelt's navigation of the Depression in New York helped him cruise to victory two years later. Of course, with a Republican in the White House, and the onset of the Depression, it is not a

that New Hampshire's March elections typically depressed voter turnout because many country roads were impassable that time of year.

[5] They were right about the linkage, but it was not enough for Republicans to win the gubernatorial election. The Republican vote increased by 4 percent over the state election held earlier in the year, but this was not enough for victory. The Democratic presidential candidate, Samuel Tilden, carried the state, and the Democratic gubernatorial candidate, Richard Hubbard, followed right along. The number of split votes was negligible: Tilden received 61,927 votes and Hubbard a nearly identical total of 61,934 (*Congressional Quarterly's Guide to U.S. Elections*, 1975).

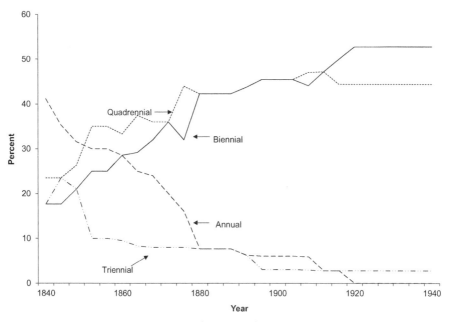

FIGURE 7.4. Gubernatorial Term Lengths

surprise that Roosevelt won his governor's race in 1930. Nevertheless, he ran
ahead of the rest of the House and state assembly Democratic ticket (Rusk
2001) that year, providing some evidence of a personal vote.

Another important institutional feature of gubernatorial elections was variation in term lengths. As Figure 7.4 shows, the length of terms ranged across
states from one to four years, and many states changed over time. In the Northeast, the original preference was for annual terms, but by the middle of the
nineteenth century most had changed to two-year terms. New York switched
from a two- to three-year term in 1876, but then changed back in 1894. The
general trend, however, was to increase term lengths.

Related to term lengths was the practice of term limits. Between 1840 and
1940, thirteen non-Southern states, at one time or another, imposed a gubernatorial term limit. Where the governor was termed out we should expect stronger
presidential-gubernatorial linkages. The removal of a visible incumbent from
the ticket presumably left voters to fall back on the default of voting a straight
ticket. Governors allowed to run for reelection may have been able to craft
a personal vote, providing them with some separation from the presidential
candidate at the top of the ticket. This effect should be even more pronounced
after ballot reform because voters could more easily cast incumbent-specific
votes.

A final institutional quirk, found in a handful of Northeastern states, was a
requirement that the governor receive a majority of the popular vote. Otherwise

the legislature selected the governor. This was not uncommon. For six straight elections, between 1848 and 1853, the Massachusetts legislature chose the governor. Used in Connecticut, Maine, Massachusetts, New Hampshire, Rhode Island, and Vermont, this electoral rule prevented the victory of the plurality winner when the legislature was controlled by the opposition. In Connecticut, the Democratic plurality winner was denied the governorship by the legislature in three consecutive elections (1884, 1886, and 1888). In each case the majority Republicans chose a fellow Republican to occupy the governor's office. In Connecticut, where Republicans were already overrepresented in the heavily malapportioned state legislature, the simultaneous manipulation of multiple electoral rules reinforced the Republican's grip on political offices.

The combination of electoral calendars, differential term lengths, and changes in ballot structure created a patchwork of electoral situations. Concurrent elections joined with a party ticket, a combination we have labeled the "consolidated party ballot," should have produced a strong association between votes for a party's presidential and gubernatorial candidates. Where elections were held separately this association should have weakened. Similarly, the spread of ballot reform should also have weakened the coattail relationship.

To test these relationships we collected all of the relevant institutional variables for every non-Southern election-state pair for the years 1840 (or date of admission if later) through 1940. This gives us an unbalanced, pooled time-series cross-sectional data structure. The dependent variable is the Democratic percentage of the total gubernatorial vote, and the key treatment variable the Democratic percentage of the total presidential vote. The presidential vote is then interacted with those institutional variables hypothesized to mediate the impact of the coattail. The model is estimated as an OLS model with state fixed effects. Also, as is appropriate for time-series cross-section data, the model is estimated with panel corrected standard errors (Beck and Katz 1995, 2004).

Table 7.1 presents the results of this analysis. Our first expectation is that the coefficient for the stand-alone presidential vote term (here representing states with a consolidated party ballot) should be significantly stronger than when it is interacted with either off-November congressional elections or ballot reform. In Table 7.1 this is what we find. The coefficient for the presidential vote is 0.76 percent when both offices were present on the ticket. Separate election calendars cut the correlation between presidential and gubernatorial voting from 0.76 percent to 0.57 percent.

Even more dramatic is the impact of ballot reform. The Australian ballot trimmed presidential coattails from 0.76 percent to 0.27 percent. Unlike some of the other offices we have looked at, the presence of a party box did not restore the impact of the coattail. The results for the ballot reform coefficients are perhaps not surprising, given the visibility of the governor's office. One should expect more split ticket voting for this higher office. This is also consistent

TABLE 7.1. *The Impact of Presidential Voting on Gubernatorial Elections, 1840–1940*

OLS (with panel corrected standard errors)
D.V. = Percent Democratic of Gubernatorial Vote

Variable	Coefficients (Panel Corrected Standard Errors)
Presidential Vote (% Dem.)	0.76**
	(0.08)
Ballot Form	
Non-November Election	9.55**
	(3.06)
Non-November Election × Presidential Vote	−0.19**
	(0.06)
Australian Ballot	13.29**
	(4.66)
Australian Ballot × Presidential Vote	−0.48**
	(0.11)
Party Box	−6.61
	(3.92)
Party Box × Presidential Vote	0.13
	(0.09)
Political Setting	
Term Limit	−3.68
	(4.17)
Term Limit × Presidential Vote	0.10
	(0.07)
Term Limit × Presidential Vote × Aust. Ballot	0.05*
	(0.02)
Lag of Governor Vote	0.05
	(0.03)
Lag of Governor Vote × Aust. Ballot	0.17**
	(0.06)
Constant	9.69**
	(3.11)
R^2	0.58
N	551
# of Groups	32
Mean Obs. Per Group	17.22

* = $p < 0.05$, ** $p < 0.01$. State fixed effects also estimated but not reported.

with research into post–World War II gubernatorial elections. Chubb (1988: 148–149), for example, examined the relationship between presidential and gubernatorial voting between 1940 and 1982 and found the connection to be negligible.

The values of the lag term provide further information about the impact of ballot reform. The coefficient for the stand-alone lag term represents the consolidated ballot era. It is not significant, yet when interacted with ballot reform it strengthens substantially. This is evidence that prior to ballot reform past election results played little role in determining outcomes (which is consistent with strong coattails).

To measure the impact of term limits we include a variable indicating whether the sitting governor was ineligible to run. If coattails were strong in term limited seats then this coefficient should be positive. We also expect this relationship to strengthen after ballot reform. This is largely what we find. When a state prevented its sitting governor from running again (the term limit variable) the coattail increased, but this effect was only significant after ballot reform.

The next question is the extent to which presidential voting and party control of the governorship were linked. To assess this linkage, Table 7.2 displays the linkage between a party winning the statewide presidential vote and control of the governorship. The top panel presents results from 1840 to 1900 and the bottom panel for elections between 1904 and 1940. In column one we list the proportion of same party outcomes for both states that held gubernatorial elections and those that did not. For example, in 1884 the Republicans won the presidential vote in Pennsylvania, but the state did not hold a gubernatorial election that year. Combining all the states in this column allows us to see, over time, any impact holding gubernatorial elections in off-year cycles may have had.

The results in the first column show that the party winning the statewide presidential vote also had control of the governorship 88 percent of the time. Notice also that of the unified cases the vast majority were instances of Republican (or Whig) victories. Also interesting to note are the few times where there was a split result. Of the split results, the majority were instances in which a Democrat held the governorship and Republicans won the statewide presidential vote.

The second column confines the results to states that held a gubernatorial election during a presidential election year (this includes gubernatorial elections held in a different month than November). Here the proportion of same party outcomes strengthens to 95 percent. Of the 329 elections, only 11 resulted in a split outcome. Finally, column three presents the results for gubernatorial elections actually held on the same day as the presidential election. In these cases, 95 percent produced a same party outcome.

The bottom panel of the table presents results for the period between 1904 and 1940 (the era of the secret ballot). Consistent with the results that show the

TABLE 7.2. *The Impact of Gubernatorial Voting on State Legislative Seats, 1840–1940*

OLS (with panel corrected standard errors)
D.V. = Democratic Seat Percent in Legislative Chamber

Variable	Lower House	Upper House
Gubernatorial Vote (% Dem.)	1.14**	1.01**
	(0.08)	(0.08)
Ballot Form		
Australian Ballot	5.21	6.51
	(4.18)	(4.15)
Australian Ballot × Gubernatorial Vote	−0.19**	−0.21*
	(0.11)	(0.11)
Political Setting		
Presidential Election Year	−4.62**	−7.33**
	(1.52)	(1.89)
Minor Party Vote	0.41**	0.45**
	(0.07)	(0.06)
Previous Democratic Seat %	0.37**	0.55**
	(0.04)	(0.03)
Previous Democratic Seat % × Aust. Ballot	−0.03	−0.07
	(0.07)	(0.06)
Constant	−28.05**	−30.36**
	(3.58)	(4.12)
R^2	0.73	0.75
N	805	802
# of Groups	34	34
Mean Obs. Per Group	23.6	23.6

* = $p < .005$, **$p < 0.01$. State fixed effects also estimated but not reported.

Australian ballot delinking gubernatorial and presidential voting, the number of split party outcomes rose substantially in this period. Nearly 25 percent were split party outcomes, compared to 12 percent in the nineteenth century. Moreover, this pattern remains consistent when we confine the analysis to same year elections (column two). In column two, 22 percent were split party outcomes. Column three presents results where gubernatorial elections were held on the same day elections. Given that almost every state had moved their elections to November, the proportion of split outcomes – 22 percent – unsurprisingly, does not differ from column two.

Overall, these results confirm a pervasive linkage between presidential and gubernatorial outcomes throughout the nineteenth century. When governors ran on the same ticket with presidential candidates there was a strong linkage. At the same time, there is evidence that governors, especially after ballot reform, were able to more easily insulate themselves from national forces than some of the other offices we have looked at. This should not be surprising given the visibility of the governor's office, which drew skilled politicians who could successfully compete for votes on their own.

Gubernatorial Coattails

Up to this point we have focused on the impact of presidential coattails on gubernatorial elections. But there is good reason to suspect that governors may have had coattails of their own that benefitted state legislative candidates. Particularly, one would suspect that in those elections that lacked a presidential nominee – elections held in non-presidential years or off-November elections during presidential election years – the governor's race would take on extra prominence. Typically, in these cases where the presidential nominees were absent, the gubernatorial candidate drew the top spot at the head of the ticket.

There is anecdotal evidence that national party leaders recognized the value of a strong gubernatorial candidate at the top of a state ticket, both to win the governorship and to provide coattails to state legislative candidates. In 1871, in the swing state of Ohio, President Grant intervened in the Republican state nominating convention. Disappointed at the Ohio Republicans' initial failure to agree on what he deemed a suitably qualified gubernatorial candidate, Grant sent a message emphasizing the spillover effects that a strong nominee could have on collective party fortunes both in Ohio and in Washington, DC. Lest the delegates fail to see what was at stake, Grant made it clear: "Give us your best man, so we will secure the legislature, redistricting of the state, [and] United States Senator" (*New York Times*, June 27, 1871). According to the *New York Times*, the mere mention of senatorial selection and congressional redistricting was all the motivation the convention needed to shape up.

To test for the presence of gubernatorial coattails, we examine the impact of gubernatorial vote shares on state legislative seats. The dependent variable is the percentage of Democratic seats in state legislative elections. The model includes all state elections that were not synchronized with the November presidential election. By construction this includes any state election held in a different year than the presidential election or an election during a presidential year but held in a different month than November. In other words, it excludes elections synchronous with the presidential elections. The main independent variable of interest is the Democratic share of the gubernatorial vote. To avoid problems associated with outliers, we excluded uncontested gubernatorial races. Like previous models in this book, we then interacted the governor's vote with an Australian ballot dummy variable. We also included the previous percentage of Democratic seats and interacted it with the Australian ballot dummy variable. The vote percentage received by any minor party was included as a further control. The model also included state fixed effects and panel corrected standard errors.

TABLE 7.3. *The Linkage Between Presidential and Gubernatorial Outcomes*

1840–1900

	All (1)	Same Year (2)	Same Day (3)
Same Party	0.88 (334)	0.95 (218)	0.95 (138)
Split Party	0.12 (61)	0.05 (11)	0.05 (7)
Both Democratic	0.26 (96)	0.23 (53)	0.23 (34)
Both Whig/Republican	0.61 (224)	0.72 (165)	0.71 (104)
Split w/Dem. Governor	0.09 (33)	0.03 (7)	0.03 (4)
Split w/Rep. Governor	0.03 (11)	0.02 (4)	0.02 (3)

1904–1940

	All (1)	Same Year (2)	Same Day (3)
Same Party	0.75 (267)	0.78 (208)	0.78 (197)
Split Party	0.25 (90)	0.22 (59)	0.22 (57)
Both Democratic	0.30 (106)	0.27 (73)	0.29 (73)
Both Republican	0.45 (161)	0.51 (135)	0.49 (124)
Split w/Dem. Governor	0.13 (45)	0.11 (29)	0.11 (28)
Split w/Rep. Governor	0.13 (45)	0.11 (30)	0.11 (29)

Note: The cells display column proportions. The actual numbers are in parentheses.

The results, presented in Table 7.3, provide clear evidence of gubernatorial coattails in the era of the party ballot. The coefficients on the stand-alone gubernatorial vote coefficients are 1.15 percent and 1.02 percent for the lower and upper chambers, respectively. This reveals a striking one-to-one relationship between gubernatorial voting and state legislative party ratios (when presidential candidates were absent from the ballot). The Australian ballot weakened the gubernatorial coattail effect for both lower and upper houses. In the lower house, the ballot reduced gubernatorial coattails by 0.2 percent, and in the upper house the reduction was 0.21 percent. In both chambers there was a positive value of the lag term but no significant interaction with ballot reform. Moreover, the minor party vote variable and elections held during a presidential year were both significant.

Another way to assess the impact of gubernatorial coattails, and how the Australian ballot may have mediated their impact, is to examine their impact on party control of state legislatures. Majority control, after all, was critical. It conferred the opportunity to select senators and potentially redraw legislative districts. Moreover, in this era of dual federalism state legislatures were often the prime incubators of public policy (B. Campbell 1995). Thus, we have estimated the results of a model with Democratic control of a state legislative chamber as the dependent variable. Because the dependent variable is binary (1 = Democratic control, 0 = otherwise), we estimate the model using logit. The key independent variable is a dummy variable indicating whether or not

TABLE 7.4. *The Impact of Gubernatorial Voting on Party Control of State Legislatures, 1840–1940*

Logit with robust standard errors
D.V. = Democrats have majority control of chamber

Variable	Lower House	Upper House
Gubernatorial Outcome (1 = Dem Victory)	4.50**	3.29**
	(0.37)	(0.31)
Australian Ballot	0.22	0.27
	(0.37)	(0.37)
Australian Ballot × Gubernatorial Vote	−1.47**	−1.27**
	(0.53)	(0.45)
Constant	−3.36**	−2.93**
	(0.32)	(0.26)
Log-Likelihood	−247.54	293.44
N	805	802

* = p < 0.05, ** p < 0.01. Robust standard errors in parentheses.

a Democrat won the governorship. This is then interacted with an Australian dummy variable. We expect a strong positive effect prior to ballot reform and a weakening after. In Table 7.3 this is what we find. Prior to ballot reform, if a Democrat won the governorship the probability of carrying the lower house was 75 percent. After ballot reform the probability dropped to 47 percent. In upper chambers the probability was 60 percent before and 35 percent after ballot reform. The reduced baseline for the upper chamber likely reflects staggered terms in many upper houses. This likely created a stronger bias in favor of the status quo and reduced the impact of gubernatorial coattails on overall control of the legislature. Nevertheless, the pattern in both chambers reveals a stronger impact of gubernatorial coattails prior to ballot reform.

The connection between gubernatorial and state legislative outcomes – in elections where the president was not at the top of the ticket (i.e., either midterm elections, elections held in odd-numbered years, or elections held in presidential election years but some month other than November) – is shown in Table 7.5. The table lists the proportion of cases where the party winning the governorship also won control of both chambers of the state legislature. The top and bottom panels list these proportions for the periods between 1840 and 1900 and 1904 and 1940, respectively. Turning first to the earlier period, notice that the proportion of unified party outcomes was 78 percent. Divided outcomes resulted only 22 percent of the time.

The third through fifth rows further break down the configurations of party control. Of the outcomes with divided government, the largest number were cases where the legislature was split between the parties. This likely reflects the staggered electoral cycles and malapportioned districts that characterized these state legislatures. Instances where a Democrat won the governorship but Republicans (or Whigs) controlled the legislature comprised the largest

TABLE 7.5. *Governor and State Legislative Matches in Non-Presidential Elections*

1840–1900

	Democratic Legislature	Republican/Whig Legislature	Split Legislature
Democratic Governor	0.89 (96)	0.08 (31)	0.52 (39)
Republican/Whig Governor	0.09 (10)	0.90 (332)	0.43 (32)
Minor Party Governor	0.02 (1)	0.02 (4)	0.05 (4)
Total Unified	0.78 (428)		
Total Divided	0.22 (121)		

1901–1940

	Democratic Legislature	Republican Legislature	Split Legislature
Democratic Governor	0.88 (43)	0.23 (50)	0.60 (18)
Republican Governor	0.12 (6)	0.77 (168)	0.37 (11)
Minor Party Governor	0 (0)	0.01 (1)	0.03 (1)
Total Unified	0.71 (211)		
Total Divided	0.29 (87)		

Note: The cells display column proportions. The actual numbers are in parentheses.

category. But even after taking these into account one finds a remarkable amount of pervasiveness evident in these numbers.

The results for 1901–1940, displayed in the bottom panel of Table 7.4, further confirm the growing disconnect in unified partisan outcomes ushered in by the secret ballot era. The proportion of unified party outcomes dropped to 71 percent, while the proportion of divided outcomes grew to 29 percent. Interestingly, the number of Democratic governors facing Republican legislatures grew during this period, while the number of Republican governors with Democratic legislatures remained small.

Overall, these results suggest that nineteenth-century governors had substantial coattails of their own. Unlike the political ciphers many of the Framers envisioned, governors became important electoral and policy standard bearers for their party. Especially in those years that lacked a presidential race and presumably pushed national issues into the background. However, much like the other offices we have studied, the strong pervasiveness of nineteenth-century elections was weakened by ballot reform. And like their presidential counterparts in Washington, DC, state executives in the twentieth century increasingly found themselves facing an opposition legislature.

Conclusion

By the mid-twentieth century, V.O. Key (1964) argued, the electoral fates of governors had become independent from the overall success of the national parties. Much of the basis for this development can plausibly be traced back to electoral law changes at the turn of the century. In particular, governors over the course of the twentieth century increasingly found themselves running in non-presidential years. So by the 1980s only trace evidence of presidential coattails could be found (Chubb 1988).

Thus, the Framers' goal of keeping governors attuned directly to local electorates seems to have been achieved. Yet there was a period in American history in which gubernatorial voting more closely tracked national level outcomes. From the mid- to late nineteenth century, gubernatorial results rose and fell with presidential outcomes. Partisan control of state government provided access to the election of senators, redistricting, and control over shaping key electoral rules (i.e., calendars, ballot format). How and why could a presumably parochial state office move in tandem with presidential elections? We have argued that electoral institutions present in the states tied together the electoral fortunes of state and national executives. The consolidated party ballot linked the fortunes of governors and presidents.

With the spread of ballot reform this connection weakened. Thus, just like the other offices we have analyzed, ballot reform weakened the overall cohesiveness of the party team. Ballot reform insulated governors from presidential coattails. Not only did these reform movements insulate governors from presidential coattails, they also worked to insulate state legislatures from gubernatorial coattails. But as we see with ballot reform, state legislatures became increasingly insulated from both gubernatorial coattails, via ballot reform, and from presidential coattails, via a combination of scheduling and ballot changes. The result was a sharp decline in the pervasiveness of party victories across the country.

8

Dismantling the Party Ticket System

One cannot say that adoption of the party ticket was premeditated. One can conclude, however, that it offered an ingenious solution to the massive coordination problems and informational costs of running a representative government in a setting ill-disposed toward successful collective action. Consider what voters faced: frequent elections to numerous offices contested by unfamiliar candidates. By the 1830s, the nation contained the largest elective office system the world had ever seen. An election might include offices for county and city governments, representatives to Congress and the state legislature, various state executives, and finally, the presidential electors. Adding to voters' challenge were steep informational costs imposed by primitive transportation and nascent communications technology.

From the perspective of party leaders, the challenge was how to send a national partisan signal across this vast mosaic of state and local electorates. Power in Washington and the state capitals – even at the county courthouses – depended on controlling multiple executive and legislative offices. A thoroughly successful election, to which all good party men in principle aspired, required winning a lot of plurality elections across many different divisions and aggregations of a state's electorate. Although politicians were most keenly attentive to winning those offices that directly affected their welfare, they all had a stake in their party's success at every level, because winning at one level conferred benefits to those at the other levels. Thus, party politicians of the nineteenth century confronted a dual problem: how to win elections both nationally and locally.

The party ticket system was an inspired solution to this formidable coordination problem. By tying elections together onto a consolidated party ballot, national and local politicians mutually benefitted from linking their fates together. If a party won the statewide presidential vote, so too would its other candidates for lower office who were listed on the slate. And if the party won the national race, it would procure a steady flow of patronage appointments to fill the coffers of state and local organizations.

But it was by no means an easy system to manage. In overseeing this multi-faceted and decentralized system, party leaders constantly walked a tightrope. They needed their followers to cooperate for the collective good of the ticket, but they lacked any legal authority to enforce contractual agreements or dictate actions among their followers. Rather than compulsion, the system was held together by a series of exchange relationships – between party leaders and supporters, leaders and officeholders, leaders and businesses, and federal, state and local politicians. As long as these exchanges remained mutually beneficial the party ticket system achieved a delicate equilibrium. But underwriting these exchanges with voter mobilization campaigns was enormously expensive. And coordinating and enforcing each actor's contribution to the collective enterprise required relentless maintenance.

Party leaders provided their supporters with jobs, patronage, and various social services. In exchange, supporters repaid the party with support on Election Day. Patronage appointees were expected to return the favor by contributing a portion of their salary to party treasuries and labor to party tasks. Politicians prized gaining control of spoils, but as a means to, not an end of, governance. Party leaders nominated candidates and delivered votes for those candidates. In exchange, elected officeholders used their offices to reward party supporters with jobs, contracts, licenses, advantageous tax assessments, and favorable legislation. Similarly, party leaders provided willing businesses with government contracts and favorable regulations. In exchange, their business partners provided the parties with campaign funds and doled out jobs to the party's supporters.

In addition, as we have emphasized throughout our inquiry, the party ticket system locked national and local politicians into an exchange-based partnership. The national label, and in particular the standard bearer at the top of the ticket, provided information to voters that redounded to the benefit of local candidates. The better presidential and congressional candidates performed, so, too, the better local candidates' chances of success. National politicians, in turn, rested their campaigns on the shoulders of state and local party agents.

As long as national and local politicians found mutual benefits in this relationship, the system held together. But tension of some form, pulling them apart, was ever present. Reneging on agreements, shirking obligations, and personal aggrandizement were threats never far below the surface of party effort. Rebellious factions might sit out an election or print up their own competing tickets. Rogue party agents might print up bogus tickets, knifing out the regular party's handpicked nominee. Factions might bolt a nominating convention and fuse with another party. Despite the many collective benefits the party ticket conferred on voters and politicians, the system never reached a stable equilibrium.

As the nineteenth century wore on, the collective action tensions pulling on the party system grew more severe. Exogenous shocks, posed by the Civil War, two massive waves of immigration, recurrent societal dislocations giving rise to third political parties, and several national economic crises required the political parties to continuously adjust their electoral and organizational strategies. But even without these intrusive forces, a stable equilibrium never amounted to more than an aspiration. Intramural competition for resources and control continuously threatened and frequently upended the multitude of fragile reciprocity agreements that tied local, state, and national party politicians together. These managerial dilemmas were compounded by the absence of recourse to an external authority that could regulate the internal activities of parties. Throughout the eighteenth and nineteenth centuries, American law treated political parties as private political associations, free to run their internal affairs as they saw fit (Epstein 1986). As a result, party leaders could not resort to the legal system to enforce agreements or mandate the actions of others. In the end, seeking a solution to these management dilemmas, party politicians dismantled the old order and constructed a new order of politics.

The push for reforming the electoral structure, and more fully involving state authority in regulating the internal affairs of political parties, emerged as a solution for those both outside and inside the political parties. Reformers saw a way to remove important discretionary decisions from base, mostly unelected party politicians. Insiders found in ballot reform a solution to the innumerable collective action dilemmas inherent in the party ticket system. Certainly, outside reform groups agitated for changes to the system, but the notion that reformers steamrolled over party politicians ignores the fundamental structural strains of the party ticket system. Rather than passively acquiescing to reform measures, party politicians played a leading role in dismantling the old order. They found in reform a short-term strategic solution to the mounting problems of managing their parties' internal conflict. Perhaps without fully realizing the consequence of their actions, they helped usher in a new political order.

The Australian Ballot as Trademark Protection

The party ticket system ran relatively well as long as the exchange relationships between national, state, and local politicians remained mutually beneficial. Yet these relationships were always tenuous and required careful maintenance. Local party operatives depended on attractive national and statewide candidates whose coattails would produce votes for local candidates. At the same time, because the ballot was printed and distributed at the local level, national and state politicians depended on local precinct captains and ward heelers to stay faithful to the regular party organization. Greater consolidation of electoral calendars in the latter decades of the nineteenth century exacerbated these problems. With different offices representing overlapping jurisdictions,

TABLE 8.1. *Factional Splits in (Non-Southern)*
State Party Nominating Conventions,
1877–1910

Decade	Democrats	Republicans
1870s*	2	1
1880s	0	0
1890s	25	8
1900s	2	2
1910s	0	3

* The data for the 1870s only covers the years from
1877 to 1879.
Sources: For 1877–1900, Bensel (2000); subsequent
years from annual editions of *Appletons Annual Cyclo-
pedia* and the *New York Times*.

tied together onto a single ticket, factional conflict became ever more difficult
to manage. And with presidential candidates being drawn into position-taking
on a growing agenda of national issues, these focal points more often transmitted the "wrong" message to various state and local constituencies.

If a nominating convention could not agree on a nominee, or a faction felt
slighted, a candidate or faction might bolt. Bolters could print "up other tickets that substituted the name of one candidate on the regular slate for that
of an opponent" (J.F. Reynolds 1988: 43). The problem of bolting reached
a crescendo during the last decade of the nineteenth century as state parties
grappled with divisions over monetary policy (Bensel 2000). In Massachusetts
in 1878, the Democratic convention split over the party's gubernatorial nominee. Benjamin Butler, a Republican congressman, was a supporter of greenback
monetary policy and sought the Democratic nomination for governor in 1878.
Although he won nomination on the first day of the convention, the State
Democratic Committee tossed out the nomination and called a separate convention, which nominated a new candidate a week later. Each side subsequently
ran its own separate ticket, with the Butler faction's ticket trouncing the regular party's ticket (although both lost to the Republican candidate). In 1892
in Nevada, the regular Republicans bolted from a convention that had been
captured by silver forces and nominated their own slate of electors pledged to
Benjamin Harrison (Bensel 2000).

The frequency of partisan infighting can be seen in Table 8.1 which collects
all reported instances of a factional fight or bolt at state nominating conventions
between 1877 and 1910. The table reveals that convention bolts occurred
regularly throughout the late nineteenth and early twentieth centuries. The peak
occurred in 1896 when splits over monetary policy led nineteen (non-Southern)
Democratic and six Republican conventions to dissolve into factional fights
(Bensel 2000). The incidence of factional splits at state nominating conventions

found in Table 8.1, while striking, only serves to underscore the severity of the problem confronting party politicians. Defections also afflicted county and city nominating conventions, where factions enjoyed the advantage over statewide factions by discretely insinuating pasters and other forms of bogus ballots to promote their favored candidates. In some states, local district captains might extort local candidates by threatening to "knife" a candidate by substituting a different name on the ticket if the candidate or local party did not pay a fee. Over time local tribute became an insurance policy against knifing (Ware 2000: 14).

The proliferation of various forms of ballot treachery resulted in higher rates of factionally induced split ticket voting, primarily at the lower end of the ballot (Reynolds and McCormick 1986; J.F. Reynolds 2006: 130–131).[1] Based on a study of precinct-level vote returns in Colorado, Reynolds concluded that split ticket voting primarily concerned local candidates:

It was the candidates for sheriff or for state assembly who usually ran well ahead of or behind the slate. Party loyalty more easily attached itself to presidential or gubernatorial nominees. It did not automatically transfer to persons running for the state legislature or for county clerk. Ticket splitting was carried out in response to local political circumstances where factional discord was most intense. (Reynolds 2006: 130)

In 1880, for instance, factional warfare almost sunk the Democrats in New York, where Tammany Hall and Reform Democrats ran separate tickets for municipal offices. The feud between the two factions opened the door to opportunistic Republicans looking to trade their local candidates in exchange for Democrats voting for Blaine at the top of the ticket.

The presence of third parties further complicated the managerial problems of party leaders. Fraying party tickets in turn made life more difficult for party leaders in maintaining each candidate's and local party's contribution to a coordinated effort to mobilize voters. In the Plains and the West, fusion tickets between Democrats and minor parties, such as the Populists, posed serious electoral problems for Republican organizations (Argersinger 1980). A number of Democratic state organizations in the West forged temporary arrangements with minor parties in which they would fuse their tickets (and sometimes without the permission of the minor party). In the Dakotas Republicans watched with alarm as Democrats arranged fusion tickets with Populist candidates (Argersinger 1992). And not all Democratic factions welcomed fusion attempts with minor parties whose ideological outlook might run counter to their own. Conservative Democrats did not always embrace Populists, and where they did not, a splinter party purporting to represent real Democracy might suddenly

---

[1] This kind of split ticket was different than the type we associate with modern politics, where voters deliberately cross party lines to register their support of, say, a congressional incumbent of one party and a charismatic presidential candidate of another party.

form. In Kansas in 1892 the Democratic state convention warded off division by agreeing to fuse with Populists (Bensel 2000).

Thus by the late 1880s the lack of trademark protection, coupled with easy entry of splinter and fused parties, presented party leaders with an array of managerial dilemmas. The state-printed Australian ballot offered one possible solution. Now, the state certified the party's nominees as official and equally important, and kept knock-off brands off the ballot. Sabotage, in the form of knifing or pasting, required alteration of the state ballot, a criminal offense carrying stiff penalties. As a result, wayward factions, bolting candidates and the "double-crossing ward heeler" (Summers 2004: 242) found that they had little option but to work through regular party channels.

In addition, supporting reform must simply have looked like good politics to many state party leaders. Good-government reformers were already pushing for reforms to the ballot. Dissatisfaction with election fraud, and corruption in government more broadly, spurred the formation of reform groups in parts of the country.[2] Many politicians also found electoral pressure from a public demanding reform. In Delaware, for instance, Republicans initially blocked the passage of an Australian ballot law in 1889. Democrats seized on this intransigence and used it as a campaign issue in the subsequent election. By the next legislative session Republicans, having been duly chastised by the electorate, reversed their position and supported passage of an Australian ballot (*New York Times*, November 24, 1889; *New York Times*, December 26, 1890).

Although the spur for change certainly included pressure from both reform groups and public opinion, party politicians in the states were ultimately responsible for crafting the new rules. And in ballot reform they found a solution to the collective action dilemmas of the party ticket. Evidence for regular party support of ballot reform can be seen in the generally bipartisan support it garnered (Ware 2002). In the 1889–1890 election cycle a third of Republican platforms and nearly half of Democratic platforms endorsed ballot reform (Bensel 2000). Bipartisan passage of reform was commonplace throughout the nation's state legislatures (Wigmore 1889).

Party leaders continued to applaud party voting, of course, and from time to time tinkered with the new state ballots in an effort to recreate a semblance of the party ticket. The precise format of the ballot, and subsequent changes, often became the target of bitter partisan battles. According to Argersinger,

The law itself and its basic provisions for a secret, public ballot did not become the object of contention (except in rare case as in New York) so much as the modifications of the Australian ballot system and the use that could be made of them did. As one opponent of subsequent ballot changes in South Dakota said, "The real trouble is the change from the law as it originally stood." (Argersinger 1992: 166)

[2] In Massachusetts, for instance, the promotion of ballot reform was almost single-handedly led by the Mugwump Richard Henry Dana III (McFarland 1975: 64).

Indeed, states commonly altered ballot formats throughout the late nineteenth and early twentieth centuries (Ware 2000; 2002). Party column ballots were substituted for office bloc ballots and vice versa; straight-ticket provisions were added or removed; and some states employed a shoestring ballot (e.g., Missouri). The latter was a state printed ballot that included strips of paper with party candidates, along with a blank page for voters to write in candidates. This format offered local parties greater control over the ballot because they could monitor, and control, the practice of pasting in preferred candidates (Ware 2002: 44). Between 1888 and 1940, twenty-six (non-Southern) states changed formats at least once, and thirteen of these altered them more than once.[3] Considerations of how the ballot format would feed national forces into state politics drove many of these decisions. In some states, parties employed the party column hoping to preserve a strong degree of straight-ticket voting. The office bloc format, on the other hand, diminished the linkage between presidential nominees and down-ballot candidates. Parties looking to shield themselves from national forces were more likely to prefer this format.

Consider the case of New York. The state first passed a ballot law in 1894, adopting the party column format. New York continued to use the party column ballot until 1913, when it switched to the office bloc at the behest of the Democratic Party. This represented a dramatic change of heart for Democrats who, with Tammany Democrats holding enough legislative seats to be a pivotal blocking group, had long opposed political reform. But short-term political calculations led them to rethink their opposition. After suffering a stinging defeat in the November general assembly elections, and losing majority control of the lower chamber, the Democratic governor called a special session of the legislature in December. In this lame-duck session Democrats hastily passed a "Massachusetts ballot" (i.e., office bloc) bill just as they were about to leave office (*New York Times*, December 9, 1913).

The Democrats had good partisan reasons for passing this midnight office bloc bill. In the years prior to 1913, Republicans consistently carried the state in presidential elections. The Democratic organization had long been frustrated by having to run against charismatic Republican presidential nominees, such as Theodore Roosevelt. In fact, they took explicit actions to detach their state ticket from the presidential candidate. In 1904, Democratic newspapers provided detailed instructions to its readers describing how to split their vote between the Republican Roosevelt at the top of the ticket and the rest of the down-ballot Democrats (Reynolds and McCormick 1986: 857). The passage of an office bloc ballot, where candidates were grouped by office rather than party, rendered this kind of split ticket voting much easier.

The fights over ballot format reveal that parties continued to tweak institutional rules for partisan advantage. But in the larger scheme of things, the

---

[3] Our numbers differ slightly from Ware in that he counts the Missouri "shoestring" ballot as a reform, while we consider this merely another version of the old party ballots.

Australian ballot, whether it was the office bloc or party column format, ushered in a new era of candidate-centered politics. The irony is that this was at the behest of the parties themselves. To extract themselves from the many prisoner's dilemmas of the party ticket, leaders delegated authority to state governments.

In this inquiry we have emphasized the role of the Australian ballot in trimming presidential coattails. But another, perhaps just as important, consequence of the ballot reform movement was the impetus it gave to state regulation of internal party affairs. Parties were no longer treated solely as private political associations. Their affairs increasingly became subject to governmental oversight in the public interest (Epstein 1986). Parties had to submit their candidate lists to electoral boards. Government officials now put an official stamp on party slates. Australian ballot reform opened the regulatory door for the states, which partisan legislative majorities exploited over the next decades. Perhaps it also eased entry into overseeing other aspects of party affairs, most notably the nomination process.

Direct Primaries: Parties Reassert Control Over Their Trademark

While ballot reform muted some of the more destructive consequences of fractious nominating conventions, party leaders still faced serious coordination issues. Nominations remained critical to constructing a party ballot the constituent parts of the party could unite behind. But nominations remained highly decentralized. Local conventions and caucuses were open to a potentially wide array of voters, some of whom might arrive with questionable loyalty to the regular party organization. Porous boundaries had always prompted party leaders to "pack conventions with their own followers and to attempt by one means or another [such as manipulating schedules] to exclude potential dissidents" (Epstein 1986: 161). Party leaders almost everywhere sought to achieve the goals ascribed to New York: "The delegates to these party assemblages were for the most part local office-holders or other individuals who had been 'handpicked' for the occasion by the state committeemen or some other local leader" Gosnell (1923: 455). As long as party leaders could monitor participation, enforce loyalty, and assuage factional divisions, the caucus-convention system gave them the wherewithal to control nominations, a key asset in inducing cooperation.

Ballot reform addressed some of the more disruptive manifestations of decentralized parties. But with dissidents no longer having a viable alternative of bolting and fielding a competing ticket, factional fights at the state conventions increased and even intensified after the passage of reform. Indeed, the peak of factional splits in Table 8.1 occurred in 1896 after a large number of states had adopted the ballot.

And other developments during this time also weighed heavily on the convention system as leadership vehicles. In urban areas, the sheer number of people who might participate in a caucus or convention exacerbated the logistics of controlling nominations (Ware 2002: 65–68). Furthermore, in states with significant urban party machines, rural interests became resentful of the influence the machine delegates wielded at state conventions (J.F. Reynolds 2006). Starting in the 1880s and continuing for the next several decades, states passed laws regulating the caucus-convention system. By and large, these reforms were designed to open access to all party voters and ostensibly weaken the hand of local party organizations (Epstein 1986). The problems of maintaining control over nominations in caucuses and conventions only increased with the passage of ballot reform.

After reform, success at the ballot box became less a product of collective effort and more a product of candidates' personal enterprise. Elective officeholders began arriving at caucuses and conventions with their own entourages. They began dominating nominating conventions while old-guard party leaders increasingly found themselves "out to pasture" (J.F. Reynolds 2006: 97). Political observers in Michigan derided the Republican state convention of 1904 as "a convention of the office holders, by the office holders and for the office holders and their allies who are too well known to require introduction" (quoted in J.F. Reynolds 2006: 97). The new styled candidates built and sustained their own personal organizations. They "circulated at conventions, lined up slates of friendly delegates, made publicized visits to their friends around the state, and injected more competition and pressure on the nominating process than it was designed to handle" (J.F. Reynolds 2006: 199). In congressional caucuses rotation practices disappeared (Kernell 1977).

As long as nominations remained the dealings of a private association, party leaders had no legal recourse to enforce boundaries on participation in primaries. The direct primary turned what had been the internal affair of a private association into a public election. Many party leaders came to believe that a state-run nominating primary would restore their control over the selection of candidates. Although it placed the choice of nominees in the hands of voters, it weakened the power of those incumbent officeholders who had deployed personal organizations at the conventions to secure nominations. Direct primaries pulled a central authority in to help resolve disputes among rivals and convey a trademark protection upon nominees that had been missing from the convention system.

Direct primary laws should be seen as a natural progression to turn to the state for aid in refereeing nominations. In printing and distributing the ballot, county and state electoral boards had to decide the rightful party nominees anyway. So, it was perhaps an inevitable next step to also develop rules for the candidate nomination process. Wisconsin adopted the first statewide direct primary law in 1903, and by 1917 most states had followed suit. The initial experience of the primary suggests that party politicians achieved their goal. Early appraisals by Merriam and Overacker (1928) found that in many states primaries had allowed traditional party organizations to reassert control over nominations through convention endorsements and even the construction of whole slates of party-certified candidates before the primary.[4] A number of states required voters to register a party affiliation as a condition for participating in a primary. Some states went even further, requiring that primary voters promise to support their party's candidate in the general election (Argersinger 1992: 60–61). Sore-loser laws also prevented candidates who lost a primary election from running in the general election. This helped thwart opportunistic behavior by dissident candidates running separate campaigns and splitting the regular party vote.[5]

In the long run, however, the influence of party organizations within the primary process waned. Ballot reform two decades earlier had deeded a competitive advantage to entrepreneurial and self-reliant politician who was already accustomed to and skilled at soliciting votes in his own behalf. Adding a primary election to the reelection gauntlet posed less a challenge for most than for challengers who sought to replace them. "The primary election method of nominating candidates for membership in the House," noted Democratic House Speaker Champ Clark (1920: 220), "helps the sitting member retain his seat if he is at all worthy of it." Over time, the evidence suggests that Clark was right, as incumbents profitably adapted to the primary system. Candidates whose appeal lay with voters could ultimately bypass party leaders. Such routes to nomination increased with the passage of state and municipal civil service laws which further sapped the importance of the payroll vote in primaries.

Unable to monitor voting, exclusive reliance on costly mobilization became too risky. And as mobilization weakened, and turnout dropped sharply over the next two decades, the large, cumbersome party organizations that required massive infusions of cash and patronage appointments and challenged the management skills of even the most astute bosses lost their electoral purpose.

A Reformed Electoral System Ushers in a New Order

With the aid of hindsight, we can see how the sequence of reforms of electoral laws at the turn of the twentieth century dismantled the institutions that manufactured responsive elections and ushered in the modern, less responsive electoral system. There is little evidence, however, that those party politicians who strategically embraced the Australian ballot fully appreciated the ramifications of their actions; they were simply following their long-standing modus operandi of tinkering with institutional rules to gain an edge in the next election. We have chronicled the numerous ways state politicians throughout the

---

[4] Moreover, they note, restricting participation in primaries, most concretely through closed primaries, further aided party organizations in the first decades after passage of direct primary laws (Merriam and Overacker 1928).

[5] Moreover, where competition receded the direct primary served to further weaken the minority party. All of the action shifted to the dominant party's primary.

nineteenth century had altered term lengths, changed electoral calendars, and redistricted with sharp pencils. But these efforts had been aimed primarily at influencing interparty competition. By contrast with the Australian ballot, and later with direct primaries, they were attempting to regulate intraparty competition. In seeking a solution to their collective action problems, party politicians resorted, perhaps myopically, to election reform. They found in popular progressive reforms a way to deal with pressing management problems, while gaining an advantage over their opponents by standing for instead of standing in the way of reform. We can only surmise that they failed to recognize that in accepting ballot reform's secret ballot they had removed the cornerstone of their edifice. The party ticket, which had joined together in a common purpose the disparate, confederal state and local party organizations, no longer provided a collective good; whereas in the past it could be challenged and corrupted by disgruntled factions and local organizations. In the reformed setting, it would fall under the jeopardy of every voter who decided whether to pull the party column or individually choose candidates from the parties' offerings.

Although it is beyond the scope of this book to assess fully the various and enormous changes the transformation of the electoral system wrought on American politics, we close by linking them to the transformation of the electoral system. They include the evisceration of political parties, the rise of officeholding professionals, rapid replacement of patronage with civil service and divided party control of Congress and the presidency.

Hollowing Political Parties

Australian ballot reform reined in disgruntled statewide factions and suborning ward bosses, just as primary reform later sought to neutralize the efforts of recently formed legions of self-reliant officeholders bent on winning renomination. But for party leaders these victories proved pyrrhic. Each entailed a major (and irretrievable) delegation of authority to state government to regulate elections and even the party's internal affairs. Piece-by-piece, unbeholden officeholders extended states' newfound regulatory authority to chip away at the institutional foundations of the mass-based political party.

Procedural powers that had long been the sole province of party leaders increasingly fell under a state's regulatory umbrella. Filing requirements, nomination procedures, delegate selection rules, campaign financing, the structure of state party committees, procedures for the selection of party officers and numerous other routine organizational activities fell under the purview of state regulators. Some states even limited party endorsement of candidates in primary elections. State governments' near continuous regulation of state parties' organizational structures and decisions over the twentieth century had hollowed out these once robust, authoritative institutions. In a summary assessment of one student of modern political parties, "State laws have created a panoply of party offices encompassing local, county, and state parties, most of which have little or no mandate to take part in the nominating of candidates for any public elective office, in running their campaigns, and certainly not in the ways they operate in government" (J.A. Schlesinger 1984: 378–379).[6]

The Rise of Careerism

Reform introduced a formidable new set of actors who challenged party leaders for control over nominations. We are referring to officeholders. Cut free from the party ticket, these politicians immediately found themselves needing to appeal directly for votes (Carson and Roberts 2012; Kernell and MacKenzie 2011; J.F. Reynolds 2006). They no longer dutifully carried the party banner, expecting to ride in or out of office on a presidential coattail they did not fully control. Now they campaigned intensely on their own behalf, as if every voter might make or end their career in office. Either explicitly or implicitly, these candidates invited a new kind of split ticket voting – one undertaken by voters instead of those generated wholesale by factions employing corrupted ballots.[7]

The incentives to campaign directly for votes elevated a new class of politicians to prominence. Shielded, somewhat, from the unpredictable winds of presidential elections, they could increasingly win and hold their office for longer stretches of time (Katz and Sala 1996; Kernell 2003; Kernell and MacKenzie 2011). They soon discovered that credit claiming for services provided to voters was more productive than diverting funds to maintaining patronage. In the late 1890s, this lesson was poignantly learned in the tentative introduction of rural free mail delivery comparable to city and village delivery services already in place. Each new route replaced the locale's fourth-class postmaster – the quintessential patronage office whose occupants distributed election materials (interspersed in voters' mail) and kept the party informed of problems in the constituency. As these routes became instant hits with rural voters, congressmen soon began clamoring for them.[8] In congressional elections the beginnings of an incumbency advantage and careers began to take root (Ansolabehere, Snyder, and Stewart 2000; Carson, Engstrom, and Roberts 2007; Carson and Roberts 2012).

---

[6] Schlesinger (1984: 389) adds, "Compared with other market-based organizations, the [American] party is seriously deficient in its ability to discipline its participants in order to meet the ever insistent market challenges. Compared with other producers of collective goods, the party . . . can neither narrow nor broaden its objectives, muddy its purposes, nor alter its timing to await the propitious moment to act."

[7] For instance, in 1892 the company Whitehead and Hoag introduced the inexpensive celluloid campaign button. It found an instant market in the thousands of candidates at every level of office as ballot reform removed them from the security of the party ticket. For the next twenty-five years, when acetate replaced celluloid, candidates distributed "several hundred million" of these buttons (Storch 1998: 3).

[8] Evidence of their political value can be found in how these initially scarce resources were allocated. The Republican Roosevelt administration piled routes in marginal districts occupied by first-term Republicans; moreover, it withheld routes from the constituencies of first-term Democrats (Kernell and McDonald 1999).

Dismantling the Patronage System

The challenges of managing patronage appointments further added to the collective action problems of the party ticket system. Allocating patronage jobs entailed a delicate political balancing act by leaders who had to negotiate among the many rival factions seeking their perceived fair share of positions. Although the first wave of civil service reform occurred in 1883 with the Pendleton Act, its scope was limited and patronage positions remained plentiful throughout the late nineteenth century. In doling out these appointments party leaders were always walking a tightrope. Government posts were finite and, as with any desirable scarce resource, competition was fierce; there were almost always more applicants than jobs. In 1890 it was estimated that there were, on average, 1,700 applicants for the 250 postal positions per House district (Fowler 1943: 215; Johnson and Libecap 1994: 16). And more than one president has been heard to rue: "For every appointment I make one ingrate and ten enemies."

Factions who felt injured or perceived that their side failed to receive their fair share of appointments might sit out an election or print up a separate ticket. During his first year in office Cleveland's imprudent handling of patronage distribution in California managed to aggravate both of the major Democratic factions in the state. Similar scenes played out in other states, and "within a year of his inauguration, Democratic organizations across the country were in open rebellion against his patronage decisions" (Williams 1973: 80). State party leaders also found disadvantages in relying too heavily on federal patronage. For instance, the return of Democratic successes in presidential elections in the 1880s led to newfound unpredictability for Republican state organizations. In the mid-1880s, for example, the Pennsylvania Republican state leader Matt Quay "realized that reliance on federal patronage had permitted national elections to disrupt their state organization, and that such a practice could no longer be tolerated" (Kehl 1981: 61).

The prevailing view of nineteenth-century party politics regards patronage as the goal of governance. Political parties and candidates suffered forbearance with "strange bedfellows" (a nineteenth-century expression) in order to assemble a team to win the Electoral College and divide up the spoils that flowed from the spigot of White House appointments. The several hundred thousand patronage appointment at its apogee during the late 1880s, the reams of coverage of patronage and related graft in contemporary newspapers and reform-inspired periodicals, and frequent displays of gloating by some party politicians, certainly convey that patronage and graft were the ends of governance for all those who engaged in this era's elections and party politics.

We shift the core motivational concerns of party politicians from the spoils of victory to the process required to win elections. At the outset of the third party system, state parties discovered that failure to link their state and local campaigns to a presidential campaign risked irrelevance for voters. Presidential candidates offered essential coordination for voters – voters divided by state boundaries, geography, and ethnicity – to decide those politicians who would control Congress and the presidency and, consequently, national policy. Those proto-parties that failed to associate with this efficient national focal point reaped none of the benefits of the party ballot system described in this book.

State and federal patronage were critical to conducting successful state campaigns under the party ballot regime. Patronage supplied the labor force to staff this continuous activity of voter contact. A party bereft of reliable patronage workers stood little chance of conducting a successful mobilization campaign. Moreover, patronage provided a kind of glue, an incentive for party politicians to resist the parochial incentives to fracture and divide. Throughout the parties' federal structure we have found party leaders distributing patronage to extinguish factionalism in state party politics and even in Congress in Buchanan's efforts to prevent the breakup of the Democratic Party.[9]

The Growth of Divided Government

Our inquiry culminates in one of the great ironies of American history. Just as presidents were emerging as national leaders – transforming the White House into a true focal point for both voters and other politicians – the states were busy dismantling the responsive electoral system that had tied all partisans to the fate of their presidential nominee. With presidents such as Theodore Roosevelt and Woodrow Wilson soon arriving on the scene, might the continuation of the party ballot regime have brought America the "more responsible two-party government" that some political scientists have long pined for (American Political Science Association, 1950)? Instead, by severely trimming coattails, the new electoral system opened the door to divided party government.

We suspect that the timing of the transformation of the electoral system and the rise of the modern presidency were more than coincidental. Both were prominent features of most progressives' reform agenda for a more professional and effective governmental system. Perhaps it was unavoidable at this moment that reformers would fail to appreciate the critical role of political parties in achieving responsible governance. We have thus far mostly ignored Progressives and consigned them a limited role in dismantling the party ballot system for the simple reason that they controlled few of the governorships and none of the legislatures that adopted Australian ballot reform. Yet sufficient numbers of voters supported Progressive and other reform candidates to require party

[9] It is beyond the scope of this book to test the relative merits of the primacy of patronage and primacy of party ballot arguments. A place one might look is in the timing of the growth and decline of federal patronage. Passage of the Pendleton Act in 1883 in some sense marks the beginning of the end of the patronage system at the federal level. Even allowing for a necessary delay in setting up job classifications and merit requirements, the growth of the number of classified jobs was gradual and uneven. Some years found reductions in even the relatively small numbers of federal merit service jobs. Meanwhile, patronage appointments continued to grow. From passage of Pendleton to the turn of the century, the single largest patronage job classification increased by nearly 75 percent (Kernell and McDonald 1999). It peaked in 1899 and subsequently declined precipitously a period shortly after ballot reform.

regulars to perfume their portfolios (i.e., party tickets) with candidates who attracted their votes. William McKinley did not like reformer Theodore Roosevelt personally and apparently had no intention to select him as his running mate. Yet he accepted Mark Hanna's advice that the ticket needed him as the vice presidential nominee in order to attract progressive voters.

Another causal connection between these opposing developments can be found in the decentralized character of America's political parties. We found the national conventions striving to identify nominees and write platforms that would minimally offend an important region for the party's success. The nominee most suited for this purpose was a politician who had weak association with controversial policies, or any policy. Yet as the turn of the century approached, presidents were increasingly consequential, and candidates for the office obliged to reveal their views on policy issues. As they did so, state parties and the candidates who resided down the list of the presidential nominees frequently found that their policy positions did not align well with the preferences of their local constituencies. The incompatibility of the old regime with the emerging new style leaders in the White House manifests a deeper systemic problem. The emergence of candidates who aspired for leadership was itself a manifestation of the emerging national community. The party ballot regime, founded on confederal accommodation, simply could not endure the nationalization of American politics.

APPENDIX

States as Bundles of Electoral Laws, 1840–1940

TABLE A.1. *Ballot Structure and U.S. House Election Laws*

State (Year Admitted)	Ballot Structure	(Year)	Party Box	House Election Calendar (Year)	Congressional Redistricting (Year)
Arizona (1912)	Office Bloc Party Column	1891 1895	1895>	Nov.	
California (1850)	Party Column Office Bloc	1891 1911	1891–1892 1903–1911	Nov. Sep.* (1859) Nov. (1864) Sep.* (1867) Nov. (1868) Sep.* (1871) Nov. (1872) Sep.* (1875) Nov. (1876)	1864, 1872, 1884, 1892, 1902, 1912, 1932
Colorado (1876)	Party Column Office Bloc	1891 1899	1891–1913	Oct. Nov. (1880)	1892, 1914, 1922
Connecticut (1788)	Party Column	1909	1909>	Apr.* Nov. (1876)	1842, 1912
Delaware (1787)	Party Column	1891	1891>	Nov.	
Idaho (1890)	Party Column	1891	1903–1917 1920>	Nov.	1918

(continued)

TABLE A.1 *(continued)*

State (Year Admitted)	Ballot Structure	(Year)	Party Box	House Election Calendar (Year)	Congressional Redistricting (Year)
Illinois (1818)	Party Column	1891	1891>	Aug. Nov. (1852)	1842, 1852, 1862, 1872, 1882, 1894, 1902
Indiana (1816)	Party Column	1889	1889>	Aug.* Oct. (1852) Nov. (1882)	1842, 1852, 1868, 1874 1880, 1896, 1912, 1932
Iowa (1846)	Party Column	1892	1892–1905 1920>	Aug. Oct. (1858) Nov. (1864) Oct. (1866) Nov. (1884)	1846, 1848, 1858, 1862, 1872, 1882, 1886, 1932
Kansas (1861)	Party Column Office Bloc	1893 1913	1901–1913	Dec. Nov. (1862)	1874, 1884, 1906, 1932
Kentucky (1792)	Office Bloc Party Column	1888 1892	1892>	Aug.* Nov. (1872)	1842, 1862, 1882, 1912, 1932
Maine (1820)	Party Column	1891	1891>	Sep.	1842, 1852, 1862, 1884, 1932
Maryland (1788)	Party Column Office Bloc	1890 1901	1892–1900	Oct.* Nov.* (1853) Nov. (1864)	1842, 1852, 1862, 1872, 1902
Massachusetts (1788)	Office Bloc	1888		Nov.	1842, 1852, 1862, 1872, 1882, 1892, 1902, 1912, 1926, 1932
Michigan (1837)	Party Column	1891	1891>	Nov.	1842, 1852, 1862, 1872, 1882, 1892, 1914, 1932
Minnesota (1858)	Office Bloc	1889		Oct.* Nov. (1860)	1862, 1872, 1882, 1892, 1902, 1914, 1934
Missouri (1821)	Party Column	1889	1891–1896 1922>	Aug. Nov. (1860)	1846, 1852, 1862, 1872, 1878, 1882, 1892, 1902, 1934

State (Year Admitted)	Ballot Structure	(Year)	Party Box	House Election Calendar (Year)	Congressional Redistricting (Year)
Montana (1889)	Office Bloc Party Column Office Bloc	1889 1895 1939	1889–1900	Oct.* Nov. (1890)	1918
Nebraska (1867)	Office Bloc	1891	1897–1898 1901–1932	Oct. Nov. (1876)	1882, 1892, 1932
Nevada (1864)	Office Bloc	1891		Nov.	
New Hampshire (1788)	Office Bloc Party Column	1891 1897	1897>	Mar.* Nov. (1878)	1846, 1850, 1852, 1882
New Jersey (1787)	Office Bloc Party Column	1911 1930		Oct. Nov. (1846)	1842, 1844, 1846, 1852, 1872, 1892, 1894, 1902, 1912, 1932
New Mexico (1912)	Party Column	1905	1918>	Nov.	
New York (1788)	Party Column Office Bloc	1895 1913	1895–1913	Nov.	1842, 1852, 1862, 1884, 1892, 1902, 1912
North Dakota (1889)	Office Bloc Party Column	1891 1893	1891–1892 1897–1925	Oct.* Nov. (1890)	1912
Ohio (1803)	Party Column	1891	1891>	Oct. Nov. (1886)	1842, 1852, 1862, 1872, 1878, 1880, 1882, 1884, 1886, 1890, 1892, 1914
Oklahoma (1907)	Party Column	1890	1890–1896 1899–1908 1910>	Nov.	1906, 1914
Oregon (1859)	Office Bloc	1891		Jun. Nov. (1910)	1892, 1912
Pennsylvania (1787)	Party Column Office Bloc	1891 1903	1891>	Oct. Nov. (1874)	1842, 1852, 1862, 1874, 1888, 1902, 1922, 1932
Rhode Island (1790)	Office Bloc Party Column	1889 1905	1905>	Aug.* Apr.* (1845) Nov. (1868)	1842, 1872, 1882, 1912, 1932

(continued)

TABLE A.I (*continued*)

State (Year Admitted)	Ballot Structure	(Year)	Party Box	House Election Calendar (Year)	Congressional Redistricting (Year)
South Dakota (1889)	Office Bloc Party Column	1891 1893		Oct.* Nov. (1890)	1912, 1932
Utah (1896)	Party Column	1896	1896>	Nov.	1914
Vermont (1791)	Office Bloc Party Column	1890 1906	1892>	Sep. Nov. (1914)	1842, 1852, 1882
Washington (1889)	Office Bloc Party Column	1890 1891	1890>	Oct. Nov. (1890)	1908, 1914, 1932
West Virginia (1863)	Party Column	1891	1891>	Oct. Nov. (1878)	1862, 1882, 1902, 1916, 1930, 1934
Wisconsin (1848)	Office Bloc Party Column	1889 1891	1891>	Nov.	1848, 1862, 1872, 1882, 1892, 1902, 1912, 1932
Wyoming (1890)	Office Bloc Party Column	1890 1911	1897–1911	Sep. Nov. (1892)	

Note: * Indicates House election held in odd years. The following states initially limited the new ballot to certain localities and later applied it statewide: Kentucky (initially applied only to Louisville, statewide in 1892), Minnesota (initially towns more than 10,000, statewide in 1891), Missouri (initially towns more than 5000, statewide in 1891), Wisconsin (initially towns more than 50,000, statewide in 1893), and Maryland (initially applied to Baltimore, statewide in 1892). The following territorial legislatures adopted a ballot law before official statehood: Arizona, Oklahoma, Utah, New Mexico, and Wyoming. New Mexico (1905–1927) and Missouri (1897–1921) provided separate ballots for each party, but these were printed, supplied by the government, and included secrecy provisions. We code these as "Party Column" ballots. For more details on ballot laws, see Ludington (1911) and Albright (1942).

TABLE A.2. *U.S. Senate and State Legislatures*

State (Year Admitted)	Senate Cycle	U.S. Senate Direct Election		State Legislative Reapportionment		State Legislative Term Length	
		Pref. Vote	Party Primary	Lower House	Upper House	Lower House	Upper House
Arizona (1912)	1 & 3	1912		1912 1934 (2)	1912	2	2
California (1850)	1 & 3	1911	1909	1850 1879 (2) 1911 1931	1850 1879 (2) 1911 1931	1(1850–70) 2(1850–70)	2(1871>) 4(1871>)
Colorado (1876)	2 & 3	1910	1910	1876 1881 1901 1913 1932 (2)	1876 1881 1901 1913 1932 (2)	2	4
Connecticut (1788)	1 & 3			1876 (2)	1903	1(<1890) 2(1891>)	1(<1850) 2(1851>)
Delaware (1787)	1 & 2			1897	1897	2	4
Idaho (1890)	2 & 3	1909	1903	1889 1890 1895 1917 1933	1889 1890 1895 1933	2	2
Illinois (1818)	2 & 3		1 1904	1870 1882 1893 1901	1870 1882 1893 1901	2	4
Indiana (1816)	1 & 3			1915 1921	1915 1921	2	4
Iowa (1846)	2 & 3		1907	1846 1921 1927	1846 1906 (2) 1911	2	4
Kansas (1861)	2 & 3	1911	1908	1861 1871 (2) 1873 (2) 1881 1886 (2) 1909	1861 1871 (2) 1873 (2) 1881 1886 (2) 1933	2	4
Kentucky (1792)	2 & 3		1907	1850 1891 1918	1850 1891 1918	2	2(<1860) 4(1861>)
Maine (1820)	1 & 2		1911	1917	1917 1931	1(<1880) 2(1881>)	1(<1880) 2(1881>)

(*continued*)

TABLE A.2 *(continued)*

State (Year Admitted)	Senate Cycle	U.S. Senate Direct Election		State Legislative Reapportionment		State Legislative Term Length	
		Pref. Vote	Party Primary	Lower House	Upper House	Lower House	Upper House
Maryland (1788)	1 & 3		1908	1851 1867 1900	1837 1851 1864 1867 1900 1922	2(<1910)	4 4(1911>)
Massachusetts (1788)	1 & 2			1939 1940 (2)	1940 (2)	1(<1910) 2(1911>)	1(<1910) 2(1911>)
Michigan (1837)	1 & 2		1907	1837 1850	1837 1850	2	2
Minnesota (1858)	1 & 2	1911	1911	1858 1913	1858 1913	1(<1890) 2(1892>)	2(<1870) 4(1871>)
Missouri (1821)	1 & 3		1907	1875 1881 1891 1901	1875 1881 1891 1901 1931	2	4
Montana (1889)	1 & 2	1912	1913	1889	1889 1895	2	4
Nebraska (1867)	1 & 2	1879	1907	1867 1920 1936	1867 1920 1936	2	2
Nevada (1864)	1 & 3	1899	1909	1864 (2)	1864 (2)	2	4
New Hampshire (1788)	2 & 3				1877 1915	1(<1870)	1(<1870)
New Jersey (1787)	1 & 2	1911	1908	1844 1931 (2)	1844	1	3
New Mexico (1912)	1 & 2			1912 (2)	1912 (2)	2	4
New York (1788)	1 & 3			1846 1894 1895 1907 (2) 1938 (2)	1846 1894 1895 1907 (2) 1938 (2)	1(<1929)	2
North Dakota (1889)	1 & 3		1907	1889 (2) 1891 (2) 1901 (2) 1907 (2) 1909 (2) 1911 (2) 1921 1931	1889 (2) 1891 (2) 1901 (2) 1907 (2) 1909 (2) 1911 (2) 1915 1921 1931	2	4

State (Year Admitted)	Senate Cycle	U.S. Senate Direct Election		State Legislative Reapportionment		State Legislative Term Length	
		Pref. Vote	Party Primary	Lower House	Upper House	Lower House	Upper House
Ohio (1803)	1 & 3	1911	1908	1861 1871 (2) 1881 1891 (2) 1901 (2) 1913 1921 1931	1861 1871 (2) 1881 1891 (2) 1901 (2) 1913 1921 1931	2	2
Oklahoma (1907)	2 & 3		1907	1907 1911 1921 1931	1907 1919 1937	2	4
Oregon (1859)	2 & 3	1901	1904	1859	1859	2	4
Pennsylvania (1787)	1 & 3			1874 (2) 1887 1906 (2) 1921	1874 (2) 1887 1906 (2) 1921	1(<1860) 2(1861>)	3(<1860) 4(1861>)
Rhode Island (1790)	1 & 2			1909 (2) 1938 (2)	1909 (2) 1938 (2)	1(<1899) 2(1900>)	1(<1899) 2(1900>)
South Dakota (1889)	2 & 3		1907	1889 1891 1897 1903 1907 1911 1913 1917 1921 1937	1889 1891 1897 1903 1907 1911 1913 1917 1921 1937	2	2
Utah (1896)	1 & 3			1896 1921 1931	1896 1921 1931	2	4
Vermont (1791)	1 & 3			1836	1836 1931	1(<1860) 2(1861>)	1(<1860) 2(1861>)
Washington (1889)	1 & 3		1907	1889 (2) 1890 (2) 1901 1930 (2)	1889 (2) 1890 (2) 1901 1930 (2)	2	4
West Virginia (1863)	1 & 2			1863 1872 1940 (2)	1863 1872 1940 (2)	2	4

(continued)

TABLE A.2 *(continued)*

State (Year Admitted)	Senate Cycle	U.S. Senate Direct Election		State Legislative Reapportionment		State Legislative Term Length	
		Pref. Vote	Party Primary	Lower House	Upper House	Lower House	Upper House
Wisconsin (1848)	1 & 3			1848 1921 1931	1848 1921 1931	1(<1870)	2(<1870)
Wyoming (1890)	1 & 2			1890 (2) 1921 1931 1933	1890 (2) 1921 1931 1933	2	4

Sources: Senate Preference Vote (i.e., Oregon plan) and *Party Primaries: Hall* (1936).
Legislative Term Length: Kromkowski (2001). *Redistricting sources: Sears* (1952). Hardy, Heslop, and Anderson, eds. 1981. Advisory Commission on Intergovernmental Relations. 1962. Walter 1941.

TABLE A.3. *Gubernatorial Elections*

State (Year Admitted)	Election Calendar (Year of Change)	Term Limit	Term Length	Majority Vote Requirement?
Arizona (1912)	Nov.	None	2	
California (1850)	Sep. (odd years) Nov. (1882 – even non-pres. years)	None	2 4 (1862)	
Colorado (1876)	Oct. Nov. (1880)	None	2	
Connecticut (1788)	Apr. Nov. (1876)	None	1 2 (1876)	
Delaware (1787)	Nov. (non-pres. years) Nov. (pres. years beginning in 1896)	1 2 (1898)	4	
Idaho (1890)	Nov.	None	2	
Illinois (1818)	Aug. Nov. (1848)	1 None (1870)	4	
Indiana (1816)	Aug. Oct. (1852) Nov. (1884)	2 1 (1851)	3 4 (1852)	
Iowa (1846)	Oct. Aug. (1850) Oct. (1857 – odd years) Nov. (1885 – odd years) Nov. (1906 – even years)	None	4 2 (1857)	

State (Year Admitted)	Election Calendar (Year of Change)	Term Limit	Term Length	Majority Vote Requirement?
Kansas (1861)	Nov.	None	2	
Kentucky (1792)	Aug. Aug. (1851 – odd years) Nov. (1895 – odd years)	1	4	
Maine (1820)	Sep.	None	1 2 (1880)	Until 1880
Maryland (1788)	Oct. Nov. (1853) Nov. (1867 – odd years) Nov. (1926 – even years)	1 None (1864)	3 4 (1851)	
Massachusetts (1788)	Nov.	1	1 2 (1918)	Until 1855
Michigan (1837)	Nov.	None	2	
Minnesota (1858)	Nov.	None		
Missouri (1821)	Aug. Nov. (1864)	1 2 (1869) 1 (1876)	4 2 (1869) 4 (1876)	
Montana (1889)	Oct. Nov. (1890)	None	4	
Nebraska (1867)	Oct. Nov. (1876)	None	2	
Nevada (1864)	Nov.	None	4	
New Hampshire (1788)	Mar. Nov. (1878)	None	1 2 (1878)	Until 1912
New Jersey (1787)	Oct. Nov. (1846)	None 1 (1844)	1 3 (1844)	
New Mexico (1912)	Nov.	1 2 (1914)	4 2 (1914)	
New York (1788)	Nov.	None	2 3 (1876) 2 (1894) 4 (1938)	
North Dakota (1889)	Oct. Nov. (1890)	None	2	
Ohio (1803)	Oct. (odd years starting in 1851) Nov. (1887 – odd years) Nov. (even years starting in 1908)	3 None (1850)	2	

(continued)

TABLE A.3 *(continued)*

State (Year Admitted)	Election Calendar (Year of Change)	Term Limit	Term Length	Majority Vote Requirement?
Oklahoma (1907)	Nov.	1	4	
Oregon (1859)	Jun. (non-pres. years) Nov. (1910 – non-pres. years)	2	4	
Pennsylvania (1787)	Oct. Nov. (1874)	2 1 (1874)	3 4 (1874)	
Rhode Island (1790)	Apr.* (1845) Nov. (1900)	None	1 2 (1912)	Until 1894
South Dakota (1889)	Oct. Nov. (1890)	None	2	
Utah (1896)	Nov.	None	4	
Vermont (1791)	Sep. Nov. (1914)	None	1 2 (1870)	Still in force
Washington (1889)	Oct. Nov. (1890)	None	4	
West Virginia (1863)	Oct. Nov. (1888)	None 1 (1872)	2 4 (1872)	
Wisconsin (1848)	Nov. (odd years) Nov. (even years starting in 1884)	None	2	
Wyoming (1890)	Sep. Nov. (1894)	None	4	

Sources: Rusk 2001, Kallenbach and Kallenbach 1977, Glashan 1979.

References

Ackerman, Kenneth D. 2003. *Dark Horse: The Surprise Election and Political Murder of President James. A. Garfield*. New York: Carroll and Graf Publishers.

Advisory Commission on Intergovernmental Relations. 1962. *Apportionment of State Legislatures*. Washington, D.C.: ACIR.

Albright, Spencer D. 1942. *The American Ballot*. Washington, DC: American Council on Public Affairs.

Alchian, Armen A. and Harold Demsetz. 1972. "Production, Information Costs, and Economic Organization." *American Economic Review* 62(5): 777–795.

Aldrich, John H. 1993. "Rational Choice and Turnout." *American Journal of Political Science* 37(1): 246–278.

———— 1995. *Why Parties? The Origin and Transformation of Political Parties in America*. Chicago: The University of Chicago Press.

Alford, John R. and John R. Hibbing. 2002. "Electoral Convergence in the U.S. Congress." In Bruce I. Oppenheimer, ed. *U.S. Senate Exceptionalism*. Columbus: Ohio State University Press, 89–108.

Allen, Philip L. 1906. "Ballot Laws and Their Workings." *Political Science Quarterly* 21(1): 38–58.

———— 1910. "The Multifarious Australian Ballot." *North American Review* 191: 602–611.

American Political Science Association (APSA). 1950. "Toward a More Responsible Two-Party System: A Report of the Committee on Political Parties." *American Political Science Review* 44: supplement.

Ansolabehere, Stephen and James M. Snyder, Jr. 2008. *The End of Inequality: One Person, One Vote and the Transformation of American Politics*. New York: W.W. Norton and Company.

Ansolabehere, Stephen, James Snyder, and Charles Stewart. 2000. "Old Voters, New Voters, and the Personal Vote: Using Redistricting to Measure the Incumbency Advantage." *American Journal of Political Science* 44: 17–34.

Anzia, Sarah F. 2012. "Partisan Power Play: The Origins of Local Election Timing as an American Political Institution." *Studies in American Political Development* 26(1): 24–49.

Argersinger, Peter H. 1980. "'A Place on the Ballot': Fusion Politics and Antifusion Laws." *The American Historical Review* 85(2): 287–306.

———— 1989. "The Value of the Vote: Political Representation in the Gilded Age." *The Journal of American History* 76(1): 59–90.

———— 1992. *Structure, Process, and Party: Essays in American Political History*. Armonk, NY: M.E. Sharpe, Inc.

———— 2012. *Representation and Inequality in Late Nineteenth-Century America*. Cambridge: Cambridge University Press.

Baker v. Carr, 369 U.S. 186 (1962).

Barnes, Harper. 2001. *Standing on a Volcano: The Life and Times of David Rowland Francis*. St. Louis: Missouri Historical Society Press.

Basehart, Harry. 1987. "The Seats/Vote Relationship and the Identification of Partisan Gerrymandering in State Legislatures." *American Politics Quarterly* 15(4): 484–498.

Basler, Roy B., ed. 1953. *The Collected Works of Abraham Lincoln*. New Brunswick, NJ: Rutgers University Press.

Beck, Nathaniel. 2001. "Time-Series Cross-Section Data: What Have We Learned in the Past Few Years?" *Annual Review of Political Science* 4(June): 271–293.

Beck, Nathaniel and Jonathan N. Katz. 1995. "What To Do (and Not To Do) with Time-Series Cross-Section Data." *American Political Science Review* 89(3): 634–647.

———— 1996. "Nuisance vs. Substance: Specifying and Estimating Time-Series Cross-Section Models." *Political Analysis* 6(1): 1–36.

———— 2001. "Throwing Out the Baby With the Bath Water: A Comment on Green, Yoon and Kim," *International Organization* 55(2): 487–495.

———— 2004. "Time-Series Cross-Section Issues: Dynamics." Paper presented at 2004 Summer Political Methodology Meetings, Stanford University.

Bensel, Richard Franklin. 2000. *The Political Economy of American Industrialization, 1877–1900*. Cambridge and New York: Cambridge University Press.

———— 2003. "The American Ballot Box: Law, Identity, and the Polling Place in the Mid-Nineteenth Century." *Studies in American Political Development* 17(1): 1–27.

———— 2004. *The American Ballot Box in the Mid-Nineteenth Century*. Cambridge: Cambridge University Press.

Bone, Hugh A. 1952. "States Attempting to Comply with Reapportionment Requirements." *Law and Contemporary Problems* 17(2): 387–416.

Boomhower, Ray E. 1997. *Jacob Piatt Dunn, Jr.: A Life in History and Politics, 1855–1924*. Indianapolis: Indiana Historical Society.

Boyd, Richard W. 1981. "Decline of U.S. Voter Turnout: Structural Explanations." *American Politics Quarterly* 9: 133–160.

———— 1986. "Election Calendars and Voter Turnout." *American Politics Quarterly* 14: 89–104.

Brady, David W. 1985. "A Reevaluation of Realignments in American Politics: Evidence from the House of Representatives." *American Political Science Review* 79(1): 28–49.

———— 1988. *Critical Elections and Congressional Policy Making*. Palo Alto, CA: Stanford University Press.

Brady, David W. and Bernard Grofman. 1991. "Sectional Differences in Partisan Bias and Electoral Responsiveness in U.S. House Elections, 1850–1980." *British Journal of Political Science* 21(2): 247–256.

Brands, H. W. 2010. *American Colossus: The Triumph of Capitalism, 1865–1900*. New York: Doubleday.

Brown, William B. 1960. *The People's Choice*. Baton Rouge, LA: Louisiana State University Press.

Bryce, James. 1889. *The American Commonwealth*. New York: Macmillan.

Burden, Barry C. and David C. Kimball. 1998. "A New Approach to the Study of Ticket Splitting." *American Political Science Review* 92(3): 533–544.

Burnham, Walter Dean. 1965. "The Changing Shape of the American Political Universe." *American Political Science Review* 59: 7–28.

———. 1970. *Critical Elections and the Mainsprings of American Politics*. New York: W.W. Norton.

———. 1974a. "Theory and Voting Research: Some Reflections on Converse's Change in the American Electorate." *American Political Science Review* 68: 1002–1023.

——— 1974b. "Rejoinder to 'Comments' by Philip Converse and Jerrold Rusk," *American Political Science Review* 68(3): 1050–1057.

———. 1981. "The System of 1896: An Analysis." In Kleppner et al. (1981, 147–202).

———. 1985. *Partisan Division of State Governments, 1834–1985* [computer file]. Ann Arbor, Michigan: Inter-University Consortium for Political and Social Research (ICPSR).

Burnham, Walter Dean, Jerome M. Clubb, and William Flanigan. 1972a. *State-Level Congressional, Gubernatorial and Senatorial Election Data for the United States, 1824–1972* [Computer file]. ICPSR ed. Ann Arbor, MI: Inter-University Consortium for Political and Social Research [producer and distributor].

———. 1972b. *State-Level Presidential Election Data for the United States, 1824–1972* [Computer file]. ICPSR ed. Ann Arbor, MI: Inter-University Consortium for Political and Social Research [producer and distributor].

Butler, Anne M. and Wendy Wolff. 1995. *Senate Election, Expulsion, and Censure Cases from 1793–1900*. Washington, DC: U.S. Government Printing Office.

Butler, D. E. 1951. *The British General Election of 1950*. London: Macmillan.

Byrd, Robert C. 1988. *The Senate, 1789–1989, Volume 1: Addresses on the History of the United States Senate*. Washington, DC: U.S. GPO. (Edited by Mary Sharon Hall).

Cain, Bruce E. 1984. *The Reapportionment Puzzle*. Berkeley: University of California Press.

———. 1985. "Assessing the Partisan Effects of Redistricting." *American Political Science Review* 79(2): 320–333.

Cain, Bruce E., John Ferejohn, and Morris P. Fiorina. 1987. *The Personal Vote: Constituency Service and Electoral Independence*. Cambridge, MA: Harvard University Press.

Calhoun, Charles W. 2008. *Minority Victory: Gilded Age Politics and the Front Porch Campaign of 1888*. Lawrence, KS: University of Kansas Press.

Campagna, Janet and Bernard Grofman. 1990. "Party Control and Partisan Bias in 1980s Congressional Redistricting." *Journal of Politics* 52(4): 1242–1257.

Campbell, Angus and Warren E. Miller. 1957. "The Motivational Basis of Straight and Split Ticket Voting." *American Political Science Review* 51(2): 293–312.

Campbell, Ballard C. 1980. *Representative Democracy: Public Policy and Midwestern Legislatures in the Late Nineteenth Century*. Cambridge and London: Harvard University Press.

_____ 1995. *The Growth of American Government: Governance from the Cleveland Era to the Present*. Bloomington: Indiana University Press.

Campbell, James E. 1986. "Presidential Coattails and Midterm Losses in State Legislative Elections." *American Political Science Review* 80(1): 45–64.

Carsey, Thomas M. and Gerald C. Wright. 1998. "State and National Factors in Gubernatorial and Senatorial Elections." *American Journal of Political Science* 42(3): 994–1002.

Carson, Jamie L., Erik J. Engstrom, and Jason Roberts. 2007. "Candidate Quality, the Personal Vote, and the Incumbency Advantage in Congress." *American Political Science Review* 101: 289–302.

Carson, Jamie L., Jeffery A. Jenkins, David W. Rohde, and Mark A. Souva. 2001. "The Impact of National Tides and District-Level Effects on Electoral Outcomes: The U.S. Congressional Elections of 1862–63." *American Journal of Political Science* 45(4): 887–898.

Carson, Jamie L. and Jason M. Roberts. 2012. *Ambition, Competition, and Electoral Reform: The Politics of Congressional Elections across Time*. Ann Arbor, MI: University of Michigan Press.

Carwardine, Richard J. 1993. *Evangelicals and Politics in Antebellum America*. New Haven: Yale University Press.

Cater, Douglass. 1964. *Power in Washington*. New York: Vintage Press.

Chandler, Alfred D. 1977. *The Managerial Revolution in American Business*. Cambridge, MA: Belknap Press.

Chubb, John E. 1988. "Institutions, the Economy and the Dynamics of State Elections." *American Political Science Review* 82(1): 133–154.

Clark, Champ. 1920. *My Quarter Century of American Politics*, vol. 1. New York: Harper and Brothers.

Claggett, William, William Flanigan and Nancy Zingale. 1984. "Nationalization of the American Electorate." *American Political Science Review* 78(1): 77–91.

Coelho, Philip R. P. and James F. Shepherd. 1974. "Differences in Regional Prices: The United States, 1851–1880." *The Journal of Economic History* 34(3): 551–591.

Cohen, Jeffrey C. 1982. "Change in Election Calendars and Turnout Decline: A Test of Boyd's Hypothesis." *American Politics Quarterly* 10: 246–254.

Congressional Quarterly's Guide to U.S. Elections. 1975. Washington, DC: Congressional Quarterly Inc.

Congressional Record. 1887. 49th Congress, 2nd Session, vol XVIII, part 2. 1885.

Converse, Philip E. 1974. "Comment on Burnham's 'Theory and Voting Research.'" *American Political Science Review* 68(3): 1024–1027.

Corstange, Daniel. 2012. "Vote Trafficking in Lebanon." *International Journal of Middle Eastern Studies* 44: 483–505.

Cox, Gary W. 1997. *Making Votes Count: Strategic Coordination in the World's Electoral Systems*. Cambridge: Cambridge University Press.

_____ 1999. "Electoral Rules and the Calculus of Mobilization." *Legislative Studies Quarterly* 24(3): 387–420.

Cox, Gary W. and Jonathan Katz. 1999. "The Reapportionment Revolution and Bias in U.S. Congressional Elections." *American Journal of Political Science* 43(3): 812–840.

_____ 2002. *Elbridge Gerry's Salamander: The Electoral Consequences of the Reapportionment Revolution*. Cambridge: Cambridge University Press.

Cox, Gary W. and J. Morgan Kousser. 1981. "Turnout and Rural Corruption: New York as a Test Case." *American Journal of Political Science* 25(4): 646–663.

Cox, Gary W. and Michael C. Munger. 1989. "Closeness, Expenditures, and Turnout in the 1982 U.S. House Elections." *American Political Science Review* 83(1): 217–231.

Crook, Sara Brandes and John Hibbing. 1997. "A Not-So-Distant Mirror: The 17th Amendment and Congressional Change." *American Political Science Review* 91(4): 845–853.

David, Paul T. and Ralph Eisenberg. 1961. *Devaluation of the Urban and Suburban Vote A Statistical Investigation of Long-Term Trends in State Legislative Representation.* Charlottesville: Bureau of Public Administration, University of Virginia.

Davis, Lance E. 1965. "The Investment Market, 1870–1914: The Evolution of a National Market." *The Journal of Economic History* 25(3): 355–399.

Davis, Lance E., Jonathan R.T. Hughes, and Duncan M. McDougall. 1965. *American Economic History: The Development of a National Economy.* Homewood, Ill.: Richard D. Irwin, Inc.

Daynes, Byron W. 1971. *The Impact of the Direct Election of Senators on the Political System.* PhD Dissertation. Chicago, Illinois: The University of Chicago.

Debates and Proceedings of the Maryland Reform Convention to Revise the State Constitution. 2 volumes. (Annapolis: William McNeir, official printer, 1851).

The Debates of the Constitutional Convention of the State of Maryland, Assembled at the City of Annapolis, Wednesday, April 27, 1864. 3 volumes. (Annapolis: Richard P. Bayly, 1864).

de Bromhead, Alan, Barry Eichengreen, and Keven H. O'Rourke. 2013. "Political Extremism in the 1920s and 1930s: Do the German Lessons Generalize?" *Journal of Economic History* 73 (2): 371–406.

DeCanio, Samuel. 2007. "Religion and Nineteenth-Century Voting Behavior: A New Look at Some Old Data." *Journal of Politics.* 69: 339–350.

Dinkin, Robert J. 1989. *Campaigning in America.* New York: Greenwood Press.

Dobson, John M. 1972. *Politics in the Gilded Age: a New Perspective on Reform.* New York: Praeger Publishers.

Dubin, Michael J. 1998. *United States Congressional Elections, 1788–1997: The Official Results of the Elections of the 1st Through 105th Congresses.* Jefferson, NC: McFarland and Company.

_____ 2007. *Party Affiliations in the State Legislatures: A Year by Year Summary, 1796–2006.* Jefferson, NC: McFarland & Company Publishers.

Duverger, Maurice. 1954. *Political Parties.* New York: Wiley.

Easterlin, Richard A. 1958. "Long Term Regional Income Changes: Some Suggested Factors." *Papers and Proceedings of the Regional Science Association* 4: 313–325, p. 315.

_____ 1960. "Interregional Differences in Per Capita Income, Population, and Total Income, 1840–1950." *Trends in the American Economy in the Nineteenth Century,* N.B.E.R., Studies in Income and Wealth. Princeton: Princeton University Press. 24: 73–140.

_____ 1961. "Regional Income Trends, 1840–1950." In Seymour E. Harris, ed. *American Economic History.* New York: McGraw-Hill Book Company, Inc., 525–547.

Engstrom, Erik J. 2006. "Stacking the States, Stacking the House: The Politics of Congressional Redistricting in the 19th Century." *American Political Science Review* 100 (3): 419–428.

———— 2013. *Partisan Gerrymandering and the Construction of American Democracy*. Ann Arbor, MI: University of Michigan Press.

Engstrom, Erik J. and Samuel Kernell. 2005a. "Manufactured Responsiveness: The Impact of State Electoral Laws on Unified Party Control of the President and House of Representatives." *American Journal of Political Science* 49(3): 531–549.

———— 2005b. "The Effects of Presidential Elections on Party Control of the Senate under Indirect and Direct Elections." In David Brady and Mathew McCubbins, eds. *Process, Party, and Policy Making: New Perspectives on the History of Congress*. Stanford: Stanford University Press, 37–52.

Epstein, Leon. 1986. *Political Parties in the American Mold*. Madison, WI: University of Wisconsin Press.

Erikson, Robert S. 1971. "The Partisan Impact of State Legislative Reapportionment." *Midwest Journal of Political Science* 15(1): 57–71.

———— 2002. "Explaining National Party Tides in Senate Elections: Macropartisanship, Policy Mood, and Ideological Balancing." In Bruce I. Oppenheimer, ed. *U.S. Senate Exceptionalism*. Columbus, Ohio: Ohio State University Press, 70–88.

Erikson, Robert S. and Christopher Wlezien. 2012. *The Timeline of Presidential Elections: How Campaigns Do (and Do Not) Matter*. Chicago: University of Chicago Press.

Evans, Cobb. 1917. *A History of the Australian Ballot in the United States*. Chicago: University of Chicago Press.

Fels, Rendigs. 1959. *American Business Cycles, 1865–1897*. Chapel Hill: University of North Carolina Press.

Fenno, Richard. 1978. *Home Style: House Members in Their Districts*. Boston: Little, Brown.

Ferejohn, John A. and Randall L. Calvert. 1984. "Presidential Coattails in Historical Perspective." *American Journal of Political Science* 28(1): 127–146.

Fishlow, Albert. 1966. *American Railroads and the Transformation of the Antebellum Economy*. Cambridge, MA: Harvard University Press.

Fletcher, Mona. 1945. *National Municipal Review* (October): 440–444.

Fowler, Dorothy R. 1943. *The Cabinet Politician. The Postmasters General, 1829–1909*. New York City: Columbia University Press.

Fredman, L.E. 1968. *The Australian Ballot: The Story of An American Reform*. East Lansing: Michigan State University Press.

Friedman, Milton and Anna Jacobson Schwartz. 1963. *A Monetary History of the United States, 1867–1960*. Princeton: Princeton University Press.

Gailmard, Sean and Jeffrey A. Jenkins. 2009. "Agency Problems, the 17th Amendment, and Representation in the Senate." *American Journal of Political Science* 53: 324–42.

Gallman, Robert E. 1966. Gross National Product in the United States, 1834–1909. In Dorothy S. Brady, ed. *Output, Employment, and Productivity in the United States after 1800. Studies in Income and Wealth*, vol. 30: 1–90. Conference on Research in Income and Wealth. New York: Columbia University Press.

Gamm, Gerald and Renee M. Smith. 1998. "Presidents, Parties, and the Public: Evolving Patterns of Interaction, 1877–1929." In Richard J. Ellis, ed. *Speaking to the People*. Boston: University of Massachusetts Press, 87–111.

Garand, James C. and T. Wayne Parent. 1991. "Representation, Swing, and Bias in U.S. Presidential Elections, 1872–1988." *American Journal of Political Science* 35(4): 1011–1031.

Garrett, Thomas A., Andrew F. Kozak, and Russell M Rhine. 2008. "Institutions and Government Growth: A Comparison of the 1890s and the 1930s." *Working Paper Series*.

Gerring, John. 1998. *Party Ideologies in America, 1828–1996*. Cambridge: Cambridge University Press.

Ginsberg, Benjamin. 1972. "Critical Elections and the Substance of Party Conflict: 1844–1968." *Midwest Journal of Political Science* 16: 603–625.

Glashan, Roy. 1979. *American Governors and Gubernatorial Elections, 1775–1978*. Westport, CT: Meckler Books.

Gosnell, Harold F. 1923. "Thomas C. Platt–Political Manager." *Political Science Quarterly* 38(3): 443–469.

———— 1924. *Boss Platt and His New York Machine*. Reprinted, 1969. New York: Russell and Russell.

Grondahl, Paul. 2004. *I Rose Like a Rocket: The Political Education of Theodore Roosevelt*. New York: Free Press.

Guenther, Scott and Samuel Kernell. 2013. "The 19th Century Party Ticket as an Extended Test of the Plurality-Mobilization Thesis." Unpublished manuscript.

Hall, Wallace Worthy. 1936. *The History and Effect of the Seventeenth Amendment*. PhD Dissertation. Berkeley, California: University of California, Berkeley.

Hamilton, Gail. 1895. *Biography of James G. Blaine*. Norwich, CT: The Henry Bill Publishing Company.

Hardy, Leroy, Alan Heslop, and Stuart Anderson, eds. 1981. *Reapportionment Politics: The History of Redistricting in the 50 States*. Beverly Hills: Sage Publications.

Harry, James Warner. 1902. *The Maryland Constitution of 1851*. Johns Hopkins University Studies in Historical and Political Science. Eds. J. M. Vincent, J. H. Hollander, and W. W. Willoughby. Series XX, Nos. 7–8. Baltimore: The Johns Hopkins Press.

Harvey, Lashley G. 1952. "Reapportionments of State Legislatures. Legal Requirements." *Law and Contemporary Problems* 17(2): 364–376.

Hasbrouck, Paul. 1927. *Party Government in the House of Representatives*. New York: The Macmillan Company.

Haynes, George N. 1905. "Popular Control of Senatorial Elections." *Political Science Quarterly* 20(4): 577–593.

———— 1906. *The Election of Senators*. New York: Henry Holt and Co.

Hays, Samuel P. 1981. "Politics and Society: Beyond the Political Party." In Kleppner et al. (1981): 243–268.

Hesseltine, William B. 1948. *Lincoln and the War Governors*. New York: Alfred A. Knopf.

Higgs, Robert. 1987. *Crisis and Leviathan*. New York: Oxford University Press.

Historical Statistics of the United States, Colonial Times to 1970. 1975. Washington, DC: U.S. Dept. of Commerce, Bureau of the Census.

Hollingsworth, J. Rogers. 1963. *The Whirligig of Politics: The Democracy of Cleveland and Bryan*. Chicago: University of Chicago Press.

Holt, Michael F. 1984. "The Election of 1840, Voter Mobilization, and the Emergence of the Second American Party System: A Reappraisal of Jacksonian Voting Behavior."

In *A Master's Due*. William Cooper, Michael F. Holt, and John McCardell, eds. Baton Rouge: Louisiana State University Press.

———— 1999. *The Rise and Fall of the American Whig Party: Jacksonian Politics and the Onset of the Civil War*. New York: Oxford University Press.

———— 2005. "Change and Continuity in the Party Period: The Substance and Structure of American Politics, 1853–1885." In Byron E. Shafer and Anthony J. Badger, eds. *Contesting Democracy: The Substance and Structure of American Politics* Lawrence: University Press of Kansas, 93–116.

Jacobson, Gary C. 2001. *The Politics of Congressional Elections*. New York: Addison-Wesley-Longman.

Jacobson, Gary C. and Samuel Kernell. 1983. *Strategy and Choice in Congressional Elections*, 2nd ed. New Haven, CT: Yale University Press.

James, Scott C. 2006. "Patronage Regimes and American Party Development from 'The Age of Jackson' to the Progressive Era." *British Journal of Political Science* 35(1): 39–60.

———— 2007. "Timing and Sequence in Congressional Elections: Interstate Contagion and America's Nineteenth Century Scheduling Regime." *Studies in American Political Development* 21(2): 181–202.

Jenkins, Jeffrey A. 2005. "Partisanship and Contested Election Cases in the Senate, 1789–2002." *Studies in American Political Development* 19: 53–74.

Jensen, Richard. 1971. *The Winning of the Midwest: Social and Political Conflict, 1888–1896*. Chicago: University of Chicago Press.

Jewell, Malcolm E. 1955. "Constitutional Provisions for State Legislative Apportionment." *The Western Political Quarterly* 8(2): 271–279.

Johnson, Kimberley S. 2007. *Governing the American State*. Princeton, NJ: Princeton University Press.

Johnson, Ronald N. and Gary D. Libecap. 1994. *The Federal Civil Service System and the Problem of Bureaucracy: The Economics and Politics of Institutional Change*. Chicago: University of Chicago Press.

Josephson, Matthew. 1938. *The Politicos, 1865–1896*. New York: Harcourt, Brace and Company.

Kallenbach, Joseph. 1966. *The American Chief Executive*. New York: Harper and Row Publishers.

Kallenbach, Joseph and Jessamine Kallenbach. 1977. *American State Governors 1776–1976*. 3 Vol. Dobbs Ferry, NY: Oceana Publishing.

Katz, Jonathan N. and Brian R. Sala. 1996. "Careerism, Committee Assignments, and the Electoral Connection." *American Political Science Review* 90(1): 21–33.

Katz, Richard. 1973. "The Attribution of Variance in Electoral Returns: An Alternative Measurement Technique." *American Political Science Review* 67(3): 817–828.

Kawato, Sadafumi. 1987. "Nationalization and Partisan Realignment in Congressional Elections." *American Political Science Review* 81(4): 1235–1250.

Kehl, James A. 1981. *Boss Rule in the Gilded Age: Matt Quay of Pennsylvania*. Pittsburgh: University of Pittsburgh Press.

Keller, Morton. 1977. *Affairs of State: Public Life in Late 19th Century America*. Cambridge, MA: Belknap Press of Harvard University Press.

———— 2007. *America's Three Regimes: a New Political History*. New York: Oxford University Press.

Kendall, M. G. and Stuart, A. 1950. "The Law of Cubic Proportions in Election Results." *British Journal of Sociology* 1: 183–197.

Kent, Frank Richardson. 1933. *The Great Game of Politics: An Effort to Present the Elementary Human Facts about Politics, Politicians, and Political Machines, Candidates and Their Ways, for the Benefit of the Average Citizen.* New York: Doubleday, Doran.

Kernell, Samuel. 1977. "Toward Understanding 19th Century Congressional Careers: Ambition, Competition, and Rotation." *American Journal of Political Science* 21(4): 669–693.

———— 1986a. "The Early Nationalization of Political News in America." *Studies in American Political Development* 1: 255–278.

———— 1986b. *Going Public: New Strategies of Presidential Leadership.* Washington, DC: CQ Press.

———— 2000. "Life Before Polls: Ohio Politicians Predict the 1828 Presidential Vote." *PS: Political Science and Politics* 33(3): 569–574.

———— 2003. "To Stay, to Quit or to Move Up: Explaining the Growth of Careerism in the House of Representatives, 1878–1940." Presented at the Annual Meetings of the American Political Science Association, Philadelphia, August 28–31.

Kernell, Samuel and Gary C. Jacobson. 1987. "Congress and the Presidency as News in the Nineteenth Century." *Journal of Politics* 49(4): 1016–1035.

Kernell, Samuel and Scott A. MacKenzie. 2011. "From Political Careers to Career Politicians." Presented to the Midwest Political Science Association, Chicago.

Kernell, Samuel and Michael P. McDonald. 1999. "Congress and America's Political Development: The Transformation of the Post Office from Patronage to Service." *American Journal of Political Science* 43(3): 792–811.

Key, V. O. 1932. "Procedures in State Legislative Apportionment." *American Political Science Review* 26(6): 1050–1058.

———— 1955. "A Theory of Critical Elections." *Journal of Politics* 17(3): 3–18.

———— 1956. *American State Politics.* New York: Alfred A. Knopf, Inc.

———— 1964. *Politics, Parties, and Pressure Groups, Fifth Edition.* New York: Thomas Y. Crowell Company.

Keyssar, Alexander. 2000. *The Right to Vote.* New York: Basic Books.

Kiewiet, D. Roderick and Langche Zeng. 1993. "An Analysis of Congressional Career Decisions, 1947–1986." *American Political Science Review* 87(4): 928–841.

Kim, Sukkoo. 1998. "Economic Integration and Convergence: U.S. Regions, 1840–1987." *The Journal of Economic History* 58(3): 659–683.

King, Gary. 1989. *Unifying Political Methodology.* Cambridge: Cambridge University Press.

King, Gary and Robert X. Browning. 1987. "Democratic Representation and Partisan Bias in Congressional Elections." *American Political Science Review* 81(4): 1251–1273.

King, Ronald F. and Susan Ellis. 1996. "Partisan Advantage and Constitutional Change: The Case of the 17th Amendment." *Studies in American Political Development* 10: 69–102.

Kleppner, Paul. 1970. *The Cross of Culture: A Social Analysis of Midwestern Politics 1850–1900.* New York: Free Press.

———— 1979. *The Third Electoral System, 1853–1892: Parties, Voters, and Political Cultures.* Chapel Hill, NC: University of North Carolina Press.

_____ 1981. "Partisanship and Ethnoreligious Conflict: The Third Electoral System, 1853–1892." In Kleppner et al. (1981): 113–146.

Kleppner, Paul, Walter Dean Burnham, Ronald P. Formisano, Samuel P. Hays, Richard Jensen and William G. Shade, eds. 1981. *The Evolution of American Electoral Systems*. Westport, CT: Greenwood.

Klinghard, Daniel. 2002. *The Nationalization of American Political Parties, 1880–1896*. New York: Cambridge University Press.

Kolodny, Robin. 1998. *Pursuing Majorities: Congressional Campaign Committees in American Politics*. Norman, OK: University of Oklahoma Press.

Korzi, Michael J. 2004. *A Seat of Popular Leadership: The Presidency, Political Parties, and Democratic Government*. Boston: University of Massachusetts Press.

Kousser, J. Morgan. 1974. *The Shaping of Southern Politics*. New Haven: Yale University Press.

Kramer, Gerald H. 1971. "Short-Term Fluctuations in U.S. Voting Behavior, 1896–1964." *American Political Science Review* 65(1): 131–143.

Kristensen, Ida Pagter and Gregory Wawro. 2003. "Lagging the Dog?: The Robustness of Panel Corrected Standard Errors in the Presence of Serial Correlation and Observation Specific Effects." Paper presented at the 2003 meeting of the Society for Political Methodology. University of Minnesota, Minneapolis, MN.

Kromkowski, Charles A. 2001. "Representative Government in the American States, 1700–2000." Retrieved from http://people.virginia.edu/~cak5u/research.htm.

Kvist, Jan F. 1995. "On Bias, Inconsistency, and Efficiency of Various Estimators in Dynamic Panel Models." *Journal of Econometrics* 68(August): 53–78.

Leach, Frank A. 1974. *Recollections of a Newspaperman: A Record of Life and Events in California*. New York: Beekman Publishers.

Leonard, Gerald. 2002. *The Invention of Party Politics*. Chapel Hill: University of North Carolina Press.

Lin, Tse-min. 1999. "The Historical Significance of Economic Voting, 1872–1996." *Social Science History* 23: 561–591.

Lipson, Leslie. 1939. *The American Governor from Figurehead to Leader*. Chicago: University of Chicago Press.

Lott, John R. and Lawrence W. Kenny. 1999. "Did Women's Suffrage Change the Size and Scope of Government?" *Journal of Political Economy* 107(6): 1163–1198.

Ludington, Arthur. 1909. "Present Status of Ballot Laws in the United States." *The American Political Science Review* 3(2): 252–261.

Ludington, Arthur C. 1911. *American Ballot Laws, 1888–1910*. New York State Education Department Bulletin No. 448: University of the State of New York, Albany.

Lynch, G. Patrick. 1999. "Presidential Elections and the Economy 1872 to 1996: The Times They Are a Changin' or the Song Remains the Same?" *Political Research Quarterly* 52(4): 825–844.

_____ 2002. "Midterm Elections and Economic Fluctuations: The Response of Voters Over Time." *Legislative Studies Quarterly* 27(2): 265–294.

Macy, Jesse. 1912. *Party Organization and Machinery*. Ann Arbor: University of Michigan Press.

Marcus, R. D. 1971. *Grand Old Party: Political Structure in the Gilded Age 1878–1896*. New York: Oxford University Press.

Martis, Kenneth. 1982. *The Historical Atlas of United States Congressional Districts, 1789–1983*. New York: Free Press.

_____ 1989. *The Historical Atlas of Political Parties in the United States Congress, 1789–1989*. New York: Macmillan Publishing.

McCormick, Richard P. 1953. *The History of Voting in New Jersey: A Study of the Development of Election Machinery, 1664–1911*. New Brunswick, NJ: Rutgers University Press.

_____ 1966. *The Second American Party System: Party Formation in the Jacksonian Era*. Chapel Hill: University of North Carolina Press.

_____ 1967. "Political Development and the Second Party System." In William Nisbet Chambers and Walter Dean Burnham, eds. *The American Party System: Stages of Development*. New York: Oxford University Press, 90–116.

_____ 1982. *The Presidential Game*. New York: Oxford University Press.

McDonald, Michael P. 1999. "Redistricting, Dealignment, and the Political Homogenization of Congressional Districts." PhD Dissertation, University of California, San Diego.

McFarland, Gerald W. 1975. *Mugwumps, Morals, and Politics, 1884–1920*. Amherst: University of Massachusetts Press.

McGerr, Michael E. 1988. *The Decline of Popular Politics: The American North, 1865–1928*. New York: Oxford University Press.

McKelvey, Richard D. and Raymond Riezman. 1992. "Seniority in Legislatures." *American Political Science Review* 86(4): 951–965.

McSeveney, Samuel T. 1972. *The Politics of Depression: Political Behavior in the Northeast, 1893–1896*. New York: Oxford University Press.

Merriam, Charles E. and Louise Overacker. 1928. *Primary Elections*. Chicago: University of Chicago Press.

Michigan Law Review Association (MLRA). 1932. "Constitutional Law: Is Redistricting of a State for Congressional Elections an Exercise of the Lawmaking Power of the State?" *MLRA* 30(6): 969–970.

Moos, Malcolm. 1952. *Politics, Presidents, and Coattails*. Baltimore: Johns Hopkins Press.

Morgenstern, Scott, Stephen M. Swindle, and Andrea Castagnola. 2009. "Party Nationalization and Institutions." *Journal of Politics* 71(4): 1322–1341.

Mott, Rodney M. 1927. "Reapportionment in Illinois." *American Political Science Review* 21(3): 598–602.

Myers, William Starr. 1901. *The Maryland Constitution of 1864*. Johns Hopkins University Studies in Historical and Political Science. Herbert B. Adams, editor. Series XIX, nos. 8–9. Baltimore: The Johns Hopkins Press.

Nardulli, Peter F. 1995. "The Concept of a Critical Realignment, Electoral Behavior, and Political Change." *American Political Science Review* 89(1): 10–22.

National Municipal League, The. 1962. *Compendium on Legislative Apportionment*. Second edition. New York: NML.

Nevins, Allan. 1924. *The American States During and After the Revolution, 1775–1789*. New York: The Macmillan Company.

Nichols, Roy F. 1948. *The Disruption of American Democracy*. New York: The Macmillan Company.

Ostrogorski, M. 1902. In Seymour Martin Lispet, ed. 1964. *Democracy and the Organization of Political Parties*. Volume II. New York: Doubldeay Anchor.

Owen, Guillermo and Bernard Grofman. 1988. "Optimal Partisan Gerrymandering." *Political Geography Quarterly* 7(1): 5–22.

Palmquist, Bradley. 1998. "The Extended Beta Binomial Model in Political Analysis." Presented at the Annual Meeting of the Southern Political Science Association, Atlanta, Georgia.

Paulin, Charles O. 1932. *Atlas of the Historical Geography of the United States.* Washington, DC: Carnegie Institution.

Perkins, John A. 1946. "State Legislative Reorganization." *American Political Science Review* 40(3): 510–521.

Peskin, Allan. 1978. *Garfield.* Kent, OH: Kent State University Press.

Petersen, Eric Falk. 1970. "Prelude to Progressivism: California Election Reform, 1870–1909." PhD Dissertation, University of California, Los Angeles.

Polsby, Nelson W. 1968. "The Institutionalization of the U.S. House of Representatives." *American Political Science Review* 62: 144–168.

Polsby, Nelson W. and Aaron Wildavsky. 2000. *Presidential Elections, Strategies and Structures of American Politics* (Tenth Edition). New York: Seven Bridges Press.

Popkin, Samuel L. 1991. *The Reasoning Voter: Communication and Persuasion in Presidential Campaigns.* Chicago: University of Chicago Press.

Powell, Lawrence. 1973. "Rejected Republican Incumbents in the 1866 Congressional Nominating Conventions: A Study of Reconstruction." *Civil War History* 19: 219–237.

Prescott, Frank W. 1950. "The Executive Veto in American States." *The Western Political Quarterly* 3(1): 98–112.

Rae, Douglas W. 1967. *The Political Consequences of Electoral Laws.* New Haven: Yale University Press.

Ratner, Sidney, James H. Soltow, and Richard Sylla. 1979. *The Evolution of the American Economy.* New York: Basic Books.

Remini, Robert V. 1963. *The Election of Andrew Jackson.* New York: Lippincott.

Reock, Ernest C. 1963. *The Population Inequality Among Counties in the New Jersey Legislature.* New Brunswick, NJ: Bureau of Government Research, Rutgers University.

Reock, Ernest C. and Alan Shank. 1966. "New Jersey's Experience with General Assembly Districts 1852–1893." Draft. New Brunswick, NJ: Bureau of Government Research, Rutgers University.

Reynolds, John F. 1988. *Testing Democracy: Electoral Behavior and Progressive Reform in New Jersey, 1880–1920.* Chapel Hill and London: The University of North Carolina Press.

———— 2006. *The Demise of the American Convention System, 1880–1911.* Cambridge: Cambridge University Press.

Reynolds, John F. and Richard L. McCormick. 1986. "'Outlawing Treachery': Split Tickets and Ballot Laws in New York and New Jersey, 1880–1910." *The Journal of American History* 72(4): 835–858.

Reynolds, Lisa A. 1996. "The Australian Ballot and Electoral Cohesion: Reassessing the Impact of Progressive Era Ballot Reform on Party Voting." Prepared for 1996 Meeting of the Midwest Political Science Association, Chicago, Illinois.

Rice, Stuart A. 1928. *Quantitative Methods in Politics.* New York: Russell & Russell.

Riker, William H. 1962. *The Theory of Political Coalitions.* New Haven: Yale University Press.

Riker, William. 1980. "Implications from the Disequilibrium of Majority Rule for the Study of Institutions." *American Political Science Review* 74(2): 753–766.

Riordon, William L. 1963. *Plunkitt of Tammany Hall*. New York: E.P. Dutton & Co.

Roberts, George C. 1994. "Indiana's Australian Ballot: Reform Tempered by the Political Environment." Proceedings of the Indiana Academy of the Social Sciences, 3rd series, October.

Roseboom, Eugene Holloway. 1970. *A History of Presidential Elections, from George Washington to Richard M. Nixon*. Madison: University of Wisconsin Press.

Rosenstone, Steven J. and John Mark Hansen. 1993. *Mobilization, Participation, and Democracy in America*. New York: Macmillan.

Roster of United States Congressional Officeholders and Biographical Characteristics of Members of the United States Congress, 1789–1996 (computer file). Ann Arbor: Inter-University Consortium for Political and Social Research.

Rothman, David. *Politics and Power: The United States Senate, 1869–1901*. Cambridge, MA: Harvard University Press.

Rusk, Jerrold G. 1970. "The Effect of Australian Ballot Reform on Split-Ticket Voting: 1876–1908." *American Political Science Review* 64(4): 1220–1238.

———— 1974. "Comment: The American Electoral Universe: Speculation and Evidence." *American Political Science Review* 68(3): 1028–1049.

———— 2001. *A Statistical History of the American Electorate*. Washington, DC: CQ Press.

Sabato, Larry. 1983. *Goodbye to Goodtime Charlie: The American Governorship Transformed*. Washington, DC: Congressional Quarterly Inc.

Safire, William. 1978. *Safire's Political Dictionary*. New York: Random House.

Schattschneider, E. E. 1942. *Party Government*. New York: Rinehart.

———— 1960. *The Semisovereign People: A Realist's View of Democracy in America*. New York: Holt, Rinehart, Winston.

Schickler, Eric. 2001. *Disjointed Pluralism: Institutional Innovation and the Development of the U.S. Congress*. Princeton: Princeton University Press.

Schiller, Wendy and Charles Stewart III. 2004. "U.S. Senate Elections Before 1914." Prepared for presentation at the Annual Meeting of the Midwest Political Science Association, Chicago, Illinois.

———— 2007. "Challenging the Myths of 19th Century Party Dominance: Evidence from Indirect Senate Elections, 1871–1913." Prepared for Presentation at the Annual Meeting of the American Political Science Association, Chicago, Illinois.

Schlesinger, Arthur M. 1986. *The Cycles of American Politics*. Boston: Houghton, Mifflin.

Schlesinger, Joseph A. 1984. "On the Theory of Party Organization." *Journal of Politics* 46(2): 369–400.

Schumpeter, Joseph A. 1939. *Business Cycles: A Theoretical, Historical, and Statistical Analysis of the Capitalist Process*. New York: McGraw-Hill.

Sears, Kenneth C. 1952. *Methods of Reapportionment*. Chicago: University of Chicago Press.

Sellers, Charles. 1965. "The Equilibrium Cycle in Two-Party Politics." *Public Opinion Quarterly* 29(1): 16–38.

———— 1957. *James K. Polk, Jacksonian, 1795–1843*. Princeton, NJ: Princeton University Press.

Shafer, Byron E. and Anthony J. Badger. 2001. *Contesting Democracy: Substance and Structure in American Political History, 1775–2000*. Lawerence: University Press of Kansas.

Shepsle, Kenneth. 1972. "The Strategy of Ambiguity: Uncertainty and Electoral Competition." *American Political Science Review* 66(2): 555–568.

———— 2001. "A Comment on Institutional Change." *Journal of Theoretical Politics* 13: 321–325.

Short, Lloyd M. 1952. "States That Have Not Met Their Constitutional Requirements." *Law and Contemporary Problems* 17(2): 377–386.

Shull, Charles W. 1961. "Legislative Apportionment in Michigan." Memorandum no. 206. Detroit: Citizens Research Council of Michigan.

Sides, John and Lynn Vavreck. 2013. *The Gamble: Choice and Chance in the 2012 Presidential Election.* Princeton: Princeton University Press.

Silbey, Joel H. 1977. *A Respectable Minority: The Democratic Party in the Civil War Era, 1860–1868.* New York: W.W. Norton & Company, Inc.

———— 1987. "The Early Nationalization of News in America: A Comment." *Studies in American Political Development* 1: 279–285.

———— 1991. *The American Political Nation, 1838–1893.* Stanford: Stanford University Press.

Skowronek, Stephen. 1982. *Building a New American State: The Expansion of National Administrative Capacities, 1877–1920.* Cambridge: Cambridge University Press.

Socolofsky, Homer E. and Allan B. Spetter. 1987. *The Presidency of Benjamin Harrison.* Lawrence: University of Kansas Press.

Starr, Paul. 2004. *The Creation of the Media: Political Origins of Modern Communications.* New York: Basic Books.

Steeples, Douglas O. and David O. Whitten. 1998. *Democracy in Desperation: The Depression of 1893.* New York: Greenwood.

Stewart, Charles H. III. 1991. "Lessons from the Post-Civil War Era." In Gary W. Cox and Samuel Kernell, eds. *Divided Government.* Boulder: Westview Press, 203–238.

Stewart, Charles H. III and Barry R. Weingast. 1992. "Stacking the Senate, Changing the Nation: Republican Rotten Boroughs, State-Hood Politics, and American Political Development." *Studies in American Political Development* 6: 223–271.

Stokes, Donald. 1967. "Parties and the Nationalization of Electoral Forces." In William Nisbet Chambers and Walter Dean Burnham, eds. *The American Party System: Stages of Political Development.* New York: Oxford University Press, 182–202.

Stonecash, Jeffrey M., Jessica E. Boscarino, and Rogan T. Kersh. 2007. "Congressional Intrusion to Specify State Voting Offices for National Offices." *Publius: The Journal of Federalism* 38(1): 137–151.

Storch, Paul. 1998. "Care & Conservation of Political Campaign Buttons." *Minnesota History Interpreter* 26(2): 3–6.

Stromberg, David. 2008. "How the Electoral College Influences Campaigns and Policy: The Probability of Being Florida." *American Economic Review* 98: 769–807.

Summers, Mark Walhgren. 2000. *Rum, Romanism, and Rebellion: The Making of a President, 1884.* Chapel Hill: University of North Carolina Press.

———— 2004. *Party Games: Getting, Keeping, and Using Power in Gilded Age Politics.* Chapel Hill: University of North Carolina Press.

Swindler, William F., ed. 1973–1988. *Sources and Documents of United States Constitutions, Volumes 1–11.* Dobbs Ferry, NY: Oceana Publications.

Szymanski, Ann-Marie E. 2003. *Pathways to Prohibition.* Durham, NC: Duke University Press.

Teaford, Jon C. 2002. *The Rise of States: Evolution of American State Government.* Baltimore: Johns Hopkins University Press.

Theriault, Sean M. 2003. "Patronage, the Pendleton Act, and the Power of the People." *Journal of Politics* 65(1): 50–68.

Tompkins, Mark E. 1984. "The Electoral Fortunes of Gubernatorial Incumbents: 1947–1981." *Journal of Politics* 46(2): 520–543.

Troy, Gil. 1991. *See How They Run: The Changing Role of Presidential Candidates, 1840–1912.* Cambridge, MA: Harvard University Press.

Tufte, Edward. 1973. "The Relationship Between Seats and Votes in Two-Party Systems." *American Political Science Review* 67(2): 540–554.

———. 1975. "Determinants of Outcomes of Midterm Elections." *American Political Science Review* 69(3): 812–826.

Turner, Frederick Jackson. 1894. *The Significance of the Frontier in American History.* Madison: State Historical Society of Wisconsin.

Turrett, J. Stephen. 1971. "The Vulnerability of American Governors, 1900–1969." *Midwestern Journal of Political Science* 15: 108–132.

Vander Meer, Philip R. 1985. *The Hoosier Politician: Officeholding and Political Culture in Indiana 1896–1920.* Urbana and Chicago: University of Illinois Press.

Walker, Jack L. 1966. "Ballot Forms and Voter Fatigue: An Analysis of the Office Block and Party Column Ballots." *Midwest Journal of Political Science* 10(4): 448–463.

———. 1972. *Diffusion of Public Policy Innovation Among the American States* (computer file). Compiled by Jack L. Walker, University of Michigan, Institute of Public Policy Studies. ICPSR, ed. Ann Arbor: Inter-University Consortium for Political and Social Research (producer and distributor).

Wallace, Leon H. 1966–1967. "Legislative Apportionment in Indiana: A Case History." *Indiana Law Journal* 42: 6.

Wallis, John Joseph. 2006. NBER/University of Maryland State Constitution Project, retrieved from www.stateconstitutions.umd.edu.

Walsh, Justin E. 1987. *The Centennial History of the Indiana General Assembly, 1816–1978.* Indianapolis: Indiana Historical Bureau.

Walter, David O. 1938. "Reapportionment and Urban Representation." *Annals of the American Academy of Political and Social Science* 195: 11–20.

———. 1941. *Reapportionment of State Legislative Districts.* PhD dissertation. Urbana: University of Illinois.

Ware, Alan. 2000. "Anti-Partism and Party Control of Political Reform in the United States: The Case of the Australian Ballot." *British Journal of Political Science* 30(1): 1–29.

———. 2002. *The American Direct Primary.* Cambridge: Cambridge University Press.

Waugh, John. C. 1997. *Reelecting Lincoln: The Battle for the 1864 Presidency.* New York: Crown Publishers, Inc.

Wesberry v. Sanders, 376 U.S. 1 (1964).

White, Leonard D. 1958. *The Republican Era: A Study in Administrative History 1969–1901.* New York: Free Press.

Wiebe, Robert. 1967. *The Search for Order: 1877–1920.* New York: Hill and Wang.

Wigmore, John H. 1889. *The Australian Ballot System as Embodied in the Legislation of Various Countries.* Boston: The Boston Book Company.

Williams, R. Hal. 1973. *The Democratic Party and California Politics, 1880–1896.* Stanford: Stanford University Press.

Wirls, Daniel. 1999. "Regionalism, Rotten Boroughs, Race, and Realignment: The Seventeenth Amendment and the Politics of Representation." *Studies in American Political Development* 13: 1–30.

Yearley, Clifton K. 1970. *The Money Machines: The Breakdown and Reform of Governmental and Party Finance in the North, 1860–1920.* New York: SUNY Press.

Index